That
Kind of
Guy

Also by Stephanie Archer

Vancouver Storm
Behind the Net (Jamie and Pippa)
The Fake Out (Rory and Hazel)

Queen's Cove
That Kind of Guy (Emmett and Avery)
The Wrong Mr Right (Wyatt and Hannah)
In Your Dreams, Holden Rhodes (Holden and Sadie)
Finn Rhodes Forever (Finn and Olivia)

Standalone Romantic Comedies
The Heartbreak Rule

That Kind of Guy

Stephanie Archer

ORION

Stephanie Archer writes spicy laugh-out-loud romance. She believes in the power of best friends, stubborn women, a fresh haircut, and love. She lives in Vancouver with a man and a dog.

For spicy bonus scenes, news about upcoming books, and book recs, sign up for her newsletter at:
https://www.stephaniearcherauthor.com/newsletter

Instagram: @stephaniearcherauthor
Tiktok: @stephaniearcherbooks

To check content warnings for any of Stephanie's books, visit www.stephaniearcherauthor.com/content-warnings

For Tim

An Orion paperback

This edition first published in Great Britain in 2024 by Orion Fiction
an imprint of The Orion Publishing Group Ltd
Carmelite House, 50 Victoria Embankment
London EC4Y 0DZ

An Hachette UK company

1 3 5 7 9 10 8 6 4 2

A CIP catalogue record for this book is
available from the British Library.

ISBN (Mass Market Paperback) 9781398724419
eBook ISBN 9781398724426

Printed in UK Clays Ltd, Elcograf, S.p.A.

www.orionbooks.co.uk

1

Avery

"AVERY, Table Four doesn't like their entrées, and they want to speak to the manager."

I looked up from the desk of my tiny office. The restaurant's bartender, Max, leaned against the doorframe in the black jeans and black t-shirt the serving staff always wore.

"Is something wrong with the food?" I asked. We didn't often get complaints. Our chef was incredible. The kitchen staff was a great team. The entire staff was top tier, from servers to hosts to dishwashers. I had hired most of them.

Max shook his head.

I leaned back in my chair. "Tourists?"

He nodded.

I stood. "It's okay, I've got it."

"Are you going to comp their meals?" He stepped back and followed me from my office to the restaurant.

I smiled at him over my shoulder. "Sure am."

"Why?"

Just before we turned the corner into the restaurant, I stopped. I had hired Max last summer as a server and noticed our bartender teaching him how to make different drinks after the restaurant closed. He was in his early twenties, had lots of energy, and was eager to learn, so I'd asked the bartender to spend a few minutes training him every shift until Max was able to work full shifts behind the bar. I'd never admit this to the rest of the staff, but Max was my favorite. He was great with customers, everyone liked working with him, and he had a genuine interest in learning the restaurant business. Tonight, he was stepping in to help with a few tables.

"Max, our purpose is to deliver a delightful experience to every customer who walks through that door. This is where people come for a break, to celebrate, to catch up with old friends or to try a new dish." In the hallway before the dining room, I could already hear the warm ambient hum of the full restaurant, filled with people eating and talking and laughing.

That sound? It made my heart happy. It made me feel like I was doing something good for the world.

"We want every single person who walks through that door to have the best damn meal while they visit Queen's Cove, and if I lose a hundred bucks to comp their meals," I shrugged, "that's okay with me. It's not worth it to piss off the customers."

It wasn't *my* hundred bucks to lose, since it wasn't my restaurant. I was just the manager. One day, though.

He raised an eyebrow, and I grinned at his skepticism.

"Maybe they're entitled," I told him. "Or maybe they're just having a bad day. Maybe they got a flat tire on the way into town, they got to their hotel late, and they're starving." I gave him my most convincing smile. "We can turn their day around. We're going to kill them with kindness." I narrowed my eyes at him. "We're going to *bury* them with our sparkling personalities."

"This is morbid. You always take this analogy too far."

"Once they see how passionate we are?" I put my fist to my chest in mock-agony. "They're going to be rolled out the door in body bags."

He pointed at me. "Yep, there it is. Alright, you're the boss. Thanks for handling it."

"Anytime. I've got your back." I walked out into the restaurant, taking in the packed house.

It was just after eight at night, and every table was full. The restaurant overlooked the harbor of Queen's Cove. On a clear night, the sunset would wash brilliant pinks and oranges and yellows across the sky, but tonight, clouds loomed and rain was beginning to trickle down. It had been sunny all day, but once in a while, these summer storms rolled in. I chewed my lip, glancing around at the busy restaurant. Hopefully it was just a little rain tonight, and no wind.

"Hi, I'm Avery Adams, the manager of The Arbutus," I introduced myself to the unhappy-looking family of four. The two boys were sulking and fidgeting, one was trying to pull the other's hair, and they wore the expressions of kids who had just been told off. "Let me grab these plates out of your way." I handed the plates to a server before placing the coloring pages and crayons on the table in front of the boys. They immediately stopped fighting with each other and turned to the pages.

The parents were in their late thirties, and just as I had suspected, they looked exhausted and irritated. Both of their jaws clenched like they expected a fight.

"I am so sorry your meals were not as you expected. Wow," I said, my gaze catching on the woman's bright red shoulder. "That sunburn looks like it hurts. Can I bring you some aloe?"

She blinked, and her irritation lifted a fraction. "Um, sure." She hesitated. "We stopped by the general store, but they were closed." She scowled and gestured outside, where the rain was coming down harder. "And now it's raining on our holiday."

"They closed early tonight because it's the owners' wedding anniversary. I'll go get you some aloe, but in the

3

meantime, are there any other entrées that interest you? They'll be comped this evening, for the inconvenience," I said with a sweet smile.

The husband blinked with confusion before studying his menu. "We were wishing we'd ordered the pizzas. The Margherita and the meatball pizzas."

I nodded. "Great choices. Can I get you a couple drinks? The blackberry gin smash is on special tonight. A local distillery makes the gin and the blackberries are local and organic."

The wife nodded, watching her sons across the table, busy with coloring, and more importantly, quiet. "That would be wonderful."

"Sure thing. Let's make your vacation a good one, shall we?" I scribbled their order on a paper, handed it to the kitchen and bar, and slipped back to my office to grab one of the travel bottles of aloe sitting in the mini fridge. Max had laughed at me when he saw this, but he stopped laughing when he saw time and time again how a stupid little bottle of aloe could turn his tables around.

"Drop this at Table Four, would you?" I said to him as he passed. "And comp their food and drinks."

He gave me a thumbs up and kept walking.

"Thanks, Max," I called after him.

I watched from the edge of the restaurant as he dropped the bottle of aloe off at the table. The woman's shoulders dropped with relief. Max and I exchanged a subtle high-five before he returned to the bar. I loved flipping customers like that. Walking up to that table, they were tired and grouchy, but now the couple were laughing and talking, their kids colored with concentration, and their vacation was off to a great start. I had turned their night around. I loved my job.

I scanned the restaurant. Tonight, there was a mix of locals and tourists. The owners of the general store were having their anniversary dinner at Table Two. The elementary school principal and her husband were at Table Six. The mayor, his wife, and their two children were at Table Eight. Their family was always polite, friendly, and well-behaved. The kids never wanted to color, they just sat in silence and smiled at everyone like little angels. It creeped me out.

The owner of a local construction company sat at Table Eleven with one of his clients. I snorted to myself, watching Emmett Rhodes schmooze and smile and ooze charm all over the table. Emmett was Mr. Popular, knew everyone in town, was all up in everyone's business, and was well aware of how handsome he was.

At Table Twelve was the owner of a couple local restaurants, Chuck, and his wife. His wife was sneering at the food, and Chuck was eyeing the place, making notes in a notebook. I rolled my eyes. I had a few tips I could give him, but he wouldn't listen.

The restaurants Chuck owned catered to tourists because the locals knew better than to go there. The food wasn't disgusting, it just tasted thawed and reheated. Even that wasn't enough to earn my disdain, though. It was the way he treated his staff. The male staff wore black t-shirts and jeans, just like here at The Arbutus, but the female staff were required to wear mini-skirts, low-cut tops, and high heels. Heels, for eight-hour serving shifts. The thought made my blood boil. He hired kids straight out of school who didn't know any better or who had no other options, so they put up with it. There were rumors he took a cut of their tips, too.

"Table Twelve giving you any trouble tonight?" I asked Max as he shook a cocktail shaker.

"Nope. They've been on their best behavior."

"Good." I watched as Chuck studied the chandelier. What was he up to?

I had been the manager of The Arbutus for two years, but I had been working here for five years, since the day I set foot in the tiny seaside town of Queen's Cove. Located on

Vancouver Island, Canada, wedged between the Pacific Ocean and the Pacific Northwest rainforest, this little town housed about two thousand residents, but because of its breathtaking beaches, dense, mossy forests, relaxed small-town vibes, and the best surfing in the country, it welcomed over a million tourists during the summer months. It was early May, and the tourists were starting to trickle in. By July, we'd be in full swing.

I was born and raised in Vancouver, but Queen's Cove was my home now. Five years ago, I came here on vacation by myself, and after going for a nice dinner at the restaurant with the best view, I fell in love. Giant windows overlooked the picturesque cove and beach. There was oak flooring, and vaulted ceilings with original beams. A menu that was modern, unpretentious, and delicious, with local ingredients. An atmosphere of warmth, community, and comfort. I mentioned the vaulted ceilings, right? Be still, my heart. I fell head over heels. The owner, Keiko, noticed how enthralled I was. We got to talking, and the next thing I knew, she offered me a serving job.

I wasn't an impulsive person. I didn't make big changes without careful consideration and weighing all the pros and cons, but somehow, this one felt right, so I headed back to Vancouver, packed my stuff, and returned to Queen's Cove.

I worked hard at the restaurant. I put everything into this job, even when I was just a server. There was something about this restaurant that was home to me. Maybe it was because Keiko's parents opened it when they moved to Canada when she was a kid. This place had history. Maybe it was that my own parents' restaurant failed catastrophically, and this was the successful restaurant I always wanted to be a part of. Maybe it was that I loved the atmosphere, that I loved making customers happy and contributing to our community.

Keiko's parents opened the restaurant in the seventies. They poured everything into this place, she told me. She grew up here, just like I grew up in a restaurant, except her parents' story was a success. They passed a few years before I moved to town, and I never got to meet them, but locals who knew them told me stories of them working in the restaurant, greeting customers, balancing the till and sweeping the floors even into their nineties. The Arbutus was the result of two generations of hard work.

One day, it would be mine. I had been saving every spare dollar for years so I could buy this place. Growing up, I always knew I'd own a restaurant. I fell in love with the busy bustle of staff, the laughter, and the mouth-watering food smells. People came to a restaurant to celebrate, to catch up with old friends, and to fall in love, and I got to see it all. My parents' restaurant went under, as did their marriage, but The Arbutus was my shot. There was no way in hell I'd screw it up the way they did.

When Keiko was ready to sell, I'd buy this restaurant. I didn't want to just be the manager, I wanted to be the owner. I wanted something that was all mine, something I could make the final decisions on, something I could be responsible for. I wanted to carry on her family's legacy and build my own. Something tangible that said Avery Adams was here on this earth. Keiko was a kind and supportive boss—she taught me everything she knew, and she trusted me, but it wasn't the same as owning the place myself. Until then, I'd continue putting every spare dollar into savings.

Outside the front door was the restaurant's namesake, a twisting, red-trunked arbutus tree. Arbutus trees were native to the West Coast, and on my walks around town to grab a coffee or meet my friend Hannah at her bookstore, I often passed tourists posing for pictures in front of this one. It always made me smile. Arbutus trees weren't the only thing that made Queen's Cove unique. It was the air here, air that flowed straight off the ocean and through our little town. It was the way everyone took care of each other, how the residents fiercely guarded the integrity of the town. No chains or franchises were allowed, only businesses run by locals. Was the town perfect? Hell, no. There were potholes in the roads, some of the sidewalks were crumbling, and windstorms often knocked over the towering fir trees, causing power outages. There was one road in and out of town, so any rockfalls or accidents on the highway had you stuck. If fog rolled into the harbor and the floatplanes couldn't take off? You were stranded.

"Getting windy out there," Max muttered to me as he moved around behind the bar, mixing drinks.

I leaned against the bar and watched as the waves crashed against the shore outside. *Come on, weather,* I pleaded in my head. *Hold up for a couple more hours, just until we close.* "Can I grab you anything?" I asked him, moving around behind the long wooden bar.

He glanced at the trays behind the counter. "Lemons, please."

"You got it."

Halfway down the hall to the storeroom, the lights started flickering. I stopped walking and sighed. The lights gave another halfhearted flicker before going out. Someone in the restaurant screamed, and I headed back to the main dining area.

"Alright, everyone," I said in a calm, reassuring voice. Max was busy lighting tea lights at the bar and placing them in lanterns, and the servers hustled them to the tables. "The wind probably knocked a tree over, and the power is out. Please stay seated while we light some candles and, in the meantime, enjoy the ambiance."

I turned and bumped straight into the hard chest of Mr. Popular himself, Emmett Rhodes.

"Hi, Adams." He cocked a grin down at me.

Irritation prickled at the back of my neck, and I pulled another lighter from beneath the bar. "I'm busy," I told him without looking at him, focused on lighting candles beside Max.

Out of the corner of my eye, his grin widened. "Need some help? I'm great in a crisis."

I rolled my eyes. This guy's ego knew no bounds. I was surprised he got it through the door tonight. I shot him a tight, professional smile. "This isn't a crisis, it's just a power outage. Please go back to your table and enjoy your meal." I was very aware of Max standing beside me, placing candles in lanterns, listening.

Emmett leaned on the bar. "What are you doing tonight?"

I gave a laugh of disbelief. "Again? Seriously? I don't bother you while you're working."

He grinned wider. "Bother? I'm not bothering you. I'm too good-looking to be a bother."

Deep breaths, I told myself. "Emmett."

He put his hands up. "Okay, okay. Going back to my table."

Emmett walked away, and my gaze followed his tall form.

The first day I met Emmett Rhodes, he dumped a girl right in front of me with zero remorse. He had come to the restaurant for a quick meal and sat at the bar. A woman about my age had spotted him and slipped onto the stool beside him, leaning toward him and gazing at him with such deep affection that when I saw the hesitant, wary expression on his face, my heart ached.

"Look, Heather," he had told her. I had my back turned to them at the bar and couldn't help but overhear. "You're great, but I'm just not interested in this whole thing. We had fun, but let's not make it more than it needs to be."

She was quiet for a second. "What?"

"I'm just not like that," he told her. "It's better this way. I don't do the wife and kids thing."

He was one of those people who you could hear from the other side of town, always talking, laughing, saying hello to everyone within sight. *Schmoozey*, that was it. Whereas I had a small circle of close friends, this guy was friends with every single person in town. He knew everything about everyone. Every time I passed by him in the grocery store or on the street, he was making small talk about somebody's business or asking how someone's kid was. It struck me as insincere, like he had an agenda.

Beside me, Max cleared his throat, a little smile on his face.

"What?" I asked him with raised eyebrows.

He bit back a grin but said nothing while he slid tea lights into the next lantern.

"Don't start," I warned.

"I didn't say anything." He lit another candle. "But you sure like to spar with him."

My mouth fell open. "He started it. He always starts it."

Max gave me a knowing look. "Mhm."

Disgust rippled through me at the notion of being romantically interested in Emmett. I had seen the way Emmett was with women—flirty, friendly, charming, and funny. He knew what he was doing. And multiple times at my restaurant, I'd seen him remind women he wasn't the guy they wanted him to be. He roped them in and spat them out when he was done with them.

My dad was like that. He was everyone's best friend until he changed his mind and disappeared. He was the brightest star in the room, the person everyone wanted to talk with and hang out with. When he was in a good mood, he brought everyone up with him, laughing and chatting and complimenting people and brightening their day. When he was in a bad mood, the clouds poured on everyone in his proximity, and he dragged everyone down with him.

I'd bet my life savings Emmett was like my dad.

Before I could respond, Max picked up two lanterns and strolled away. I laughed to myself before glancing back at

Emmett's table, where he was deep in conversation with his client. He glanced up, and we made eye contact before he winked.

I rolled my eyes again before turning back to the lanterns.

I didn't know Emmett Rhodes in high school, but I had heard all about him. Heartbreaker, ladies' man, Casanova—just a few of the names people had used to describe him back then. I believed it. The guy was six-four, lean but muscular, with olive-toned skin, dark hair that he kept short and stylish, and a sharp jawline. His eyes were a pale gray, like all the Rhodes men. The guy could have modeled for cologne ads if he wanted to. He made whatever he was wearing look designer. Tonight, he wore slim black jeans, brown leather boots, and a white t-shirt, but he looked like he'd stepped out of the Red Wing Shoes catalog. He was a walking advertisement for clothes, he made them look so good.

Not that I was interested. Yes, the guy was Henry Cavill's doppelgänger, but I wasn't in the market for someone who I could barely get within ten feet of without rolling my eyes.

Emmett Rhodes was what happened when a man grew up too attractive. He thought he had the world at his fingertips. I had spent the last five years avoiding Emmett Rhodes.

He liked to play this little game where he'd ask me out and I always said no. He had been doing this for years. He didn't like me. He loved the chase. He only messed with me because I was the only person in town immune to him.

One of the candle flames singed my fingers as I placed it into the lantern and I swore under my breath. No more thinking about Mr. Popular. I had a job to do.

Within a few minutes, soft candlelight illuminated the restaurant.

"We need a generator," Max told me.

"Find me the money," I responded. "We're making do with what we have." I tilted my chin to him. "I'll take care of the bar. You know what to do."

He grinned and slipped out from behind the bar, tossing me his apron. I glanced over the receipts from the servers and began making a whiskey sour. Servers dropped off more drink receipts and delivered the last of the dishes from the kitchen to their respective tables. In the corner of the restaurant, Max took a seat and balanced his guitar on his knee. He began playing, and diners watched and listened with little smiles on their faces. I pulled out my phone, took a sneaky pic of him playing, and posted it to our social media.

"The power's out but nothing will stop us from having a great night at The Arbutus." I typed out the caption and hit *post* before slipping my phone back into my pocket and getting to work on the drinks.

In the summer, the power went out about once a month, but in the winter, outages occurred at least once a week. We couldn't close up shop every time we lost power or we'd be in the red, so over the last couple years, I figured out ways to stay open. No music? Max was a musician, and a damn good one. No lighting? Candlelight in the restaurant and propane lanterns in the kitchens. Our kitchen had gas stoves so we could finish dinner service. Because we didn't know how long the outages would last and didn't want a week's worth of food going bad, we kept our fridge and freezer stocks low. The Arbutus was all about fresh, local food anyway, so this wasn't an issue.

We made it work. Whatever happened, we always made it work.

Hours later, after the last customer had left, the servers counted up their tips, Max packed up his guitar, and I flipped chairs onto the tables as the staff left. Candles still illuminated the space in their lanterns, and I moved around the empty restaurant, tidying and sweeping and closing up. Some people wouldn't want to be here alone so late, but I wouldn't be anywhere else. Late at night, when everything was quiet and still, was when I was most at home. The charming place felt like mine during these moments.

One day, when I had enough money and Keiko was ready to sell, The Arbutus would be my restaurant. My legacy. The success story my mom never had.

A light knock on the door shook me out of my thoughts. It was after midnight and we were closed, but maybe someone had forgotten their phone or wallet under a table.

Keiko's smiling face peered through the glass door. She was wearing her bright yellow raincoat and gave me a cheery wave.

"Hi, what are you doing here so late?" I asked and opened the door. "You have a key. You don't need to knock."

She followed me in and locked the door behind her. "I didn't want to startle you. I knew you'd be here still."

"Want something to drink? I can put the kettle on."

"That would be nice." She threw me a soft smile as she pulled a bar stool down.

In the kitchen, I filled the kettle and put it on the stove in the dim light from the lanterns. Keiko didn't often pay me visits, but I savored the moments I had with her, just the two of us. My previous bosses didn't have the time or interest to teach me the industry, but Keiko had taken me under her wing and taught me everything she knew. When I took over as manager and she saw I had things under control, she began to step back from the business. Her daughter had just had a baby, so Keiko spent several weeks at a time in Vancouver, visiting her. I still sent her monthly reports of the restaurant's financials, although I doubted she read them anymore.

I returned with our mugs of tea. "So, what brings you to our beautiful establishment tonight?"

"Thank you," she said, accepting the mug and blowing the wafting steam off it. "I want to chat with you about something."

"Is everything okay?" I frowned and slid onto the stool beside her. "Are you okay?"

She nodded. "Don't worry, everything is fine, no one is dead, and I'm healthy as a teenager."

"It's all that yoga you do."

"Every day. I'm thinking about doing my teacher training."

"Oh, really? You're going to be a yoga teacher?" I asked, a big smile spreading across my face. Keiko would be a perfect yoga teacher, with her calm, grounding presence.

She shook her head. "No, it's just fun to keep busy and keep learning. Something new." She took a breath and patted my hand. "Speaking of something new."

My eyebrows shot up. "Mhm?"

She hesitated, like she didn't know which words to use. "I think it's time for me to move to Vancouver to be with Layla and the baby."

I blinked, taking a moment to digest this. "Moving. Wow." Queen's Cove was a three-hour drive to Victoria, the biggest city on Vancouver Island, and then another three hours to Layla's place via ferry and highway. "I guess that makes sense. I'm sure it's a pain, going back and forth on the ferry all the time." I sagged a bit, bummed I would be seeing even less of Keiko. "We're going to miss you around here. Are you going to move into Layla's place?"

She took a sip of tea and shook her head. "No, actually, a townhouse in her complex just went up for sale, and I would like to buy it."

"Wow, that's lucky," I told her. "Layla's place is pretty small, right?"

She nodded. "Two-bedroom. Too small for me to move into." She gave me another soft smile and pressed her lips together, watching me. Something in Keiko's expression told me she wasn't finished.

"I feel like there's more."

"Well," she said and took a deep breath. "Avery, I know you love The Arbutus, and I know it's as special to you as it is to me."

"Of course." Zero hesitation.

"The townhouse in Layla's complex costs more than my home here by a lot. Vancouver real estate is quite expensive."

I had heard about this. Even Vancouver Island prices were rising. Young families struggled to purchase homes without their parents' help. I knew about the issue but wasn't concerned by it, because I had no intention of buying a home anytime soon. My sole focus was saving to buy The Arbutus one day.

"Are you going to sell your home here?" I asked her.

She nodded and flattened her lips. "I'm listing it tomorrow. It'll be hard to leave the place I've lived in for thirty years, but it's time." She smiled again at me and nodded. "And I'll be selling the restaurant as well."

My pulse stopped. I blinked. "Selling the restaurant?"

She nodded, watching me. "That's the plan. My financial advisor thinks it's better if I sell both to pay for the town-home." She nodded again to herself. "And I'm ready. It's time for the next phase of life, being a grandmother." She smiled.

"I have to ask—who are you selling it to?"

"You, if you're interested." There was a sparkle in her eye.

My mouth gaped open. "Of course I'm interested!"

She laughed. We had never spoken about me buying the place, but there always seemed to be an unspoken understanding about it.

"I was hoping you'd say that," she said, taking another sip of tea and smiling at me over her mug. "I was disappointed when my Layla didn't want anything to do with the place, but you waltzed in and answered my prayers."

My eyes stung, and I smiled at her. I had worked in the restaurant industry for five years before moving here and never had I found a mentor like Keiko, someone who was kind to their staff, someone who taught me everything about how to run a restaurant. To hear her tell me she wanted me to buy The Arbutus made me even more resolved to make her proud.

A thought struck me. Did I have enough savings for a loan? I thought I had more time. I thought Keiko would retire in five or ten years. This was a surprise, but I could handle it. I had handled surprises before, and I had everything under control. I was going to buy the restaurant.

"I hope you know I love this restaurant, and I will do everything in my power to ensure it is a success," I vowed, leaning in. "I'll go to the bank tomorrow. I'll talk to them about a business loan."

"Wonderful," she sang with a bright smile. "Absolutely wonderful."

Later, after we finished our tea and I had said goodbye to Keiko, my gaze lingered on a framed photo in my office of me and my mom, taken about twenty years ago. My thumb brushed the frame, and I studied her young, smiling face, full of hope and optimism. My dad took the photo on opening day of her restaurant, before everything went downhill.

That wouldn't happen to me. I'd make sure of it. No one was going to grab the wheel from me. I'd learned my lesson, watching my parents.

I set the picture back down on my desk, locked up, and headed home to my tiny, crappy apartment. The rain and wind had stopped, and the air smelled saturated and earthy. I lived in the loft apartment of a house a few blocks from the restaurant. The landlord had subdivided the house into five different units and often rented to people who came to work in Queen's Cove for the tourist season. I opened the door of my place and flicked the lights on. It was one in the morning, and I could hear music from the downstairs neighbors through the floor. This summer's tenants liked to party.

"Hello, shit hole," I murmured as I tossed my bag and

keys on the counter of the poky little kitchen. I had lived in this apartment my entire time in Queen's Cove, and because of the cheap rent, had no intention of moving. I got what I paid for, though. There were water stains on the ceiling, the carpet was worn and thin, and I could almost hear my downstairs neighbors breathing. I'm sure they could hear every cough and sneeze from me, as well.

My stomach rumbled and I realized I'd left my dinner on the counter of the bar, back at the restaurant. I pulled my phone out and ordered a pizza.

After my stomach was full and I had showered, I crawled into bed. Keiko's words replayed in my head, and I wiggled my toes with excitement. I grinned to myself in the dark. After all these years of hard work, I was going to buy the restaurant. This was my shot, and I wasn't going to let anything get in the way.

2

Emmett

THE CONSTRUCTION SITE was bustling when I arrived. A couple weeks ago, the crews had been pouring the concrete foundation, but now the structure was up, and men and women in hardhats and steel-toed boots moved through the doorways with tools and drawings in hand. In three months, this site would open as the new Queen's Cove community center.

"Hey, Emmett," Sandra, one of our civil engineers, said as she passed. "Holden's in the atrium."

"Thanks, Sandra. How about that game last night?" I grinned at her. Her beloved hockey team, the Toronto Maple Leafs, had lost to the Vancouver Canucks in overtime the night before.

"I don't want to talk about it," she replied, making a mock sad face.

I laughed and waved goodbye before heading inside. As I passed through the site, I made note of the job progress. I spotted Holden and waved to get his attention before gesturing for him to follow me outside where it was quieter.

My brother Holden ran the construction side, and I was the business guy. Whereas he was on construction sites, managing the crews and working with contractors, I was in the office, taking care of the financials. Occasionally, our tasks would overlap, like when we needed to quote a big job, or when we met with potential clients. Holden wasn't a personable guy. Out of the four Rhodes boys, he was the grouchiest. Wyatt and Finn were almost as personable at me. Almost. I was the charming one. I always had been. I liked people, liked talking to them and fixing problems and making people happy. Wyatt owned a surf shop and was training to go pro as a surfer and Finn was a firefighter, often spending summers around the province fighting wildfires.

Holden and I had made a name for ourselves in this town with Rhodes Construction. People were skeptical when I returned from university with an MBA and a degree in environmental science and convinced Holden to start a company with me. Two brothers, twenty-three and twenty-two, start a construction company with no clients? Good luck. But Holden had worked in construction for four years and saw how disorganized and low-quality our competitors were. I saw how climate change was affecting our planet and knew we had an opportunity to offer customers solutions that would save them energy and money. Rhodes Construction was born, and we haven't looked back since. The first years weren't easy, but we turned those skeptics around.

He had sent me a text this morning with two words: Call me. My brother was a man of few words, so I wasn't concerned, and the job site was on my way to our office so stopping by was convenient. Also, I liked to walk our job sites, say hello to the crews, and show my face. Our business had grown from the two of us, but I didn't want to be one of those guys who hid in the office while everyone did the work for them. That wasn't leadership. Leadership was showing your face, knowing your employees, and knowing the ins and outs of your business.

"Everything okay?" I asked as we pulled the earplugs out of our ears.

He shrugged. "SparkPro didn't show up this morning, and they aren't answering calls." SparkPro was an electrical contractor we used when our electricians were tied up with other projects.

I frowned. "Cal confirmed the crew would be here today." I slipped my phone out of my pocket and scanned through emails until I found the one I was searching for. "Tuesday morning, seven on the dot. Six electricians."

Holden put his hands up and shrugged, as if to say *I don't know what to tell you.* "I need to start wiring today or the crew will need to work overtime to stay on schedule."

"I'll call them." This had happened before. I had an idea of what was going on but didn't want to say anything until I called Cal.

"If they don't show up, I need to call someone else."

"Don't call someone else. I'll call them right now and fix it."

I scrolled through my contacts until I found Cal.

"SparkPro," the older guy rasped. He had been a long-time smoker, and his voice was like phlegmy gravel.

"Cal, it's Emmett."

He grunted his hello. Cal wasn't a small talk guy, so I cut straight to it.

"We expected your electricians this morning at seven," I said in a concerned tone. "Did something happen? Or maybe I missed an email from you."

In my years of working with hundreds of clients, crews, and personalities, I had learned one thing: assume innocence. I had a sneaking suspicion another client had thrown money at Cal to get the electricians to their site, and Cal had conveniently forgotten to tell me. But electricians were scarce in our small town, and we needed Cal's people to help keep our job on track.

"They got held up."

"Hmm." I moved out of the way as some of our crew moved beams into the community center. "Well, the thing is, Cal, we need to start wiring today or we'll have to delay everything else. We gave you our word we'd use you as our electrical contractor, and I want to stick to that. Your people do quality work. I don't know the other contractors, and I don't like to use people I don't know."

I let that sit for a moment. I was about to ask Cal what I could do to make this work, but he grunted another acknowledgment.

"They'll be there within an hour," he promised.

"You're a good guy, Cal." We said our goodbyes before hanging up.

I found Holden reviewing drawings with the architects. "SparkPro will be here in an hour. Call me if they aren't here by noon."

He nodded. "Thanks."

"No problem." I clapped him on the shoulder, pride pinging in my chest. I loved fixing problems like that. I loved it when I could smooth something over and make everyone happy.

Holden turned to me. "I forgot to ask, everything go okay with Will this morning?"

My good mood popped like a balloon, and my mouth pressed into a firm line as I nodded. "Yep."

Will was my best friend. We had grown up next door to each other here in Queen's Cove. This morning, Will, his wife, and their four-year-old daughter, Kara, moved to Victoria, a city three hours away. My chest wrenched every time I thought about it. It wasn't right.

"Do he and Nat need any help with their place?"

I shook my head. "I've got it covered. Renters are moving in tomorrow."

He nodded, thinking. "Sucks."

"Yep. See you later."

I made my way back to the office, walking instead of driving since it was only a few blocks and I enjoyed seeing the town this way. I pushed thoughts about Will and his family out of my head as I neared the main street and ran into several people I knew. I said hello to the bookstore owner, chatted with a teacher from the high school, and stopped to say hi to Keiko, the owner of a local restaurant.

"Everything okay with the power outage last night?" I asked her. "I always worry when the power comes back on the surge will damage something in the kitchen. You should let my crew take a look in there to make sure everything's okay."

Way back in the sixties, Queen's Cove housed a population of about five thousand people. With the extra load on our electrical grid from the tourists in the summer, and the tall trees falling onto power lines during big winter storms, the town seemed to be enduring more power outages, more often. And sometimes, for a day at a time.

Keiko waved a hand. "Oh, yes. Avery always has it handled."

Right. Avery Adams. The corner of my mouth tugged up when I thought about how irritated she was when I asked if she needed help.

Avery Adams was a curious one. Early thirties, shoulder-length auburn hair in a cute, choppy cut, and bright blue eyes the color of the pen I wrote with. Great body. Gorgeous smile, although she never shined it at me, only other customers and staff. She was cute—super cute—and she couldn't stand me, which only made me want to talk to her more.

I think it was that women didn't usually find me irritating. They found me funny, charming, helpful, interesting, handsome...

But never irritating.

I wasn't sure what my end game was, annoying her like I did. It wasn't like I wanted a relationship. I wasn't like Will.

Will had always been that family kind of guy, even when we were kids. Me? Not so much. I had my business, I had my friends, and I had my brothers and parents. Relationships got complicated.

Now, if Avery could do a casual kind of thing, then we'd be in business.

"Emmett?" Keiko asked, and I got the impression I had spaced out while she was talking. "How is Kara doing?"

"Who?"

"Kara. How is she doing with the move?"

My heart sunk again, and I thought about Kara growing up in Victoria, away from her grandparents and all the people who helped Will and Nat with raising her. Queen's Cove was the village committed to raising Kara, just as it was for everyone who had grown up here.

"She seemed okay," I told Keiko, thinking about Will driving away this morning with Nat in the passenger seat and Kara waving at me from the backseat. "The power outage last night just reinforced their decision to go."

I remembered the day Will told me Kara was sick. It was renal failure, and the doctors were putting her on dialysis until they could find a donor. That was a bad night. I sat with Will at his kitchen table while he found solace in the bottom of the bottle, a rare indulgence for him. It wasn't fair, but there wasn't a single thing we could do.

I thought they were managing okay with dialysis. It wasn't ideal, but they were managing. Then Nat let it slip that the power outages added another layer of stress to their already upside-down life. Will had bought his parents' house and the wiring was old. They'd installed a generator, but a surge damaged it. They couldn't win, and finally, they gave in.

My chest wrenched with frustration. I hated that there wasn't a damn thing I could do about this.

I had spent years building a successful construction company with my brother. We had started with nothing. I'd done well for myself. I was in my mid-thirties, I had a nice car and a beautiful, custom-built home. I had more money than I needed, but I was powerless against this, and I couldn't do a thing to help them.

Keiko sensed my mood and patted my arm. "It's going to be okay."

I nodded at her, but I wasn't sure about that. "Thanks. I've got to run. See you later, Keiko."

I made my way to the office down the street, thinking about the power outages the whole time. They affected the entire town, not just Will and Kara. Every business had to either close or come up with a solution. Every resident had to have their flashlights ready every time a tree swayed. It had been like this for as long as I could remember.

I approached town hall and frowned to myself. The power outages never came up in town hall meetings. No one seemed as frustrated with the outages as I was. Everyone just accepted that this was part of living in Queen's Cove and we couldn't change it.

One person could change it, though.

"Is Isaac available?" I asked the receptionist inside town hall, a young woman smacking her gum and staring at her phone.

She shrugged. "Probably. Go on in."

"Thanks." I flashed her a grateful smile before heading into the office behind her.

Isaac Anderson, mayor of Queen's Cove for a decade, sat at his desk, reading the local paper. He glanced up with surprise when I entered.

He was in his early forties, always pleasant to everyone, but something about him irked me. His wife never spoke, she just smiled at his side. He was always too perfectly groomed— not a single hair out of place. His kids were so well behaved that they seemed like robots. And for the last decade, nothing in our town seemed to change.

"Emmett." He blinked. "Did we have a meeting?"

I shook my head. "Nope, just thought I'd stop by to chat."

Isaac blinked again and put the paper down, leaning over to read his calendar. "Sure, but I think I have a meeting soon—"

"This won't take long." I took a seat across from him. "Let's talk about the power outages."

His eyebrows went up. "Okay. What about them?"

"What is the city doing to fix them?"

He frowned and shook his head. "Emmett, as you know, our grid is from the sixties. It just isn't designed for how many people live here."

I gestured at him to go on. "And?"

"And that means we're out of luck." He shrugged. "What can we do?"

I frowned. "Cities expand all the time. I'm not an electrical engineer, but can't we upgrade the power grid?"

He gave me a sympathetic look. "That would be costly. There's just nothing we can do."

I frowned deeper. His first sentence proved his second sentence wrong. I watched as he sat back in his chair, his expression resolved.

"People are moving away from town," I told him. "The town spent money on a new tourist center two years ago, but we can't spend money on the residents themselves?"

Isaac shrugged again and shook his head. "What can I say, Emmett? My hands are tied. Just consider it part of our small-town charm."

It was like he didn't want to fix it. My chest was tight with irritation. The role of the mayor was to take care of the town and work hard for the people who lived here. Isaac didn't seem like he cared about the town or the people. I swallowed and stood.

"Thanks for your time." My voice sounded curt.

I spent the rest of the morning in my office with the door

closed, catching up on paperwork, emails, and client calls. I kept my head down and worked to keep my mind off Will and Isaac and the power outages.

———

"HEY, DIV," I called out my open office door later that afternoon.

He appeared at my office door, phone poised and ready to go. "Yes?"

Div, short for Divyanshu, was in his mid-twenties and wore a full suit every day. I'd made it clear he didn't have to dress up for work, but the guy insisted. Div was a good assistant—punctual, memory like a steel trap, tech-savvy, and often knew my schedule without consulting my calendar. He could wear whatever he wanted, as far as I was concerned.

"Did Holden submit his invoices yet?" I asked him.

Div pointed to a corner of my tidy desk. "Right there."

"Ah. Thanks." I scooped up the papers and shuffled through them until I found the one I was searching for.

"I'm ordering lunch."

"Nothing for me, thanks. Hey, can you send Cal at SparkPro a bottle of the whiskey he likes?" We still had six months left on the community center project. Staying on Cal's good side would prevent misunderstandings like this morning.

On the bottom of the pile of Holden's invoices sat a business magazine I had done an interview with a couple months ago. I cringed at my image on the cover, leaning against the railing of one of our custom-built homes. Holden never wanted to be involved with this kind of thing, so I took care of it. I didn't want to be involved either, but it helped our reputation and our business. We had employees to keep busy and mouths to feed.

"Your mom wanted ten copies," Div told me. He didn't dare laugh but his eyes gleamed.

I rolled my eyes with a snort and tossed the magazine in the recycling as Div left to answer the phone.

My email pinged with a newsletter from the town journalist. He retired a few years ago but ran a blog with town events.

One of the articles mentioned Will and his family. My gaze snagged on a picture of Kara, holding a stuffed toy I had bought her. A panda. I grinned. She looked so damn cute, missing that front tooth. My chest tightened as I realized this was my relationship with Will and his family for the foreseeable future—photos, texts, emails, and FaceTime.

It wasn't right, Kara growing up in the city three hours away. Both Will and Nat's parents lived here, all her friends at school were here, and my heart broke every time I thought about her not having the carefree, small-town childhood Will and I had.

I thought about Nat and my chest panged for her. Kara was her world, and she was trying so hard to create a great life for her. Although she hadn't spoken to me about this, I knew moving was hard on her. She didn't want to leave either, but it was the right choice for their family.

I had to fix this.

I kept skimming the newsletter, and something caught my eye.

Mayoral election scheduled for July 2.

I frowned, trying to remember the last election we had, but came up with nothing.

"Hey, Div," I shouted out the door.

"What?" he called back, appearing at the door moments later.

"When was the last mayoral election?"

"About four years ago." He shrugged. "This town has a low voter turnout."

"Why?"

"Isaac doesn't campaign because no one ever runs against him."

An idea struck me. Money poured into the town in the summers—it was a hot tourist destination with world-class accommodations, dining, and the most beautiful, scenic nature in the world. Businesses couldn't keep up with the crowds in the summer. Residents and businesses alike paid millions in taxes to the city every year and yet the town hadn't done anything about the power outages.

If Isaac Anderson continued on as mayor, nothing would ever change. The old, outdated electrical grid would continue to endure power outages and Will and his family would never return to town.

I was on to something. I grinned at Div.

He frowned with concern. "What? What is it now?"

"I have a great idea."

His nostrils flared. "Emmett, whatever it is, I'm going to caution you to think about it for a moment. You can sometimes be a little impulsive—"

"I'm going to run for mayor."

His head fell to his chest. "There it is."

I nodded, mind racing with ideas. "Yep. This feels right. I'm going to run for mayor. Call the printers, call the graphic designer, and let's get some campaign swag going. Oh, and I guess we should tell town hall."

Div gave me a long look before he sighed. "I'm on it."

"Thanks, Div," I called after him as he returned to his desk.

Suddenly, this day didn't feel so awful. So Will left town, sure, that was a bad start, but I had a plan. I was going to fix this.

Avery

"THEY TURNED YOU DOWN?" Hannah asked later, her blue eyes wide behind her glasses as we sat in the back of Pemberley Books, the bookstore she ran with her dad.

We often hung out back here, behind the bookshelves and the towering stacks of books. Hannah's mom had started Pemberley Books in the nineties with Hannah's dad. After she passed in Hannah's teenage years, her dad took over, but Hannah ran the store full-time after she graduated university.

My cheap apartment smelled like hot dogs and Hannah lived with her dad in a tiny house a couple blocks away, so once the customers were gone and Hannah had locked the door, the bookstore was the perfect place to chat. Sometimes, on Friday nights, we put Spice Girls music on and drank wine. This dusty little store was my favorite hangout spot in town.

I slid further down the big squishy chair, breathing in the familiar paper smell in the store. Hannah sat across from me in an identical chair. "Yep. A big red rejection stamp, right on my forehead." A pang of frustration hit my gut. "I don't have enough savings to pass the business loan stress test."

Hannah chewed her lip and watched me. "What are you going to do?"

An older man poked his head out of the book stacks. "Do you have any books on wood?" he asked Hannah with a frown.

Hannah paused, thinking. "We have a book on oak trees."

He shook his head. "Not trees. Wood."

I stifled a laugh while Hannah looked confused.

"And don't even say they're the same thing like the other place," the man told her, and I hid my grin behind my hand. When Hannah looked perplexed, the man disappeared into the book stacks.

"I have no clue what I'm going to do," I told her. "Do you have a couple hundred thousand dollars lying around?"

We glanced around the shabby bookstore. There was dust on every surface. The place was dark, with the only daylight peeking in behind the floor-to-ceiling bookshelves in the windows. The carpet beneath our feet was worn. As if the bookstore heard us, one of the shelves behind Hannah's head broke and books clunked to the ground.

"Oh my god, are you okay?" I asked.

She rubbed the back of her head. "Ow. Yes. And no, we don't have a couple hundred thousand dollars lying around or this place wouldn't smell like that."

I grinned at her. "All I smell is old books."

She studied me out of the corner of her eye. "That's good."

We laughed.

The man's head popped out from behind the book stack again. "Any books on termites?"

Hannah shook her head. "We don't have any books on termites right now, but if you have a specific one you were searching for, I can order it in."

The man made a *forget about it* gesture, grumbled something, and wandered off.

Hannah was my best friend, and I had spent many hours sitting with her in the back of Pemberley Books. I met her shortly after I moved to town. She was a few years younger than me, very shy and quiet with most people, but I had worn her down by stopping by her bookstore on a weekly basis and asking her to track down several hard-to-find books on antique jewelry. I was not a rich lady, and I had been saving my ass off for years to buy the restaurant, but I had one teeny tiny indulgence—antique jewelry, specifically from the early nineteen-hundreds.

I exhaled through my nose and the pang of frustration hit me in the gut again. I couldn't believe how naïve I'd been this morning at the bank. I figured because I had worked hard and saved, didn't have any debt, and had always been responsible with my credit card, I could just put my hand out, ask for some money, and the bank would sign it over.

Not the case.

"I either need to find a way to make way, way more money," I told Hannah, "or I need to find another way to get a loan. Or I need a cosigner."

She cocked her head at me.

The loan specialist had told me I could get a business loan if I had a cosigner sign on the loan for me. The loan would be for both of us, and if I chose not to pay it back, that other person would be on the hook for the money. Ideally, this would be a person with high income, exceptional credit, and deep pockets.

"What about your parents?" Hannah asked, and I snorted.

"With his credit, I don't think my dad could borrow a book from the library, and I don't want to put my mom in that position." After the restaurant went under, my mom found out how much money my dad had borrowed while they were trying to make it work. They were in the red. Really, really red. Then my dad took off and because they were married, it wasn't just his debt. It was her debt, too. I still remembered her expression when the letters began to arrive, all stamped OVERDUE and LAST NOTICE in big red letters.

A shiver rippled through me. There was no way I was going to ask her to cosign on my loan, even if I would fight like hell to prevent her from having to pay a cent. I just couldn't do that to her.

Off Hannah's uncertain expression, I sat up straighter and gave her a confident smile. "I'm going to figure this out."

She nodded. "Is there anything I can do to help—"

"Nope," I said, cutting her off. "I've got it."

The bell on the front door rang as a customer walked in. Hannah stood. "Be right back."

I stood as well. "I've got to get to the restaurant. Thanks for listening."

"Anytime," she said over her shoulder, giving me a smile and disappearing into the book stacks to say hello to the customer.

On the walk back to the restaurant, I mentally ran through my options, coming up short on any solutions. I couldn't get a smaller loan and offer Keiko less money—that wasn't fair to her. She had put years into this business and selling it was her retirement fund. Offering her less would put her in an awkward position, because I had a feeling she would accept. She wanted me to have the restaurant, but I couldn't sleep at night knowing I short-changed her.

The second I turned the corner and the restaurant came into view, I forgot all about Keiko, the restaurant, and the loan. I had a brand-new problem.

In front of the restaurant, there was a small stretch of grass with some gardens and foliage. The restaurant's name-sake Arbutus tree grew at the right of the entrance. A path led through the garden area to the restaurant and in the evenings, lanterns lined the walkway. Benches sat around the entrance among the flowers and plants to seat diners waiting for their tables. I loved this front exterior design—it was beautiful, inviting, and serene.

But I didn't feel the serenity as two men pounded wooden

stakes into the grass, installing an enormous blue sign with Emmett Rhodes' face on it.

Rage clouded my vision.

Vote for Emmett Rhodes, the sign read. It was ten feet tall and blocked the windows to the restaurant so pedestrians could view the monstrosity. Instead of seeing the town's quaint street and people-watching, diners would have a view of the back of Emmett's sign.

I barked a humorless laugh. Of course he was running for mayor. The guy thought the sun shined straight out of his ass, *of course* he wanted to get into politics.

I sure as hell wasn't going to help him, and I wasn't going to let him scare off customers with a picture of his face the size of an elephant.

The men were putting the finishing touches on the structure as I stalked up.

"Good morning. Let's talk about this." I gestured at Emmett's stupid smiling face. His teeth were so freaking white.

The men looked uncertain. One of them climbed down his ladder. "Emmett Rhodes hired us to install this."

I nodded at them. "I understand you're doing your job, but this is a business, and you don't have permission to do this. Please remove it."

Emmett appeared at my side, studying the sign. "Great work, guys."

They began to pack up and leave, and I turned to Emmett, crossing my arms over my chest. "Get rid of it."

He studied the sign, ignoring me. "I thought it would be bigger."

I inhaled and rubbed my temples. This guy. I couldn't believe him. "This can't be here. Who said you could put the sign up?"

He gave me the same winning smile that was on the sign. "Keiko."

My nostrils flared. "Keiko told you it was okay to put a *billboard* in front of her restaurant?"

He nodded, smiling and watching me with an expression that was equal parts curiosity and amusement. "She sure did. See, Adams, when I'm mayor, I'm going to upgrade the electrical grid. That means no more power outages, and business owners love that idea just as much as residents." He gestured at the sign. "Keiko was happy to let me install this here."

I shook my head. *Keiko, you're too good to be wooed by this guy and his false charms*. "Unbelievable," I scoffed. "Your ego knows no limits, does it?"

He gave me a cocky grin. "I'm just trying to do the right thing, Adams."

Right. The right thing. I knew guys like Emmett Rhodes. Slippery, schmoozey, friends with everyone until you needed them or they needed to be accountable for their choices.

Keiko had said yes to him, and I didn't own the restaurant. A twist of nerves hit me in the gut when I remembered my bank loan rejection this morning. I had bigger problems than this sign.

"Remove it by the end of election day," I said, turning and walking up the path to the restaurant. "Or I'll draw devil horns on it and show people who you really are."

Emmett's low laugh followed me, and my jaw clenched.

"I hope I can count on your vote, Adams," he called after me.

"When hell freezes over," I called back before disappearing inside the restaurant.

"Avery," Max's voice stopped me in my tracks the second I stepped inside. It was busy, most tables were full, and Max had a frantic, wide-eyed look to him. "Bea called, she has a cold. I told her we'd cover it. That's okay, right?"

I nodded, glancing out at the back of the campaign sign. What an eyesore. "I'll handle her tables," I told Max, and he sagged with relief.

I missed serving sometimes. The good parts at least, like keeping busy, interacting with people on vacation and locals enjoying their day, and watching the cogs of this restaurant turn.

"Table Three, order up," the line cook called, and I used cloths to scoop the plates up before hustling them out to the table.

"Hey there," I said to Elizabeth, one of my favorite people in this town. She sat at a table near a window by herself, chin on her palm, gazing out at the ocean with a gentle smile.

Elizabeth Rhodes was in her sixties and was one of the kindest, most astute people I knew. She had raised four boys, including Emmett, so she took no bullshit from anyone. She had a grounding presence about her, and the second I stepped into her proximity, I didn't have to be anyone but myself. She was one of those people who made everyone around her feel special. I couldn't explain it.

Don't ask me how someone like Emmett came from someone like Elizabeth. I had no clue.

She beamed up at me. "Avery, what a nice surprise."

"I have a salmon burger with a side salad and a chickpea bowl."

She held her hand up. "Chickpea bowl here, please."

"The salmon burger is for me," Emmett said at my side, slipping into his chair. He flashed me a big grin, and I stared at him blankly before turning back to Elizabeth with a pleasant smile.

"Can I get you anything else?" I asked her, ignoring her son.

She shook her head. "No, thank you."

"I'll have another coffee," Emmett added.

"We're out," I said without looking at him.

"Oh, did you hear the news?" Elizabeth asked me. "Emmett here is running for mayor."

I snorted, and my gaze flicked to him.

Elizabeth stood. "Excuse me a moment, I want to wash my hands before I eat."

When she disappeared, I looked around wildly in mock confusion. "Hey, why's it so dark in here?" I kept my voice low so only Emmett could hear me. "I didn't know we were due for an eclipse—oh, that's just your campaign sign blocking out the sun."

An amused grin spread over his features.

"Isaac Anderson has been mayor a long time," I told him.

"I'm aware," he replied, and I saw a flash of indignation in his eyes. "Too long, don't you think?"

"What does that mean?"

"It means I'm tired of the problems in this town, and it's time we had some fresh blood in town hall." He leaned forward and rested his elbows on the table, watching me intently. "Aren't you sick of having to throw out everything in the freezer every time your kitchen loses power?"

I paused. He had a point. We had refined our ordering so we kept as little food on hand as we could, but it wasn't the most efficient process. It would save me time and money if I could buy more food in bulk and store certain things longer.

The image of Isaac and his perfect little family eating at the restaurant the other night flashed into my head. "So, you're going to dethrone Isaac."

"Yep," Emmett confirmed. "I am."

"You should hire someone to play your dutiful little wife," I told him. "Maybe a couple child actors to play your perfect cyborg children. That's the only way you're going to win." I looked him up and down. "No one's going to trust the town bachelor with their tax money."

That got a reaction. He frowned and opened his mouth to say something but shut it when Elizabeth slipped into her seat across from him.

"Avery, I heard about Keiko selling the place," she said, a

sympathetic expression settling on her features. "That's too bad about your loan."

My eyes widened. How did she know? Someone must have overheard Hannah and me in the bookstore this morning. Or maybe someone saw me leaving the bank, looking pissed off.

I nodded, giving her a tight smile while my stomach twisted. Goddamn, this small town. I loved this place, but word spread fast. A knot formed in my stomach at the mention of the loan. "It's unexpected."

She reached out and touched my arm. "I know how much The Arbutus means to you."

I gave her another tight smile. I hated that people knew I couldn't get a loan. Shame boiled in my gut. "I'll figure something out."

Emmett's phone buzzed. "Hi Div," he answered, standing and walking away from the table.

I shook my head after him. So rude. Polite men didn't answer the phone while having lunch with their moms. Especially not moms like Elizabeth.

Through the windows that weren't blocked by the world's largest campaign sign, I spotted a group of people outside, gathering around someone.

"What's going on out there?" I asked.

Elizabeth glanced over. "One of the kids in Ms. Yang's class at school is taking care of the class turtle for the week. Don't tell Emmett, he hates turtles. Avery, honey, did you see the magazine Emmett is on?" She lifted it up to show me, and I studied his image.

Damn, he was good-looking. Too bad his outsides didn't match his insides.

Wait. "What do you mean, he hates turtles?"

She shook her head. "Can't stand them. He ran into one with his bike when he was a kid and crushed it, poor thing."

I wasn't sure whether her *poor thing* referred to Emmett or the turtle, but I had spent enough of my day thinking about him so I gave her another warm smile. "Okay, well, enjoy your food."

Once the lunch rush died down, I retreated to my office and closed the door. I slumped into my chair and let out a long sigh. The bank was concerned I couldn't make payments in the event that the restaurant had to close. I either needed to find another source of income or get a loan from elsewhere.

A wave of despair and hopelessness washed through me, and I sucked a sharp breath in through my nose. I closed my eyes. I would *not* feel sorry for myself, and I would not give up. I was going to find a way to get that money.

4

Emmett

"HI, DIV," I answered with my phone against my ear, walking away from the table.

"The poll numbers are in."

I stepped outside, where it was quieter. "And?"

"Isaac is ahead of you by a full twenty points."

I choked. "Twenty?" My eyes narrowed, and I wandered down the path before taking a seat at one of the benches. "It's early. Our campaign just started. People need time to process the information. Did they say what it was in particular that made them hesitant to vote for me? Is it my experience? Because I have ten years—"

"—experience running a multi-million-dollar construction company, yes, everyone is aware. They saw the magazine cover. It's been very popular on our social media, especially with women twenty to forty."

Realization hit me. "I know what the issue is."

He sighed with relief. "Good. I'm glad it's clear to you, too."

"I'm too handsome to be mayor. People don't trust someone attractive to also be smart and capable."

Damn my parents for passing on their good genes.

Div made an impatient noise. "No, Emmett, this may come as a surprise to you, but being good-looking is helping you in the polls."

I could hear his eyes roll, and I grinned to myself.

"It's that you're single."

Record scratch. I frowned and ran my fingers along the outside of the window. Single pane. I frowned deeper. Single pane windows were really energy inefficient. These must have been part of the original structure of the building. They would let a lot of heat out in the winter and would let the heat in during the summer.

Wait, single? People didn't want me to be mayor because I was single?

"What does that have to do with anything?" I asked Div, shaking my head. "How does my relationship status affect my ability to do the job?"

"It factors into how reliable, trustworthy, and responsible you are," he told me. "Deep down, people figure if someone is willing to date you long-term or marry you, you must be a somewhat decent guy." He cleared his throat. "And you have a long history of—how did Tessa Wozniak put it—hit it and quit it."

I choked out a laugh. "That is not what I do."

"That's what it looks like to everyone."

This was unbelievable. My shoulder muscles tightened, and I shook my head again. "Just because I haven't done the relationship thing doesn't mean I'm irresponsible. That's just not what I want, and it's not what the women I hang out with want."

"I know, I know," Div said. "I'm just giving you the information. Your relationship history and single status are knocking your numbers down."

My mouth pressed into a tight line, and I exhaled through my nose. "Politics are stupid."

"I know," he agreed as if he were a mother consoling a child. "They're very, very stupid."

Irritation twisted in my stomach. I couldn't believe after spending most of my life here except for college, this town still judged me by something as ridiculous as my relationship status. Unbelievable. Why was I even doing this?

I remembered Will's face from a couple days ago when we had packed the boxes into his car. How he looked determined but sad as we scanned through the house to make sure he hadn't forgotten anything.

Right. Will. My best friend. I was doing this for Will, for Nat, and for Kara, so they could move back here, and Kara could have the childhood Will and I had had. She should be growing up here, where her family and community were, not in some apartment building in the city where no one knew each other.

I took a deep breath and rolled my shoulders out. "So, what do we do?"

"We need to find a way to make you look responsible. You'll be volunteering at the food bank next week."

"Great." I narrowed my eyes and grimaced. That wasn't enough, though.

What did Isaac Anderson have that I didn't?

A wife. A family.

Will. What the town wanted was someone like Will. I snorted. That wasn't me. Sure, the idea of a family was nice, for some people—people like Will, people like Isaac. Not people like me.

I didn't buy into the idea that there was someone for everyone, and that everyone needed to be in a relationship. I liked my space. I enjoyed living alone. I liked my things where I left them. I liked my tidy house, and not having to clean up after anyone. I liked coming home whenever I chose to, and not having to check in with anyone. I tried being someone's boyfriend once, and it crashed and burned. It wasn't who I was.

Avery Adams' words flashed into my head.

You should hire someone to play your dutiful little wife.

A slow smile spread over my features. I might be handsome, but damn if I wasn't a genius as well.

"Div, I'm going to need you to reach out to a talent agency in Victoria. We need a woman around my age."

He was silent on the other end.

"Div? You still there?"

"I'm still here." His tone was flat. "I'm afraid to ask, but why do we need a woman from a talent agency?"

"We're going to hire someone to play my girlfriend."

Div groaned, and I grinned. "I'm on it," he said with reluctance.

"Great. Thanks, buddy."

We hung up, and I headed back into the restaurant as a few people were leaving.

"Did you hear Keiko is moving to the mainland?" a woman asked her friend. "She's going to sell the restaurant to Avery."

The other woman shook her head. "No, Avery tried to get a loan this morning, and they rejected her. She doesn't have a high enough income."

The other woman's mouth dropped. "That poor thing."

I watched the women walk away, and I remembered my mom mentioning this inside the restaurant.

Avery Adams wanted to buy this restaurant but couldn't get a loan.

Huh.

My eyes narrowed.

I didn't know much about Adams, besides the fact that she couldn't stand me, but even I knew how hard she worked. Back when she was a server, everyone wanted to be seated in her section because of how attentive she was, how the food always showed up quick and exactly as ordered, and how personable she was. Anyone could see she loved the restaurant, the way she thrived on keeping customers happy, how she took pride in the place.

I thought again about what she had said inside, how Isaac Anderson had a perfect wife and perfect family, and how she said I should hire someone to play my wife.

My skin prickled with that funny feeling I always got at work when I was onto something. When I could sense an opportunity. I didn't build Rhodes Construction to what it was by ignoring my instincts. They always told me when there was an opportunity in front of me.

Avery Adams needed to buy this restaurant, and she didn't have enough money. I needed to win this election, and I didn't have a dutiful little wife to make me look responsible.

She was perfect. Cute, hard-working, independent, and well-liked in town. She was exactly the kind of person people would believe I'd date.

A big grin spread across my face.

———

THE NEXT DAY, I returned to the restaurant. "Is Avery here?" I asked Max.

He shook his head. "Nope, she'll be back soon." He pulled out his phone and checked the time. "In about an hour."

I couldn't wait an hour, I wanted to talk to her now. "Any idea where I can find her?"

"We forced her to go to a movie."

My eyebrow ticked up. "You forced her?"

Max nodded. "Sometimes, she needs encouragement to take a break from this place."

So, Adams was a workaholic. Zero surprise there. I thanked him again and made my way down the street to the theater.

"One, please," I told the teenager working there.

She blinked at me with a bored expression. "The movie's half over."

I nodded. "That's fine. I won't be here long."

She rolled her eyes and took my money before handing me a ticket.

It was dark in the theater, and an old movie from the sixties flashed across the screen. There weren't many people inside, so it didn't take me long to spot her.

"Hi," I said, taking a seat beside her, and she flinched behind her giant tub of popcorn.

She gave me a look that said *ugh, you.* I grinned at her. I loved a challenge.

"What movie is this?" I whispered, reaching over and taking a handful of her popcorn.

She slapped my hand away. "What are you doing?" she whispered back. "Here to convince me to vote for Emmett Rhodes?" She snorted. "Desperate," she mocked in a sing-song whisper.

I tilted my head at her. "You don't like me, do you?"

She gave me a flat look out of the corner of her eye and turned back to the screen. "No."

"What are you doing tonight?"

She gave me an *are you serious* look. "Really? Oh my god, this is so sad. This is beneath you."

"What?" I asked with a frown.

"Asking women out in order to garner votes? Don't you think that's going to catch up with you?"

A laugh choked out of my throat. "That is *not* what I'm doing here."

"Oh, really?" She put on a low voice and jutted her jaw out. "I was looking for you, Avery. What are you doing tonight, Avery? Let me just cross my arms so my biceps pop out."

A huge grin spread across my face, and I glanced down at

my bicep and flexed. "Thanks for noticing all my hard work at the gym. Is that what I sound like?"

Someone shushed us.

"I'm very busy," she whispered. "Please leave."

"I know how you can buy the restaurant."

Her expression changed, and satisfaction settled in my chest.

"What are you talking about?" She watched me, chewing her lip.

Someone shushed us again.

"Harold, you've seen this movie six times!" Avery called over her shoulder. She turned back to me. "What are you talking about?" she whispered again.

I gave her my most charming smile. I wasn't going to tell her yet. Marketing 101 taught me people don't want to give up what they already have. That's why free trials were so effective. I would let Avery mull all afternoon about the possibility of having her restaurant, and by this evening, she wouldn't want to give it up, so she'd accept my deal.

"Do you remember where I live?" I asked.

She frowned. "Emmett. What are you talking about?"

I stood. "Seven o'clock."

"Just tell me now," she hissed after me as I walked out.

"Seven o'clock," I repeated over my shoulder. "Don't eat before."

Outside, I caught my reflection in the glass, and smiled to myself. I was a genius. A handsome goddamn genius.

———

THERE WAS a knock on the door as I filled a pot with water to boil the linguine.

"Come on in, Adams," I called and placed the pot on the stove.

"Adams?" my brother Holden asked, walking into the kitchen.

I turned and frowned. "You can't stay. I have a thing." He didn't need to know the details.

It wasn't unusual for Holden to drop in like this, my brothers and I did this all the time. I didn't want him to hang around and scare Avery off, though. Not before she knew what I could offer.

"Avery Adams?" He tilted his head at me and took a seat at the quartz counter, his gaze skimming over every surface, every plumbing connection. We had installed most of this kitchen ourselves a couple years ago, and he wouldn't let us cut a single corner, even though it was only me living here and I never planned to move or sell this place. "I thought you didn't allow women in your home."

I salted the water. "What? That's ridiculous. Mom comes over all the time."

"*Single* women. You said inviting women over tells them you want a relationship."

That did sound like something I would say. "This is different." I turned and gave him a look. "Did you come here to harass me? Because I have a stack of invoices of yours from four months ago we can talk about."

Holden grunted. "I came to pick up my drill." He glanced at the painting Kara had done a few months ago, pinned to my fridge with a magnet. "How are Will and Nat settling in?"

I shrugged and focused on chopping shallots. "Fine."

"I saw the renters moved in." We had told Will we'd keep an eye on the place and help out if there were any issues.

I swallowed and chopped the shallots into tiny bits. "Yep. Haven't heard about any problems, though."

Holden grunted again.

"What are you making?" he asked, watching me chop.

I gave him an exasperated look. "You're not staying."

"Because Avery's coming over?"

There was another knock on the door and Holden's eyebrows went up. I pointed at the back door. "The drill is in the garage. Out. Now."

His mouth hitched, and he strode out the back door while I dropped the pasta into the boiling water, set a timer, and made my way to the foyer.

She stood on my front step with a hand on her hip and a scowl on her face.

"You showed up," I noted with a grin.

She raised an eyebrow and crossed her arms over her chest. She seemed pissed. Maybe my plan to have her mull things over for the afternoon had backfired.

"Come on in," I said, and she followed me inside without a word. I led her into the kitchen, where I pulled a bottle of white wine out of the wine fridge and worked at removing the cork.

"Why am I here?" she asked, studying my kitchen. She'd never admit it, but I knew a look of admiration when I saw it.

"Take a seat." I gestured at the bar stools and poured her a glass of wine. "Kick your feet up. Relax. You've had a long day."

She glared at me.

I turned my back to her to hide my grin and stirred the pasta in the boiling water. I had my work cut out for me with Avery, but I loved a challenge. The last decade of my life had taught me the bigger the challenge, the better the payoff. Holden and I had worked for months to win a contract to rebuild the hospital a couple towns over. I spent weeks on those job proposals and attended countless meetings, answering question after question. The project manager on their side tested my patience, but eventually, we won the project.

I had been running for mayor for less than a week, and it was already proving to be an uphill climb, but I knew it would be worth it.

The timer for the pasta dinged. I drained it in the sink while she watched. "You're a closed book, Avery. All I know is you don't like me."

She shifted on her stool and glanced between me and the pasta. Steam billowed into the air between us. I tilted my chin at her. "See? Can't stand me. You can barely be in the same room with me. Why is that?"

She glanced around my kitchen, gaze snagging on the top-of-the-line gas stove, fully stocked wine fridge, and bar cabinet with an extensive supply of liquors that rivaled her restaurant. "Get to the point, Emmett." She took a sip of wine.

I checked my sauce over the stove, dipping a spoon in. "You should be my fake girlfriend."

She choked and nearly dropped the glass, catching it with the other hand just in time. I smiled and watched her reaction flip from surprise to confusion to disbelief, to finally, humor.

She barked out a laugh. "What are you talking about? Did you inhale too many paint fumes on a job site?"

"I don't work on job sites, my brother does all that. Here." I carried the spoon of sauce over to her. "Taste this." On instinct, she opened her mouth, and I slipped the spoon between her lips. She blinked in confusion. "Enough salt?"

"No. What?" She sputtered and blinked, and I returned to the stove to add more salt. "Can we go back to the part about me definitely not being your fake girlfriend?"

"I thought you wanted to buy The Arbutus." I glanced at her over my shoulder.

Something flashed across her face. Focus. Determination. Shame. She stared at her wine glass. "I do."

"Everyone in town is talking about how you got rejected for a business loan."

Her nostrils flared and her expression could have singed my eyebrows off. "Everyone is *not* talking about it."

I raised my eyebrows at her.

She glanced down at her wine, and for a moment, I almost

felt bad for her. But then I remembered I was going to offer her a mutually exclusive deal that would give her what she wanted.

"What does this have to do with me not being your fake girlfriend?"

She watched as I plated the pasta—a pesto white wine sauce with sun-dried tomatoes and prawns. It had everything delicious—salt, fat from the olive oil and pesto, sweetness from the tomatoes. Her fingers toyed with the stem of her wine glass.

"I have you to credit for my genius idea, actually," I told her, sliding the plate toward her and pulling forks from the cutlery drawer. "Isaac Anderson has something that I don't— a perfect family of robots." I took the seat beside her and gestured at her food. "I mean, at least try it."

She gave me a withering look out of the corner of her eye, picked up her fork, and ate a bite. "Cyborgs. Max and I call them cyborgs because they're all so perfect," she said and reached for another bite. "I'm not dating you."

I laughed. "Of course not, not for real. It'll all be for show. I just need to show the town I'm a responsible, reliable guy."

"You want to lie to everyone."

I blanched. "Of course not. I *am* a responsible, reliable guy, but people can't seem to get over the fact that I'm single."

"Why would I do this?"

"Because I'm going to loan you the money for the restaurant." I took a bite of pasta and flavor burst on my tongue. "Damn, I'm a good cook. It's the wine, it always makes food better."

She didn't answer. Her fork hovered over her food, and she stared at her wine glass.

My mouth hitched, but I stayed quiet. She was thinking about it. She was turning it over in her mind, inspecting it from all angles, and weighing her options. She had no other choice. I had her right where I wanted her.

Her mouth twisted. "No one is going to believe us."

I had her. She was in, but I kept my expression neutral. "Sure they will."

She shook her head. "It's not going to work. This town knows us. They know we—" She flicked her finger back and forth between us. "—would never."

"Don't say that about yourself, Avery, you're a very attractive woman."

She looked murderous. "That was more about you than me."

"No one is going to believe *you* wouldn't sleep with *me*."

She put her head in her hands. "Oh my god. This isn't happening." She looked up and shook her head. "I'm not doing this. I'm not lying to everyone. It won't work, and it'll blow up in our faces."

I set my elbows on the counter and leaned toward her, resting my chin on my palm, looking into her eyes. "What's your grand plan?"

Her chest rose and fell but she stayed silent. She had nothing. She stabbed her fork into the linguine and took another huge bite. It was good, and she *hated* it was good, and something about that made me very, very happy.

She shook her head. "No. No one is going to believe two people who can't stand each other are together."

"It's only *you* who can't stand *me*," I pointed out. "People believe what they want to."

She stood, making her barstool scrape against the floor. "I'm not doing this." She strode out of the kitchen, so I got up too and followed after her.

"Adams, come on," I told her. "I'm happy to loan you the money. Is it a pride thing? No one will know but me, and I won't even tease you about it."

She shot me another withering look as she opened the door. "I don't need your help."

"You're friends with the Nielsens, right?" Frank Nielsen

owned the bookstore, and I had seen Avery with his daughter, Hannah, a quiet, soft-spoken woman about Avery's age.

Her back stiffened. "Yes."

"Frank uses a CPAP machine at night to breathe. The morning after the last power outage, he wasn't feeling well. I remember him saying he had a headache." This was true, I was talking to him in the hardware store about it. "He had a headache because his brain wasn't getting enough oxygen the night before. Next time the power goes out, he could *die*."

"Oh, shut up," she said, shaking her head. "Frank Nielsen isn't going to die."

I held a solemn expression as I nodded. Yeah, I was reaching, but she put up more of a fight than expected. "Frank might die, and then you'll have to tell Hannah it was your fault. But if we do this and I'm elected mayor, I'm going to upgrade the electrical grid, the power outages will stop, and Frank will live a long, happy life."

"You are so full of shit." She pointed at me and narrowed her eyes. "I knew it from the day I moved to town. You are so full of it, and no one can see past it but me. I would *never* date you."

She closed the door and through the window beside it, I watched her stride down the path to the street.

Well, that didn't go as planned. I rubbed my jaw. Why was she being so stubborn? I opened the door.

"Come on, Adams," I called after her. "You know there's no other way for you to get the restaurant."

She stopped in her tracks, and I smiled at the back of her head twenty feet away. Fucking bingo. Her hands made fists at her sides, and I knew she was picturing terrible, terrible things happening to me. Once she got home, she'd stab needles into a voodoo doll of me.

She faced me and crossed her arms over her chest. The cogs turned in her head. She ran through every single scenario she could think of, any possible option other than giving me what I wanted. Her chest rose as she took a deep breath.

"I'll figure it out," she told me, and fire flashed in her eyes. My eyebrows went up. There was something in her expression that turned me on a little, the fierceness, the determination.

Huh. That's interesting.

"Well, when you do," I told her, "I'll be here waiting."

She walked away, and I pulled out my phone.

"Yes?" Div answered.

"Cancel the actors. I have a better idea."

5

Avery

THE NEXT MORNING, once I had glanced around the street outside the restaurant to make sure no one was watching, I flipped my middle finger at the billboard of Emmett's face as I passed.

I still couldn't believe what he had asked me to do. The ego on him was unparalleled. I laughed out loud at the idea of us pretending to be a couple. I pictured him trying to put his arm around my shoulders while I gagged and pulled away. A snort escaped me. I didn't have the acting skills to pull this off.

Even if I was willing to step into his radius of sickening charisma, no one in this town would believe I would date him.

No one.

In my office, a yellow sticky note sat on my computer screen. *Call Keiko!*

My stomach sank. If Elizabeth knew about me not being able to get a bank loan, Keiko knew, too. Was she going to tell me she found another buyer? Anxiety rippled throughout me at the idea of not only losing the restaurant but someone else owning it.

Emmett's words from last night replayed in my head, and my hands clenched. That guy. I thought about him and his stupid, cocky, knowing grin from the second I got home last night until the moment I fell asleep. I had a terrible sleep, thinking about his stupid deal. There was no way I'd ever agree to play his girlfriend so he could win an election. The thought was revolting. No one would believe us. He'd have better luck convincing people by lugging a blow-up doll around town and naming it Avery.

Not to mention, we would be lying to the entire town. I couldn't do it.

Regarding Isaac Anderson, he had a point. Isaac didn't seem to do much as mayor. The town hosted a million tourists a year and yet there was never enough money for things we desperately needed. Business owners often resorted to crowd-funding or paying out of pocket to fix fallen trees near their property or crumbling sidewalks.

How immoral was it for Emmett to lie to the town if he was doing it for a good reason?

No, I told myself. I would *not* empathize with someone like Emmett Rhodes. Blegh.

That still left me at square one regarding the restaurant. I picked up the sticky note and studied it. Maybe it wouldn't be so bad.

A spike of determination hit me, and I laughed out loud. No way. No freaking way. I was going to figure this out. I just didn't know how yet, and that's what I would tell Keiko.

I dialed her number.

"Hi, sweetie," she answered.

I took a deep breath. "Keiko. Hi. I'm sure you've heard already—"

"That Emmett Rhodes is running for mayor? I know. Interesting."

I frowned. "No. I mean, yes, he is, I don't know who he thinks he's fooling, but it'll be entertaining to watch him try."

Keiko laughed. "You'll have to keep me updated once I'm

in Vancouver. I put an offer in on the townhome yesterday, and the seller accepted."

My eyes widened. "Wow. You put the offer in before selling the restaurant?"

"The real estate agent put a couple conditions in the contract, 'subject to purchase of existing assets'," she told me. "So, I won't be bound to fulfill the contract unless I sell my house here and the restaurant. Standard real estate stuff. I put my house up for sale today, and I already have three offers! Can you believe that?"

"Wow," I repeated. This was moving forward, and it was very, very real. Keiko hadn't mentioned anything about my bank loan rejection. Was it possible she hadn't heard?

"All that's left is for you and me to meet at the bank, and I'm good to go," she said.

She definitely hadn't heard about me getting rejected.

"I was asking them about it this morning when I transferred the deposit for the townhouse," she continued. "The paperwork to sell you the business will be simple."

"Deposit? You put money down on the townhouse?" My stomach turned, and it was as if it was full of rocks. I swallowed.

"It's standard to put down five percent of the purchase price when making an offer. If the deal falls through, the owners keep the deposit. The deal almost never falls through, though. Everyone wants to get paid. I have two months to get everything in order, which is less time than usual but I want to get moving on everything."

My knee bounced up and down and my stomach twisted again. With purchase prices in Vancouver, five percent was a significant amount of money. Keiko would lose that money if she couldn't sell the restaurant in two months.

I didn't have a lot of time to figure things out.

"That's great," I croaked. "So great, Keiko."

"I'm a bit busy this week with the townhouse, but can we set up a meeting at the bank sometime next week?"

"Mhm. That sounds great." I pictured walking back into the bank and them chasing me out, yelling *shoo! Get out of here! We already said no!*

"Wonderful. Talk to you soon, honey."

"Bye, Keiko." I hung up the phone, tossed it onto my desk and put my head in my hands.

Keiko was selling the restaurant, and she was selling it fast. If I didn't figure out a solution soon, she would have no choice but to sell it to someone else.

Emmett's cocky grin flashed into my head, and I groaned.

———

"THERE'S MY SWEETHEART," Emmett grinned as he opened his front door that evening.

I scowled at him.

I hated this. I'd been here for seven seconds, and I hated it. I hated everything about his smug, annoying face. His knowing expression, like he expected me to accept his deal and knew I'd come crawling back because I had no other options. I hated relying on someone else, and I especially hated relying on him because I got the sense he loved it.

But I wanted the restaurant, and I wanted to make things as smooth as possible for Keiko. So, I was doing this.

"Okay," I forced the word out of my mouth.

His eyebrows went up. "Okay?"

"Okay."

He beamed at me and extended his arms. "Let's do a practice hug."

I put aside my rage and focused on plotting Emmett's slow, painful death. "You can hug me in your mind," I told him, walking past him into his home.

"We're going to need to practice affection if we want to sell this," he called after me, closing the front door.

A few minutes later, we sat in the living room. Giant windows overlooked the forest around the house. Anywhere else, I would have wondered if the room would get too hot in the early evening sun, but the towering, two-hundred-year-old fir trees kept the place shaded and cool. The decor throughout the house was mid-century modern, all dark woods and clean lines, with the occasional interesting painting or vase, and big leafy plants. Photos of Emmet's family popped up once in a while. The whole place had a Mad Men vibe to it and I wondered if he had chosen the decor himself. Probably not. Men like Emmett paid people to do things like this.

"The election is in two months," Emmett informed me. "You know this town, as soon as they find out you and I are dating, they're going to go nuts."

He was right. Something like this would be all over town.

"When do you need the money? I can have the lawyer draft up a loan contract," he said, pulling out his phone.

I shook my head. "I'd rather you cosign on my loan." After this was all over, I'd rather pay the bank directly instead of him. Paying him would feel like I was on the hook long after this was all over. This deal was already humiliating enough, and I wanted to part ways with him as soon as I could.

He shrugged and put his phone away. "Sure, that's fine."

"And I'll be the sole owner of the restaurant," I told him.

He snorted. "I have no desire to get into the restaurant business. It's all yours, Adams."

I nodded, and the tension in my chest eased a little. I may be selling my soul to the devil, but at least he was agreeing to my terms.

"Five public appearances a week," Emmett said.

I rolled my eyes. "Public appearances? Who are you, a nineteen-year-old popstar?"

"We can call them dates if you prefer." He winked at me.

"One *public appearance* a week."

"We'll split the difference. Two a week." He didn't wait for me to agree. "How much PDA are you comfortable with?"

In my mind's eye, I pictured Emmett and myself making out on a park bench like teenagers. I was straddling his lap, and his hands were in my hair. I blinked and shook it out of my head. *That* would not be happening.

"What?" he asked, frowning. "What's that face?"

"Nothing." I swallowed. My cheeks warmed. "Light hand holding."

He laughed. "*Light* hand holding? What does that even mean? How is that different from regular hand holding?"

Er, I wasn't sure. "I just want to avoid your politician's death grip."

He grinned at me. "Adams, no one is going to believe I'm dating a woman who will only allow some 'light hand holding' in public."

I sighed. He was right. "Okay, public affection is fine, just don't be gratuitous about it, alright?"

He raised an eyebrow at me. "Are you sure? I'm serious about this, I don't want to make you uncomfortable."

I gave him a flat look. "I'll be fine. If you make me uncomfortable, I'll let you know."

He leaned back in his chair, balancing his ankle on his knee, regarding me. "There's one more thing. I need a pair of your underwear."

I choked on my wine, almost spitting it out onto Emmett's couch. "What? Why?"

He grinned devilishly. "You'll see."

I shook my head. "So people can catch you sniffing them? No, thanks."

His devilish grin widened. "My brothers are always over at my place. What better way to sell them on us than them finding evidence of us getting it on?"

I gagged. "Never say *getting it on* and *us* in the same sentence ever again."

He looked at me expectantly.

"A sock," I relented. "I'll give you a sock."

He put his hands up. "We'll work our way up to underwear. Buy the nice stuff instead of whatever three-pack budget brand you wear."

My mouth fell open. "I do *not* wear budget underwear."

His mouth hitched again and he raised his eyebrows, watching me. "Oh, yeah? Tell me more about your underwear. This is great practice."

My face heated, and I took another long slug of wine. "Is it a bad sign I'm regretting this so early on?"

He laughed. "Eye on the prize, Adams. You'll get your restaurant soon enough."

He was right. The restaurant deal was a sure thing for me, but there was no guarantee for Emmett. I cocked my head at him.

"What if you don't win?"

He leaned on the armrest of his chair, smiling at me. "I will."

"I just want to make sure if you don't win, because people see through your extra-schmoozey smiles and faux questions of concern, my deal isn't going to fall through."

He glanced out the window. "I'm going to win." He leaned forward, resting his elbows on his knees, and looked at me. "And as my girlfriend, you're going to need to believe I'm going to win, too, otherwise no one in town will buy this." He gestured back and forth between us. "But let's say some meteor hits Queen's Cove, wipes out the entire population except for the Andersons, and I don't win."

I held back a grin. I would *not* laugh, mostly because I didn't think he was joking.

"You'll still get your restaurant." He shrugged. "I know you're good for the money. You have too much pride."

The sun was setting, and the warm light caught his gray eyes and gave his skin a golden hour glow. He watched me with a knowing expression, like he could see beneath my skin. The back of my neck prickled. I didn't like how naked I felt when he looked at me like that.

But a tiny, minute fraction of me *did* like it. I brushed that feeling aside as fast as I could.

"So, after the election, we tell everyone we've broken up," I tell him.

He nodded. "I figured we'd stop going on dates—"

"Public appearances," I corrected.

"We'd stop going on public appearances, and then after a month or two, break the news we had broken up."

"We should tell people we've been together for a while and wanted to keep it secret," I mused.

His eyes lit up. "Great idea."

"What about dating?"

"That's what we're doing."

"No, I mean, dating other people." I sent him an emphasized look. "You aren't known for being celibate."

He barked a laugh of disbelief. "Neither are you."

My brows furrowed. "What are you talking about?"

A muscle in Emmett's jaw ticked. "You usually date summer workers. Elizabeth mentioned you seeing some guy last summer, some guy who worked at Wyatt's surf shop." He surveyed me. There was something hard in his gaze. Irritation. "Seems like you always date people who have a defined date to go home, is that right?"

I was speechless. My mouth opened and closed, and I looked around the room. "Okay, so? I'm not looking for anything long-term and—" I shrugged. "—I'm a human and sometimes I need to get laid."

The irritation faded from his eyes and a grin spread across his face. He looked absolutely delighted. He loved this conversation. He'd probably write it in his diary and re-read it again and again.

"Is there anything wrong with that?" I asked, defensive.

"Of course not." His gaze skimmed over my form so briefly, I could have blinked and missed it. "Sex is important."

My skin heated. "Great. I think if we're discreet and no one finds out about it, it's okay for us to date on the side."

He shifted on the couch and rested his arm up along the back of it. So casual, except his eyes, narrowed on me. "No."

"Excuse me?" My eyebrows shot up.

He shrugged. "Too risky." He was very interested in something out the window, and kept his gaze glued there as he rubbed his jaw.

"You expect me to stay celibate?"

Look, I'd done it before. Of course I had. It wasn't a big deal. It was two months. But the second I was told I couldn't have something, I wanted it.

His gaze cut to me. "Didn't know you were such a horndog." The corner of his mouth tugged up but his jaw was still tense.

I stood. "That's my cue to leave."

That amused look was back. "Adams, I'm happy to provide as many boyfriend services as you need." He followed me out of the living room to the foyer. "Day or night."

I shook my head to myself. This was a mistake. Huge mistake. "Don't wait by the phone." I opened the door and stepped outside without another word.

"Avery." Something sober in his voice made me pause, and I turned. He leaned against the doorframe with a thoughtful expression. Thick, dark lashes rimmed his eyes, and a tiny white scar sliced through his upper lip, barely noticeable. "I only go into business with people I trust." He watched me, crossing his arms over his chest. "Can I trust you?"

I let the question hang there in the air. "I don't feel good about lying to everyone, but if you're going to fix the grid like you say you will…" My words trailed off. "Yeah, you can trust me." I pointed a finger at his chest. "Can I trust you?"

He flashed me that wide politician's smile with all his white teeth. "Of course you can trust me."

I rolled my eyes. "Jesus Christ, you need to do better than that if you want to be mayor."

His laugh followed me as I walked down the path, out of his yard. What had I gotten myself into? By the time I unlocked my door, I knew there were no other options. Besides, it was a couple months. I could do this. I'd be busy with the restaurant and they would pass faster than expected.

And at the end of it, I'd have my restaurant.

I smiled to myself, closing my eyes with excitement. The Arbutus would be mine, and it would be in my hands to carry on Keiko's family legacy. No one could take it from me, no one could override my decisions, and no one could derail my dream. I'd be in full control. This ridiculous fake dating thing with Emmett was one tiny steppingstone to the rest of my life, and in five years, I wouldn't even remember it.

6

Emmett

BLOOD RUSHED in my ears and my feet hit the path, one after the other. My lungs burned as I ran, and I focused on my breathing and on the light peeking through the trees.

I was on my morning run, and today was tougher than normal. Last night, I was too excited to sleep. She said yes.

I couldn't believe she said yes.

To be fair, she didn't have much of a choice. A pang of guilt wrenched in my chest as I remembered the anguish on her face when she realized I was her only option. Everyone needed to be happy for deals to work, and even though I was doing this to win the election, I truly wanted her to walk away feeling like she got what she wanted.

I shrugged my guilt off. She'd get her restaurant. I was cosigning on a loan for someone who was almost a stranger. She'd walk away happy, it might just take a few weeks.

The revulsion on her face when I asked for a pair of her underwear still made me laugh, though.

My watch beeped, indicating my heart rate was getting too low and that I needed to pick up the pace. I groaned and pushed myself harder, carrying myself through the forest paths toward the beach.

When I reached the sand, sweat poured down my face and my hair was soaked. I slowed to a walk and took a seat on a log, staring at the ocean as the waves crashed on the shore. Damn, this place was gorgeous. I shook my head and admired the brightening sky with its sunrise tones.

I unlocked my phone and saw I had a missed call from Will.

My throat tightened. Something was wrong. Something had happened with Kara or Nat.

"Hey," he answered when I called back.

"Is everything okay? What happened?"

"Everything's fine," he told me. "Relax. I was up early and just wanted to say I heard the good news, Mr. Mayor."

I exhaled my relief and grinned. "I'm not mayor yet."

"Yeah, but you will be. That town worships the ground you walk on, always has."

I thought about my low poll numbers. "How's the family doing?"

"Good, we're setting up the apartment and unpacking still. Kara misses her Uncle Emmett."

I propped my elbow on my knee and leaned my chin on my palm. "I miss that kid, too." My mouth pressed into a line as I stared at the water. "I'm going to fix the electrical grid, Will. It might take a couple years, but I'm going to do it. Kara should grow up here in Queen's Cove, where her family is. She should grow up the way we did."

"It's not so bad here," Will said, but I could tell he was putting on a brave face and trying to stay positive. "I hope you're not—" His voice broke off.

"What?"

"I hope you're not running for mayor just for us. I could never ask you to do that. You have a business to run. You have a life. Being mayor is a big commitment."

Was I doing this for Will? Of course, I was. He was my

best friend. He'd do the same for me in an alternate universe where the situation was reversed.

The more I thought about being mayor, the more I campaigned, created my platform, and spoke with locals, the more I wanted it. I wanted to fix Queen's Cove. It wasn't just for Will, it was for everyone who lived here. I wanted this magnificent place to shine the way it should.

Will's situation was just the catalyst.

"You guys moving gave me the idea," I admitted. "But I want to make this town what it should be. The business is doing well, and I trust my management team. I'm ready for a new challenge. I want this."

"Well, for what it's worth, Rhodes, I appreciate it." Will's voice was thick.

"Don't get all sappy on me. You can cry when I win."

He laughed. "Asshole."

A big grin pulled across my face.

"Well, I should get going," he said. "Just wanted to say congrats. Let me know if I can do anything, okay? Do you need help with the website?"

"Nah, my team has it handled. Thanks, buddy. Talk to you soon."

We hung up, and I sat there on the beach, watching the sky become brighter as the sun rose higher, thinking about what the next month had in store for me. First, I had to make my relationship with Avery known to the town. There was a town fair starting tomorrow night. A thrill of excitement hit my chest, and I grinned. I wasn't a relationship kind of guy, not like Will, but dragging Avery around town and enduring her eye rolls and irritation was going to be fun. Something about her made me laugh.

Deep in my mind, a little spike of nerves hit me. I had always had a little *thing* for Adams. She was fun to irritate. It was too easy with her. The woman just did not like me, not one bit. She always held that wall up.

Now, we'd be spending time together and pretending to be a couple. My knee bounced at the thought of it. It was dangerous.

Good thing it would all be fake. Avery would keep that wall up and nothing would happen. Things would stay the same as they always were. I'd carry on, become mayor, and fix this town, while she'd get her restaurant, and both of us would walk away happy.

I made my way off the beach, back into the forest, and ran home with a renewed sense of energy.

7

Avery

"WE HAVE to make the town suspect something." I was back at Emmett's place, standing at the patio door in his living room, looking out into the forest behind his house. A thick canopy of emerald-green towered over the small backyard. Two blue jays zipped in and out of a tree. My eyes narrowed. "We need to get the Queen's Cove rumor mill going."

Over on the couch, he cocked an eyebrow at me. "Nothing stays secret in this town. What are you thinking?"

"Phone Ricci's Pizza and order a medium pizza with dairy-free cheese, pear, and arugula. Make sure you specify no mushrooms."

He winced. "That's your order? What's wrong with you?"

I gave him a knowing look. "That's what Mateo says every time I order it. He tells me I'm insulting his family's Italian heritage with that pizza. Also, order it after midnight. I always call when I'm on my way home from the restaurant."

He noted down my order before reaching into his wallet. He fished out a little paper ticket. "My dry cleaning should be ready tomorrow."

I choked in disbelief. "You're kidding."

"What?"

"I'm not picking up your dry cleaning."

"That's what girlfriends do."

Oh my god, this man. "Maybe in the fifties."

"I thought you were supposed to be dutiful." A smug grin pulled at his mouth.

I snorted. "You picked the wrong girl for that." I tapped my chin with my finger, thinking. "How about I pick up your campaign signage at the post office?"

The print shop for our little town doubled as the post office.

I walked over and leaned against the back of the couch. "There's always a lineup at lunch when everyone is on their break. I'll go then and everyone will see me running an errand for you."

This seemed to satisfy him. "Perfect. We'll give it a few days, and then Friday, we'll walk through the town fair together."

Right. The town fair, where this bizarre ruse would begin. I was dreading it. All those eyes, watching and whispering about us made my stomach churn, but there was no other way to get my restaurant than to dive into this, head-first.

I nodded, taking a deep breath. "Friday."

———

"STOP JERKING YOUR HAND AWAY," Emmett whispered. "We're supposed to be in love."

I could feel the eyes watching us, lingering on our backs as we wandered through the vendor booths. This year's fair theme was mushrooms.

Yeah, mushrooms.

The fair happened twice a year, sometimes three times if the town's Fair Planning Board felt like it. The theme usually revolved around food (apples, pumpkins, cherries, peaches), and sometimes holidays (Halloween, Christmas, Valentine's Day).

I regarded the tray of stuffed mushrooms at a booth run by a local caterer and bit back my revolted expression. The Fair Planning Board must have run out of ideas.

I freaking hated mushrooms.

Emmett slipped his hand into mine again, and I fought the urge to yank it away. We had agreed on doing one quick loop of the fair, just to be seen, and then I could go home. I tried to relax my hand.

"There you go." He grinned at me. "Just like that."

Deep breaths, I told myself as irritation spiked on the back of my neck.

"Emmett." A woman appeared in front of us, a big grin on her face. Her eyes glowed with excitement, darting between our hands, myself, and Emmett.

"Hey, Miri." He turned to me. "Avery, do you know Miri?"

I nodded and smiled at her. "Hi, there."

Miri Yang was in her early forties and was a teacher at the high school as well as an active volunteer around town. The woman was a social butterfly, constantly meeting friends for lunches and helping with town events. She was always in a cheerful mood, consistently polite, and tipped my staff well.

My hand twitched, but Emmett held firm.

Miri's gaze returned to where my hand connected with Emmett's. "Oh, yes, I see Avery all the time at The Arbutus."

"How's Scott doing?" Emmett asked.

She dragged her gaze up again to his. "He's good. You know him, he always wants to keep everyone happy, but it's impossible." She shrugged and shook her head. "He just has such a good heart." Her eyes flicked back to our hands. "So, the rumors are true."

Emmett squeezed my hand, and I ignored it.

"Rumors?" His voice was innocent. "What rumors?"

Miri's gaze snapped up, and she smiled brightly. "That you two are together. I didn't believe it."

I pressed my lips together, hiding a grin. I liked Miri more by the second.

"Believe it." Emmett let my hand go and wrapped an arm around my shoulder. "I finally convinced this one to go public."

I just stood there.

"Right, honey?" Emmett dropped his head to catch my gaze.

I nodded at Miri. "We're so in love." My tone sounded flat.

She clapped and clasped her hands together. "I knew it."

Don't laugh, I told myself. *You'll blow this whole thing*.

"We need to get dinner together." Miri pulled out her phone and flipped through her calendar. "Scott will be so happy to hear you're settling down, Emmett."

"Absolutely." He pulled out his phone as well. "Sunday?"

Miri's eyes lit up. "Sunday it is!"

"Great. See you then."

Miri twiddled her fingers at us as she left, and Emmett turned to me. "We're so in love?" He repeated my words from earlier. "Can you sound more convincing?"

My mouth dropped open. "What about you? *Honey?*"

There was challenge in his eyes. "Miri ate it right up."

He had me there.

"Let's keep walking." He grabbed my hand again and pulled me toward a booth. "We need to circulate."

I let Emmett lead me through the fair while his hand grasped mine. It could have been worse. His hand could have been sweaty. It wasn't, though. His hand was big and warm, and I fit into it perfectly. It was almost comfortable. I was almost having an okay time.

Someone gasped.

Almost.

"I knew it." Mateo, the pizza shop owner, shook his head at us. "I friggin' knew it. The second you called in that order, Emmett, I told my guys, those two are sneaking around." He shook his head at us. "I friggin' knew it."

His wife, Farrah, beamed at us. "I hoped it was true." She squeezed a plush toy to her chest. "How sweet. I'm so happy for you two."

"Thanks, Farrah." Emmett returned her smile. "Nice toy."

She beamed again and nudged Mateo. "My husband won it for me."

And that was how we ended up at the darts booth.

"We agreed on one loop of the fair." I gave him a flat look.

"This is what people in a relationship would do." Emmett pulled a twenty out of his pocket before he exchanged it for a handful of darts. "I'm going to win you a dumb little toy, and you're going to carry that thing around all night."

I scoffed. "Wow, macho much? The caveman's stick hit you extra hard."

He glanced around to make sure no one would overhear us. He wore a little grin on his face when he leaned in, and I got a clear view of his light gray eyes, filled with humor. The little scar on his lip quirked. "Dutiful," he reminded me.

That was it. I yanked my wallet out of my bag.

"What are you doing?"

"You want to win something for me?" I pulled a bill out of my wallet and handed it to the teenager behind the booth. "I'm going to win something for *you*. And you also have to carry it around all night."

I had never played darts in my life, but something about Emmett got to me. Maybe it was that smug expression. Or maybe it was that little scar on his lip that kept capturing my attention.

The teenager handed me some darts, and I gestured at Emmett. "Are we on or what?"

A big grin spread over his face. "Absolutely. Whatever I win for you, you have to cart around all night."

I nodded. "And if I win that enormous mushroom——" I pointed at the massive stuffed toy hanging from the roof with the rest of the toys. It must have been bigger than me. "——you have to carry it around all night."

"Great." His eyes shone with competition and challenge.

"Wonderful." I gave him my most confident smile.

"Ladies first."

I positioned my feet in a way that felt right and closed one eye as I threw my first dart at the board.

It bounced off.

Shit.

"Don't worry about it, Adams." Emmett aimed for his own board. "The first one's just to loosen you up." He threw the dart and hit the bull's eye. My mouth fell open, but I closed it as Emmett shot a satisfied grin over his shoulder at me. "Your turn."

I swallowed.

"So," he asked the teenager, "if I hit three bull's eyes, I can pick whatever toy I want?"

The teenager shrugged. "Yep. Anything."

Emmett pointed at a mushroom toy with a big hole in it. "Even that hat?"

Oh my god. A strangled noise came out of my throat. It was a mushroom *hat*. Oh my god. No. I could feel myself grimacing. Wearing that would be complete humiliation.

The teenager nodded. "Sure, but no one ever wants that one."

"I wonder why." My gaze bored into Emmett, but he threw me a winning grin.

"Go ahead, Adams. You're up."

Behind us, a group of people gathered to watch. I took a steadying breath and threw the dart. It hit the board near the edge.

Better, but not good enough.

Emmett whistled. "Close."

"Shut up."

He aimed his dart and tossed it like it was nothing. It hit the bull's eye, and the crowd applauded behind us. I could feel my mood souring but wouldn't give Emmett the satisfaction of it. I rolled my shoulders.

Emmett threw darts with ease. I just had to throw it like he did. I shook out my arm before I let the dart fly.

It whizzed past the teenager's shoulder, but he jumped out of the way. "Hey!"

"Sorry." I winced. There were murmurs in the crowd behind us, and more people stopped by to see what the fuss was about.

Emmett shook his head. "Adams, you punch above your weight, and I like that." He threw the dart and again, it connected with the bull's eye.

The crowd behind us erupted, and I rolled my eyes.

He looked like a kid on Christmas. "One mushroom hat, please." Delight dripped off his words.

The teenager pulled the stupid thing down and handed it to Emmett. He shook it out to fluff it up and took a step toward me. It was red and brown and white, all poofy. It was horrifying. This was the stuff of nightmares.

I took a step away from him. "No."

His grin widened. "Adams, I thought you were a woman of your word."

"I am." I glanced between him and the hat.

"Put the hat on so I can take a picture, and then I'll go get us some mushroom ice cream."

I made a face.

"We can leave as soon as you put the hat on."

I sighed and grabbed it out of his hand. The second I yanked it onto my head, I regretted it.

"Avery, don't you look adorable!" Miri trilled, her phone in front of her as she snapped pictures. "This is going to go straight on the Queen's Cove blog."

"I will make you pay for this," I murmured to Emmett as he wrapped an arm around me, posing for Miri's picture. I glared at her camera.

"I look forward to it, Adams."

8

Emmett

"AVERY, it was so nice running into you at the fair," Miri told her. "I hardly see you outside The Arbutus."

The four of us—myself, Avery, Scott and Miri Yang—were out for dinner Sunday night at Bob's Barbeque. Scott Yang was the head of the local trade union. Holden and I had known the guy since we started our company and always took him and Miri out for dinner around Christmastime. He was a nice guy to work with, never lost his temper, and was punctual. On the rare occasion there was a dispute with any of the trades guys regarding Rhodes Construction, he brought it to us immediately and was straight with us. He was fair, always willing to share the responsibility, and he was well respected by the couple hundred members of the union—which was why I needed to secure his endorsement in the election.

Miri was no slouch in the influence department, either. She knew everyone and was liked by all. She was also extremely talkative and effusive, and if we nailed this tonight, she'd be a major advocate of the validity of our relationship.

"The restaurant keeps me busy, but I love it." Avery glanced between Miri and the menu. "I feel like it's my baby I'm leaving with a babysitter for the first time."

Miri laughed. "I've been there many times, and you have that place running like a navy ship."

"Oh, I don't know about that." Avery smiled into her menu.

"It's true." Scott nodded at her. "I'll send you some of my younger trades guys, you can scare them straight."

Avery's expression turned devious, and we all laughed.

I watched her. She was a fucking natural. I should have known.

And me? I was a fucking genius. Never again would I bring Holden along to one of these dinners. I loved my brother, but the guy was a terrible conversationalist. There was no small talk with that guy, no polite questions, no inquiring about how someone's work was going. He always just sat there, ate his food, and listened while I chatted away with whoever we were eating with.

But now? I was never taking another client or potential endorsement out for dinner again without her by my side.

My gaze snagged on Avery's neckline and the smooth skin of her collarbone. She had nailed it in the "looking sharp" department, with a white silk t-shirt, black jeans, and black suede heels. I was no women's fashion expert, but she had dressed nice enough to show respect to our dinner guests but not so over the top that it made Miri uncomfortable. Her ass looked amazing in those jeans.

"That is a gorgeous necklace," Miri noticed, and Avery's hand came to the old-looking silver pendant hanging around her neck.

Avery nodded with enthusiasm. "Oh, thank you, it's vintage," she told Miri. "If there's ever anything you're looking for, let me know. I know all the good vintage sites, and I have a few friends in Victoria who give me a heads-up when they get new stock in."

Miri's eyes lit up. "That would be amazing."

I was a goddamn genius. Who knew Avery could be so

likeable? Not me. She was friendly, sweet, Miri and Scott already liked her, she asked all the right questions and she laughed in all the right parts of the story. Was this what it was like to not have to carry the conversation? I grinned to myself. *Isaac Anderson, I'm coming for you*, I thought.

"Well, Avery," Scott said, interrupting my barrage of self-congratulations. "You've got a good one here. Emmett is a good man." He nodded at me. "Works hard to make sure his employees are happy and always does the right thing."

She raised an eyebrow at me in disbelief. "Oh, does he?"

I nodded at her with a look that said *play along*. "Yep. I'm a good guy, Avery." The side of my mouth hitched. "That's why you're dating me, right?" I gave her a wink, just to push her boundaries a little.

I thought about her in that mushroom hat and nearly burst out laughing. Okay, I wasn't a good guy, but it was worth it to see her wearing that hilarious hat.

She watched me for a beat with eyes narrowed but a small smile on her lips. "Exactly. That's why I'm dating you."

"A partner is a great thing, Emmett." Scott put his arm around Miri and she gazed up at him in adoration. "Eleven years in, and I can't imagine my life without Miri."

I nodded and smiled at them. "That's sweet."

Miri nudged Scott. "He had to convince me, but best decision I ever made."

Avery's mouth twisted. "Oh, there was some convincing on Emmett's part."

Scott leaned forward. "I have to say, I was surprised to hear about you two. Emmett, you never seemed like you wanted to settle down." He nodded at Avery. "Until now, of course."

I still didn't want to settle down. The idea of a wife and family turned my stomach. It was great for Will. Will always wanted a family. But me? I liked being alone.

But Scott didn't know that.

"What can I say?" I reached out and grabbed Avery's hand on her lap. "I found my soulmate." I squeezed her hand, and she returned my squeeze with a death grip. I grinned at her. She did *not* like that soulmate comment. "Right, honey?"

"Right, darling," Avery replied through gritted teeth.

"You're so in love." Miri let out a wistful sigh.

Avery nodded with pressed lips. "Mhm. We're *so* in love."

"Avery, you're from Vancouver, right?" Scott asked.

"Yep, moved here about five years ago."

"Do your parents live there?" Miri leaned forward and rested her chin on her palm. "Are they still together?"

"They still live there, but they divorced years ago."

Miri gave her a sympathetic look. "Aw, I'm sorry to hear that."

Avery shook her head adamantly. "Don't be, getting divorced was the best choice they ever made."

Huh. Interesting. I had never thought about Avery's family before, but now my curiosity was piqued. Maybe this had something to do with her never having anything long-term, relationship-wise, in town. I watched her for a moment.

"I have a pitcher of Bob's Margaritas," the server said as she placed it on the table.

Avery gave the server a grateful look. "Thank you." She poured out four glasses.

Miri clasped her hands together with excited eyes. "Tell us the story of how you got together."

Avery and I glanced at each other with uncertainty. We hadn't covered this when we hashed out the details.

"Well," Avery started, at a loss for words.

I said the first thing that came to mind. "She was surfing."

She blinked at me, and I held back a laugh. I would bet my yearly salary she had never been on a surfboard in her life, despite it being one of Queen's Cove's major tourist attractions.

She nodded, holding a pleasant expression but boring into

me with her eyes. I'd pay dearly for this later. "Exactly. I was surfing."

I turned to Miri and Scott. "I was with my brother Wyatt at his surf shack, and we noticed the wind picking up."

Scott's head was tilted in interest, and Miri nodded with wide eyes, leaning forward, hanging on to every word. She looked to Avery. "Were you alone out on the ocean?"

I put a hand on Avery's upper back, wincing and nodding. "She was. Classic beginner mistake." Under my hand, her shoulder muscles tensed. "Wyatt was busy with customers, so I grabbed a board and ran out there to make sure she was okay."

Scott nodded with approval. "Good man."

"That's so sweet," Miri cooed. "I hope you put a wetsuit on, that water is so cold."

I shook my head at them with a *whatcha gonna do* expression. "There was no time, and I had to make sure she was okay."

Avery made a choking noise in her throat, and I turned to her, rubbing her back. "Are you okay, sweetheart?"

The look she gave me could have burned my corneas off. "I'm great, honey. So great," she managed. She tensed her shoulder muscles again, and I knew this was her way of saying *get your fucking hands off me.*

"Anyway," I said, turning back to Miri and Scott, leaving my hand on her back. "I got out on the water, and it was really choppy. The wind was picking up, the swells were getting bigger and there were some gnarly waves coming in, as Wyatt would say."

Miri chewed her lip, and Scott frowned with concern.

I leaned in toward Miri. "I spotted Avery just as a wave knocked her off her board."

Avery dropped her head into her hand in exasperation.

"Oh, no," Miri breathed. She was leaning so far toward me, she was inches from lying on the table.

I nodded at her. "Oh, yeah. I paddled over as fast as I could on my board. Avery was nowhere to be found." I shook my head. "I saw her board floating, but she wasn't there. At this point, I was so scared. The tie strap around her ankle must have come loose when the wave knocked her off. I had to find her."

"Where was she?" Miri urged.

"I was heartbroken, thinking she had drowned. Just then, she surfaced beside my board, gasping for air," I told them.

"Thank god," Scott said, shaking his head.

"She looked up at me, coughing and gagging up water—"

"Okay," Avery interrupted, but I cut her off.

"She grabbed my board and said—"

Miri's eyes bugged out of her head. "What? What did she say?"

"She said, 'Is that you, Henry Cavill?'"

Out of the corner of my eye, Avery turned to stare at me dead on. I didn't dare look at her. I would either start laughing and never stop, or burst into flames from the intensity of her gaze.

I took a deep breath and let it out, rubbing my hand on her back again, still not looking at her. "And that's when I knew I was in love with her."

Miri pressed her lips together and clasped her hands over her necklace. "You are so brave. What a story! Isn't that an incredible story, Scott?"

Scott shook his head in amazement. "It sure is." He held up the margarita in front of him. "Let's do a toast. To love."

"To love," Miri and I chorused after him.

Beside me, Avery chugged her drink until only the ice remained.

The food arrived, and between Avery and I, we managed to steer the conversation away from us and to the town, and eventually, the power outages.

Scott shook his head. "It's tough on the older folks when

the power goes out, especially in the winter when it's damp and cold as hell."

I nodded. "It's disruptive, and I think a lot of people in town have just gotten used to it and accepted it." I sat back. "Anytime discussion about upgrades come up at town hall meetings, they're shrugged off as too expensive, too much work." I squeezed my napkin in my hand, frowning. "That doesn't feel good enough to me, so I'm doing something about it." Scott was listening intently, and I could see he was trying to stay neutral. "I know you're in a position where you feel you can't get involved with the election, and I'm not asking you to. I don't know your relationship with Isaac. All I know is any work on our electrical grid will be done using your tradespeople. These won't be short employment stints where they're back looking for work in a couple weeks. Some of this work will take years."

Scott nodded and studied his plate, thinking.

Miri shrugged. "I'm not head of the union, and I can do whatever I want. I'm voting for you, Emmett."

I gave her my most winning smile. "Miri, I do adore you, I hope you know that."

She grinned and blushed.

"You're right that it's usually recommended I don't get involved in local politics," Scott said, crossing his arms over his chest.

I raised my hands in surrender. "That's fine, and however you vote, it won't affect our friendship or working relationship. Rhodes Construction is committed to using high-quality labor through your union, regardless of the outcome of the election."

Scott shifted in his chair. "I usually abide by that recommendation, but you're right." He shook his head at all of us. "I'm sick of these problems. I tell our guys every morning, *see a problem, fix a problem*. It's irresponsible to just sit by and watch this happen to our town and not do anything about it." He glanced between Avery and me. "I used to think you were just out to have fun and make some cash, but I've always thought Avery had a good head on her shoulders, so if you're good enough for her—" He reached across the table to shake my hand. "Emmett, you've got my vote."

Pride swelled in my chest, and I tried to stay calm. This was big. This was an enormous win for me and the campaign. Winning the election was one step closer.

I accepted Scott's crushing handshake with my most modest, bashful smile. "Scott, you have no idea how much I appreciate that. I look up to you, how you manage your guys and how they respect you. I hope I can make you proud as mayor."

"I bet you will." The server started clearing our plates and Scott looked around the table. "How about dessert to celebrate the happy couple?"

"That would be great. Sweetheart, would you like to split some cheesecake?" I asked Avery. Splitting dessert, what could be more romantic than that?

She shook her head. "I'm lactose intolerant."

"What?" I blanched. "That's awful." I remembered her favorite pizza had dairy-free cheese on it, and now it made sense.

Miri sent me a chastising look. "Emmett, you need to remember things like this. You sound like you hardly know her." She laughed. "Imagine that."

Avery cocked her head at me, a little grin forming on her pretty mouth. "Yeah, Emmett, it's like I'm a total stranger to you."

I raised my eyebrows at her in challenge. Did she forget how easy it was to embarrass her? I did it earlier with that stupid surfing story, and I'd do it again. And I'd enjoy every second of it as she got embarrassed and tried to disappear into the floor.

"Quick," Miri clapped her hands. "Let's play a game."

Our heads whipped toward her. "What game?" Avery and I asked in unison, both with a heavy dose of suspicion.

"The newlyweds game. It's easy and *so fun*. I'll ask you questions about each other, and you write down the answers." She flagged down a server for some paper and a couple pens.

I had a bad feeling about this. We didn't think there was going to be a *test*, for Christ's sake.

Avery exhaled slowly out of her nose. "Sounds super fun."

"Okay," Miri said once Avery and I had the paper in front of us, wiggling her eyebrows. "Name each other's birthday."

Avery and I sat there in silence, staring at our papers.

"February…" I winced. "…fourteenth?"

She snorted. "That's Valentine's Day."

"You're supposed to write it down," Miri reminded us.

"It can be both," I said defensively. "People are born on Valentine's Day. And you don't know my birthday. It's January 27th."

"I was just about to say that."

"Right. And when is yours?"

Miri cleared her throat. "You don't need to say it, you write it down, and I'll read the answers."

"September 12th."

I pointed at her. "That was my second choice."

We turned back to Miri and Scott, who were watching us with hesitation.

"Next question," Avery demanded, her voice heavy with competition.

"This is just supposed to be a silly, fun game," Miri said, laughing. "We don't need to—"

"Next question, Miri," I told her.

Her eyes widened a fraction. "Favorite movie."

I narrowed my eyes at Avery, sizing her up. "Something with Audrey Hepburn. What's that one where she goes to France?"

Her head whipped toward me, and she regarded me with suspicion. "*Funny Face*. How did you know that?"

I shrugged. "You kind of look like Audrey Hepburn, and I took a wild guess."

Miri squealed and clapped, and a smug smile settled on my face. I gave Avery an arch look. "Too easy. What's mine?"

Her mouth twisted as she thought. "*Top Gun*."

My mouth fell open. "What? How did you know *that*?"

Miri hyperventilated.

"Breathe," Scott murmured to her, putting a glass of water in front of her.

Avery laughed and waved her hand in my general direction. "You just seem like a *Top Gun* kind of guy."

I was speechless. My brothers and I had watched that movie countless times growing up. I shook my head.

"Ooooh, this is getting good!" Miri beamed at us, clasping her hands together.

At least we were getting some of the questions right now, instead of looking like a pair of people who only agreed to get together based on strategy.

"Favorite animal," Miri prompted, leaning forward.

"Hamster," I shot, saying the first thing that came to mind.

Avery grimaced. "No one's favorite animal is a hamster. All they do is sleep and poop. My favorite animal is a dog."

"Everyone likes dogs," I added, rolling my eyes. The only people who didn't like dogs were sociopaths.

"Unless they're a sociopath," she added.

I frowned.

"Avery, what's Emmett's favorite animal?" Miri asked. She had lost a bit of her enthusiasm.

Shit. We needed to save this. Whatever animal Avery said, I'd agree to. Avery was watching me with a funny expression on her face. Her eyes were narrowed, and the corner of her mouth twitched up.

"Turtles." She leveled me with her gaze. "Emmett's favorite animal is the turtle."

My stomach dropped. She knew. How did she know?

Miri's mouth dropped in shock. "Is that true?"

I nodded, suppressing a grimace. I fucking hated turtles. In my mind, I heard the crunch of my childhood friend's turtle shell as I accidentally rode over it with my bike, and my stomach churned.

I gagged thinking about it. I'd never touched one, but they were so slimy and gross. Their heads were all wrinkly and gooey, like a decaying thumb.

My stomach lurched again. I was going to be sick. I swallowed and focused on Miri.

"I *love* turtles," I told her. "Love them. Can't get enough of them." As long as they stayed far away.

Miri reached out and slapped my arm lightly with a chiding look. "How come you've never visited my turtle rehabilitation center?"

I blinked at her. Beside me, Avery's chest convulsed once before she propped her elbow on the table and hid her mouth with her hand.

"I'm sorry," Avery managed. "Your what?"

Miri beamed at her. "I run a turtle rehabilitation center."

Scott put his arm around her and gazed at her with affection. "They rescue turtles who have been hurt by boats in the harbor, nurse them back to health, and then release them into the wild. They also take pet turtles."

"Emmett," Miri said, "you have *got* to volunteer with us. Oh my god, you would love it. You get to hold the turtles, wash the turtles, feed them, play with them, tell them all your secrets."

She said it like those were good things.

"Would I have to touch them?" I asked.

She threw her hands in the air with joy. "Of course you would get to touch them. Turtles produce oxytocin, the cuddle hormone, just like people do. We always need volunteers to help at the rehab center. It's just like those programs at the hospitals where people hold newborn babies."

"Except they cuddle turtles?" Avery asked.

Miri lit up. "Exactly! You get it. Some people don't get it."

I pictured myself holding a turtle. My skin ran hot and cold, like when I had the flu last year.

Scott gave me a sidelong look. "It would be great campaign press."

Avery nodded at me, barely containing herself. She was vibrating, she was so excited. There was a flash of something in her eyes, and I remembered her hissed words from Friday from beneath the mushroom hat.

I will make you pay for this. Revenge, thy name is Avery.

Her eyes danced over my face. "It would, Emmett, and it would be great for you to take a break and do something you love—touch turtles."

Miri was radiating with excitement. "Come touch turtles with me, wouldn't you?"

There was no getting out of this one, not at this moment at least.

"I would be honored to," I told Miri, "and Avery would too."

"What?" Avery blanched. "I'm busy that day."

Miri shook her head, still smiling. "We haven't set a date yet."

So we set a date for the following week for Avery and me to drop by and help out at the disgusting turtle rehab. While Miri and Avery talked more about Miri's volunteer organizations around town and Scott told me about the renovations he was doing on their kitchen, I made a mental note to ask Div to schedule conflicting meetings that day that I couldn't possibly get out of. Avery would be stuck holding the slimy creatures all by herself. Served her right.

I glanced over at her, smiling and listening attentively. Her fingers toyed with her necklace, and her eyes sparkled in the light as Miri talked.

I had to admit as I sat there watching her, she was the perfect person to be my fake girlfriend, not just because of her people skills and an equal desire on her part to make it look real, but because she was beautiful. I knew what I looked like, and the two of us together? People would watch us walk by, my arm draped over her shoulders, and they'd comment on what beautiful kids we'd make. Exactly what I wanted them to think.

It helped that I didn't mind the idea of draping my arm around her, either. Not one bit.

As we departed the restaurant later, Scott gave me another firm handshake.

"Congratulations, Emmett," he said, nodding at me. "You've done alright for yourself."

"I sure have," I told him. Everything was going to plan.

Miri gave us a conspiratorial look. "Do we hear wedding bells in the future?"

"What? No," I said before I could catch myself.

"No way," Avery said quickly, and Miri looked crushed.

"I mean," I began. Shit, I had to save this. "Who knows." I smiled at Miri, and her mouth fell open with a knowing look.

Avery and I exchanged a glance. What had I just done?

"Miri, can you take a picture of us?" I asked.

"Of course." She waved between us. "Get closer."

I handed her my phone and put my arm around Avery's shoulders. She fit right against me, and I could feel the warmth of her skin through her clothes. I could smell her hair, light and sweet. My cock twitched, and I inhaled sharply.

Jesus Christ, Rhodes. Get yourself together. I hadn't been turned on so fast since I was a teenager.

"Give each other a kiss," Miri suggested.

"Uh," Avery startled.

I leaned down and gave Avery a kiss on the cheek. Her skin was soft, like velvet.

"No, a real one," Miri pressed.

Avery cleared her throat. "I have garlic breath."

I don't know what happened, but one second, I was standing there with my arm around Avery, and the next one, I was pulling her toward me, about to press my mouth to hers.

She turned and I got her ear and a mouthful of hair.

"What the hell, Adams," I murmured in her ear.

"What the hell, yourself," she murmured back, her gaze blazing. "A little warning next time?"

"Well," Miri chirped, handing my phone back to me. "We'll see you two lovebirds later. Have a great night. Avery, I'll email you those details about the schoolwork program."

"Goodnight," Avery said.

"What was she talking about?" I asked her on the way to the car. "The school program."

"There's a work program at the local high school that places queer teens in accepting and welcoming work environments. We could use some summer workers at the restaurant."

Something clicked in my head. Avery was the only straight woman unrelated to me, that I'd ever met who wasn't attracted to me. She didn't date much—only hookups, from the sounds of things. And now Avery was showing a lot of interest in an organization for queer youth in town.

My pulse stilled. Avery was *gay*. This made so much sense. Of course. Jesus, why didn't I realize this before? Perhaps she just wasn't ready to come out to our community, or didn't plan to.

Disappointment flickered in my chest that things with Avery and I would never go further. It would have been fun to have a couple hookups, if she ever warmed up to me. At the same time, relief settled in my chest. I wasn't losing my mojo. I wasn't aging out of being attractive. Avery not liking me had nothing to do with *me*. It was all about her. Completely out of my control.

I slid into the driver's seat and turned to her with a sympathetic look.

"It'll be our little secret," I told her.

She gave me a strange look. "Yeah, I know."

I started the car. "I hope you know Queen's Cove is an incredibly liberal place, and no one would treat you any differently."

She narrowed her eyes at me. "What are you talking about?"

I gave her a *duh* look. "Avery, you're gay."

She gave me an amused look. "Am I?"

There was an inkling of hesitation inside my head. "That's why you don't like me. Because you're gay." My gaze cut from the road to her. "Right?"

She burst out laughing. "Wow."

"What?"

"Is your ego so massive you can't believe a straight woman doesn't like you?"

"No." Yes. The frown settled on my face. "But you're getting involved with—"

"I'm getting involved because I think it's a great cause, Miri seems nice, and last week, a customer told Max he was a sinner, so it was a perfect opportunity."

"That's awful."

"About the customer telling Max he's a sinner or me not being gay?"

The light ahead of me turned yellow, and I slowed to a stop just as it turned red. "Both."

She snorted. We were quiet as I drove down the town's main street.

She narrowed her eyes at me. "When Miri brought up the wedding bells, you couldn't say no fast enough."

My gaze cut to hers as I turned onto her street. "Nothing to do with you."

"I wasn't worried about that."

I shrugged. "I just don't see that life for me." I glanced at her. "You were pretty quick to say no, too."

"I know."

"So, your parents are divorced."

"Yep." She stared out the window.

I didn't say anything for a moment, but she let the silence hang there. I guess that was all I was going to get out of her tonight.

I pulled the car over to the curb in front of her house. Alright, this was enough serious talk. I gave her my best seductive smile, the one that worked every time. "Well, if you're not gay," I said in a low voice before looking up at her, "can I come in?"

She snorted and opened the car door. "No."

I grinned. I didn't *really* want to go inside, I was just trying to get a rise out of her. Pushing her buttons was my new favorite hobby.

Okay yes, yes, I did want to go inside. I had been sporting a half-boner since that awkward kiss outside the restaurant. It was because Avery didn't like me. That's why I wanted more.

"Alright, next time then. We can work on practicing that kiss."

"Nope." She shook her head before closing the door. Her face was going red.

I watched her as she walked up the path to her home. When she was just about to go inside, I stepped out of the car.

"How did you know about the turtles?"

She turned and gave me a conspiratorial look. "Elizabeth told me."

I groaned and watched as she turned and continued up the path.

"Goodnight, sweetheart," I called to her, loud enough so everyone in town could hear.

She looked around to see if anyone was out on the street before shooting me a disapproving look, and I grinned big at her, wiggling my eyebrows. More payback for that stupid turtle rescue stunt she pulled. She disappeared inside, and I waited until a light turned on upstairs to drive away.

9

Avery

I WOKE the next morning to my phone buzzing.

"Hello?" I asked. My voice was raspy with sleep.

"I have a great idea."

I rubbed my eyes. "Emmett?"

"Are you still sleeping? Adams, it's nine in the morning."

"I know, it's nine in the morning, and you're calling me. So rude."

"I get up at six every day. We should get married."

I narrowed my eyes, replaying the words I must have mistakenly heard. "No, thank you."

"It's working, Adams. My polling numbers shot up the second you and I stepped out together. Also, Miri sent herself that picture from last night and posted it on social media."

"The second one?" I remembered the way his mouth brushed my cheek right before he got a bunch of my hair in his mouth. His stubble had scraped my skin so gently. Why did I keep replaying that?

"No, thank god, the first one. My phone has been ringing all morning with people around town wanting to congratulate us."

I pulled my phone away from my ear and saw a few phone

calls and missed texts. I didn't care what most people thought, but there were a select few in town I didn't like lying to, including Hannah, Keiko, Max, and Elizabeth. I winced. I didn't think about Elizabeth when we made this deal, I just thought about myself. But now, I'd have to lie to Elizabeth about dating her son, and I liked and respected her. I chewed my lip and stared at the trees outside my bedroom window, thinking.

"We wouldn't have to actually get married, we could just get engaged," Emmett was saying. "People love weddings. This would create so much buzz. You saw how Miri reacted and that was just us dating. Imagine if we got engaged, she'd lose her mind."

Married. Blegh. My stomach churned. My initial reaction to Miri's mention of a wedding last night was accurate—I had no desire to get married, especially after what I saw my parents go through. What they made me go through.

I had worked my way up from the bottom. I would never allow myself to give away half of what I had, especially when things inevitably went south. I would never allow someone to do what my father did to my mom.

"Emmett, you already said it was working, why do we need to get engaged?"

"I don't have this in the bag yet. Isaac is still ahead."

"I'm not doing it."

I hung up on him, and my head dropped back on the pillow. My phone began to buzz a second later.

"No," I answered.

"Double-paned windows."

"What?"

"The Arbutus still uses single-paned windows. Do you know how energy inefficient those are? I could cut thirty percent off your utility bills in the summer and winter by switching them out."

"You're going to give me free double-paned windows if I

pretend to get engaged to you?" I rubbed my eyes again and stared at the ceiling. It was way too early to be agreeing to a fake engagement. "How romantic."

"Mhm."

While Emmett talked about how it would work, I slipped out of bed and padded over to the kitchen to make coffee. It wasn't that different from what I was already doing—try to smile at him, not jerk my hand away when he reached for it, pretend to like him. The wedding would never happen. We'd quietly break up sometime after the election, and everyone would go back to their business.

I watched the coffeemaker drip caffeine into the pot. "Fine."

Emmett made a satisfied noise on the other end. "Excellent. I'll drop by the restaurant to say hi later."

"No, don't—"

But he had already hung up.

———

"I'LL TAKE THAT," I told Max that evening during dinner service, handing him a full pitcher of water and taking the empty one from him.

He accepted it with relief before heading back out into the restaurant, and I went back to watching Chuck in front of me, seated at the bar. He was glancing around the restaurant and making notes in a notebook in between mouthfuls of the linguine pasta I had reverse-engineered to the best of my ability with the chef yesterday.

"How's your food, Chuck?" I asked. He had a big grease stain on the front of his shirt.

He stared at me for a second before making a note in his notebook. "Too salty." He shoveled another bite into his face.

My eyebrows rose, but I kept my customer service smile

pasted on my face, reserved purely for people like Chuck. If only I could see what he was writing in that book.

"You have a lot of staff," he commented, reaching up and digging into his ear before wiping it on his cloth napkin. I suppressed a gag.

"It's our busiest night," I told him with a shrug. "All hands on deck."

It was Thursday night, and I was standing behind the bar, doing what I could to help keep things moving along as the restaurant was bursting at the seams with customers. Thursday nights were when locals visited the restaurant. Visitors from Vancouver, Victoria, and Seattle often swarmed Queen's Cove for weekend vacations, so locals knew to avoid us on weekends. During these summer months, most locals worked weekends anyway. Summer tourism was how Queen's Cove made money, either through the bars and restaurants, the outdoor activities like surfing or kayaking tours, or the kitschy gift shops with mugs, t-shirts, and fridge magnets with our town's name on them. Thursday night was the locals' weekend.

Chuck sent a wry glance at Max, who stepped up beside me to make drinks. "Heard you're trying to buy the place."

"I *am* buying the place," I corrected him.

He made a disapproving noise in the back of his throat and wrote something down. My shoulders tensed, and I shrugged it off. Whatever he was writing in his notebook—people to fire, dishes to remove from the menu, changes to the decor—none of it would come to fruition because the plan Emmett and I had cooked up, it was going to work.

Keiko walked in the front door, and the hostess greeted her. I gave her a cheery wave. Chuck wrenched around in his seat to see who I waved at, and when he saw Keiko, he hopped up to go over and say hi to her.

His notebook lay open on the bar.

Read it, the devil inside me whispered.

I snorted. Emmett must have been rubbing off on me.

Before I could change my mind, I whirled around and left the bar area. I didn't need to see whatever was in that book. I was better than Chuck. I was hardworking, treated my employees with respect, and I had enough business smarts to run this place. Keiko knew this, and I didn't need to worry about whatever was written in that book.

I spotted Hannah and her father at a nearby table.

"Hey, you two. Frank, so good to see you," I said to her father, who I rarely saw around town. He was a shy, quiet man.

He gave me a quick wave and a warm smile. "Hello. Hannah convinced me to put the book down and go out for a nice meal tonight."

"I'm thrilled that she did," I told them. "Can I get you anything?"

Hannah smiled softly up at me and shook her head. She and her dad had the same smile. They were splitting our paella with a few glasses of white wine. "Everything is great. Thanks, Avery."

Frank looked across the table at his daughter with affection. He gestured outside at the setting sun on the water, splashing oranges and pinks across the sky. "And what a view."

Hannah smiled again and raised her eyebrows at me. There was a glint of *something* in her eye I hadn't seen before. Mischief.

"What's that look?" I asked her, frowning. "What do you know that I don't?"

She shook her head and smiled into her napkin. "Nothing, nothing. It's nice to be here."

I clapped my hands together. "Alright, well, please let me know if you need anything else, and enjoy your dinner." I noticed the empty bread basket on the table. "I'll send over some more bread."

I bumped straight into Elizabeth Rhodes on my way back to the bar. She had just stepped in the door.

"Oh, Elizabeth." I put my hand on her arm. "Nice to see you. Hi, Sam," I said to her husband, Emmett's dad. It suddenly struck me how he looked like an older version of Emmett, with his thick, short hair, strong nose, and light gray eyes. Behind him stood Wyatt and Holden. "It's a whole gaggle of Rhodeses tonight." The whole Rhodes family was here except Finn. I could see various women throughout the restaurant sending glances their way. They were all over six feet, and all handsome in their own way. Emmett in his chiseled Ralph Lauren way, Holden in his beard scruff, plaid-clad, gruff but polite mountain man way, and Wyatt with his sandy blond hair that was perpetually in need of a haircut, and lazy, overly confident smile.

I glanced around for the host, Rachel, but she was seating another group at their table.

Elizabeth beamed at me. "Emmett suggested we all go out for dinner here, isn't that nice?"

Emmett appeared at my side and put his arm around my shoulder with a smile. "Avery, looking gorgeous as always."

My face prickled, and I ignored the warmth and weight of his arm on my shoulder.

"Rachel," I said to her as she returned. "Can you please seat the Rhodes family at Table One?" I smiled at Elizabeth. "Let's give you a view, shall we?"

"Actually," Emmett interjected, "we'd prefer a table in the main dining room. Right in the middle of the action."

My eyes narrowed at him. What was he doing? "Table One has a much better view of the harbor."

He grinned down at me and my gaze snagged on the tiny white scar on his lip. Annoying, meddling, tall man. "We'd like to be in the main room with everyone else."

Elizabeth waved a hand. "Oh, honey, it doesn't matter where we sit."

Emmett stared at me intently. "I insist. Give Table One to someone else."

I met his gaze, glaring at him for a moment before I broke. "Rachel, please put the Rhodes family at Table Ten. Right smack dab in the middle of the dining room." I turned to Emmett with my most pleasant, polite smile. "Happy?"

His amused grin was sincere. "Absolutely. Thanks, *sweetheart.*"

"Anytime, *darling.*" I then looked at everyone. "Enjoy your dinner."

Rachel gestured at them. "Follow me."

Emmett gave my shoulder a squeeze and quickly winked, and the family followed Rachel, except for Elizabeth, who wrapped me in a tight hug. She smelled like roses, and I relaxed against her.

"What's this for?"

She pulled back and beamed at me. "I can't tell you how excited I was to hear the news about you and my Emmett. I always thought you didn't like him!"

She gave my arm a light slap, and I laughed nervously.

"Oh, ha-ha. Got you," I said in a joking tone.

"You two fooled me." She shook her head at me.

Elizabeth, you have no idea.

Later, when the dinner rush was in full swing and the bar was stocked, I headed to my office.

"Where are you going?" Max asked the second I stepped into the hallway, blocking my path.

I pointed behind him. "I'll be in my office if you need anything."

"We need you out here tonight."

"I'm just getting in the way," I dismissed him. "Is there something in particular you need?"

Max stood his ground. He sent a glance over my shoulder. "There's a customer who wants to complain about something?"

I frowned at him. "Who, Chuck?"

There was the tinkling sound of someone clinking their glass, and the entire restaurant quieted down behind us. I stepped back out into the restaurant, curious.

Emmett stood at his table with his glass raised.

Oh my god. My gut wrenched with panic, my lungs constricted, and I remembered the conversation we had a few days ago, right after I woke up.

I had forgotten about it.

My mind began to race. Here? No. Tonight? He was going to do it *tonight*? But we had only talked about it a couple days ago. There was supposed to be more planning involved. The guy could have given me some warning. I spun around, intending to sprint back into my office, lock the door, and slide the filing cabinet in front. Max, however, the little brat, blocked me again.

"No, you don't," he said, turning me back around. He locked his arm around my shoulders to hold me steady.

"What are you doing?" I hissed at him. "Whose side are you on?"

He continued smiling at Emmett while whispering to me out of the corner of his mouth. "Emmett slipped me a hundred bucks to make sure you were here for this."

That bastard. A tiny fraction of me was impressed. I shouldn't have been surprised. The guy was always strategizing, always scheming. The deal we cooked up? It had come to him so naturally. He had everything figured out before I even said yes. Of course he had this timed to the minute.

"Most of you know me," Emmett was saying to the restaurant. "I was born and raised here in Queen's Cove, and you know my parents, Elizabeth and Sam." He tipped his glass to them and smiled. "This town means more to me than most of you will ever know. I've traveled all over, but I've never met a finer group of people."

Wow, he was laying it on thick. My pulse picked up speed. Maybe this was just a toast to his campaign.

"I love this town, and I love the people who live here, that's why I'm running for mayor. The people of Queen's Cove are important, and I'm going to do everything I can to protect them, including upgrading the electrical grid so those power outages are a thing of the past."

People started clapping, and he waited for them to finish. I rolled my eyes. In Emmett's head, he was Jesus Christ himself, here to save our sad little town. Annoying.

Emmett nodded. "You know me as the Queen's Cove boy who caused trouble with my brothers, you know me as the upcoming mayor, but there's a side of me you don't know."

Emmett, the showman he was, let this last sentence settle in the room. There was a ripple of curiosity throughout the restaurant. My stomach was in knots, twisting and churning, and adrenaline dripped into my bloodstream from the anticipation. His family exchanged curious glances. Not a soul made a noise.

"I'm also a man in love."

Every woman in the room except me swooned. My face tingled, and I couldn't tell whether it was from exasperation, nerves, or nausea. Diners watched me with big smiles. They must have seen Miri's photo of us online.

Emmett gave them all a bashful look. "That's right. I've fallen head over heels for the last person I expected." He set his wine glass on the table and reached into his pocket.

I closed my eyes. Why, *why* did I agree to do this? This was mortifying. No one was going to believe it. They'd take one look at my face and know it was a complete load of crap.

Emmett pulled out a small, navy-blue velvet box, and a chorus of gasps rose up around the room. He looked straight at me, and Max's grasp on my shoulders tightened in response. My throat was thick. Even as Emmett inflicted this mortification on me, I couldn't look away from him. He was an anchor. He was the only person who knew the truth, and we were in this together.

He gave me a soft smile and walked across the restaurant to me. The slow thump of his boots on the hardwood echoed as everyone held their breath.

Max shoved me forward to the center of the restaurant. Everyone could see me.

"Avery," Emmett said, and behind him, Elizabeth clutched her hands to her mouth in elation. "I know you're scared, and you wanted to keep us a secret." He reached out and took my hands. "But baby, I'm crazy about you, and I want to tell the world. You make me a better man. I want to spend the rest of my life with you." He dropped down to one knee and more gasps rose up around the room.

"Oh my god!" Max squealed behind me.

My head was about to explode. A nervous laugh sat right below my vocal cords, ready to bubble up at any minute. My stomach twisted back and forth. My hands shook in Emmett's. Everyone stared at me. Every single person I considered a friend was here tonight, watching me, watching this happen.

On bended knee in front of me, Emmett opened the box.

My mouth fell open.

It was a vintage diamond ring from the 1920s, Art Deco style. I'd seen similar styles online. It sparkled brilliantly, catching the light from every angle. The center diamond was a soft gray, just like the color of Emmett's eyes. A halo of tiny white diamonds encircled the larger diamond, with baguette-style gems cascading from the halo.

It was gorgeous. It was complicated, unique, over the top, and yet dainty. My heart squeezed.

How did he know what I would like? The only person I had told about this was—

My gaze cut to Hannah, who gave me a soft smile while biting her lip in anticipation. She wiggled her eyebrows at me.

I swallowed again and my gaze returned to Emmett. His

money and influence knew no bounds in this town, it appeared.

"Avery Adams, will you marry me?" he asked softly, but just loud enough for everyone to hear.

The whole restaurant was silent, waiting for my answer. Emmett watched me with a gentle, reverent look on his face. I was frozen. My thoughts moved through jello, slow and sluggish. The longer I was silent, the more the tension grew. Shit, what was I doing? I had to say something. I had to say yes.

Out of the corner of my eye, Chuck fidgeted in his seat before checking his phone, like he was bored.

The restaurant. I was doing this so I could get the restaurant. Emmett and I were in this together, and I always kept my word. I always held up my end of the bargain.

Uncertainty flickered through Emmett's eyes as he waited for my answer. His Adam's apple bobbed.

"Yes," I whispered.

"Yes?" His eyebrows shot up, and I could tell he was relieved I didn't fuck it all up. "Yes?"

I nodded and smiled despite myself. It was fun, playing with Emmett's sanity and emotions like this. "Yes."

He slipped the ring on my finger, stood, and before I realized it, stepped into my personal space and put his mouth on mine.

I stopped breathing.

His arms wrapped around me. Emmett was kissing me.

Around us, applause and cheering exploded. Emmett was kissing me. A champagne bottle popped behind the bar. Emmett was kissing me.

His mouth was warm, soft, and I felt the lightest scrape of stubble on my skin, which sent a little shiver down my spine. I could smell his masculine scent, and my hands instinctively came to his chest. I shivered again when his fingers tangled into my hair.

Before my brain could make sense of what was happening,

he pulled back and smiled down at me. "Nice work," he murmured into my hair.

We were immediately surrounded by happy friends and family, wishing us well and congratulating us. Even though we kept getting pulled apart for hugs and handshakes, Emmett stuck by my side like glue, one hand always on me, whether it was my elbow or my hand or my shoulder or the small of my back. It was loud, noisy, and chaotic, and I didn't have time to think while smiling and thanking people and shrugging with a quick smile when people told me they had no idea.

After everyone settled down and went back to their tables, and the staff had gone back to work, I returned to my office and closed the door before sitting down, closing my eyes, and putting my head in my hands.

I let a long breath out. My pulse slowed but my mind still raced. I couldn't believe we did it. We pulled it off.

Elizabeth's jubilant expression projected in my mind. She had raced over and given me another hug after Emmett proposed, beaming at me with tears in her eyes. She was over the moon about us. Her oldest son was getting married. This was everything she wanted.

Guilt washed through me, and I winced. I didn't like this, and I didn't like lying to her. She was a nice woman, and I could already picture the disappointment on her face when she learned Emmett and I hadn't worked out.

But then I thought about what would happen if I didn't go along with this charade. Emmett wouldn't cosign on my loan, I'd be out of luck, and Chuck would swoop in and buy the restaurant from Keiko. He'd turn it into a strip club or something.

Was I doing something wrong? Yes. But it was the lesser of two evils, so what choice did I have?

And if the lesser evil meant wearing this ring for a couple months, I was on board. It caught the light as I tilted my hand to and fro. Every tiny diamond was placed with intention and care. I had never seen a ring quite like it.

"Just gorgeous," I breathed.

There was a knock at the door before Emmett stuck his head in.

"Good work, Adams," he said with approval, stepping in, closing the door behind him, and leaning against the filing cabinet.

I stared at him a beat.

He made a face and crossed his arms over his chest. "What? What do you have to be cranky about now? That went better than I could have imagined. That little hesitation before saying yes?" He shook his head with wistful satisfaction. "You're a natural. *Who, me? Marry you? Well, I don't know…*" he mimicked in a high-pitched voice and bit his lip.

"That wasn't for show. I was debating whether buying the restaurant is worth taking a one-way trip to hell with you."

His mouth hitched, and his gaze settled on me. My skin prickled, remembering the way our eyes met when we were inches apart. "You're funny. Did you know that?"

I nodded. "Yes."

He winked. "And modest. Looks like we have that in common." He straightened up. "Engagement party at my house, Sunday." He paused and looked at me out of the corner of his eye. "Wear that lipstick you wore to dinner with Miri and Scott."

He gave me a devilish grin, and I stood, placed my hands on his chest, then gently shoved him out of my office.

"Out," I told him.

He laughed and put his hands up. "Okay, okay. Good-night, Adams."

I closed the door and flopped down in my chair. He was still thinking about that red lipstick, huh? I thought about the way his gaze lingered on my mouth the other night, the way heat flashed in his eyes before he blinked it away, and how it sent electricity straight down between my legs.

I shook my head to myself and woke up my computer. Emmett was trickling into my thoughts more and more, but it was only because I was spending so much time with the guy. Also, I hadn't been laid in a while. This was natural. Of course I was thinking about him, he was a handsome man who I was pretending to date. My body didn't know the difference.

My brain did, though. This was just a deal. Emmett wasn't interested in me, or he would have made a move years ago. Not that I would have done anything about it. So all I needed to do, if I wanted this whole agreement to go smoothly, was keep a cool head.

Easy peasy.

10

Emmett

"EMMETT," Miri called from outside the low older building, just off the highway before the town border. Across the parking lot and down the hill was a small cove. This one was rockier than the other beaches and not as calm, but I knew from some of my morning runs that the most spectacular sunrises could be viewed from here. I always enjoyed running past this area.

Until I learned this building housed creatures of the underworld.

"Emmett," Miri called again, and I got out of my car.

Look, I liked Miri. She was a lovely person, very sweet, and did a ton of charity work in Queen's Cove. She was an incredible asset to our community. I couldn't think of a bad thing to say about the woman.

She was persistent, though, I'd give her that. When Miri phoned with the details about the turtle rehab, I had told her that regrettably, Div had already booked me a visit with the local hospital. She said she had *already confirmed with my assistant*.

Miri might be an evil genius.

"Good morning." I put on a bright smile as I approached, my stomach churning.

Miri clasped her hands together. "Good morning, handsome. Your darling is already inside."

"My who?" I asked, frowning. "Oh. Avery."

Miri laughed and slapped my shoulder. "Come on, let's go in. The reporter is already here."

I stared after her as I held the door open, and she breezed past me. "The who?" I asked for the second time.

"Emmett," Don O'Rourke greeted as I walked into the lobby of the small office. Don was the reporter for the local paper and news blog. It was a small paper run by one guy, who usually hired a summer student during the busy season. His camera hung around his neck, and he gave me a big grin. "Ready to get up close and personal with some turtles?"

I rubbed the back of my neck and swallowed. On the drive over, my stomach had tightened into a knot.

Beside Don, Avery pressed her lips together and glanced down, trying not to smile. She had done her hair differently; it was tied up into a ponytail instead of down around her shoulders like usual.

"Can't wait," I told him, giving him a quick, tense smile and stepping over to Avery. I wrapped my arm around her shoulder and pulled her to me, pressing a quick kiss onto the side of her head. Her hair smelled amazing, that freshly washed scent of women's hair products. "Hello, sweetheart."

"Hello, darling." Her tone was dripping with self-satisfaction.

Miri caught sight of the ring and gasped, reaching for Avery's hand. "I haven't seen the ring yet. Oh my god." Miri gave me a flat look. "It's gorgeous. Emmett, you have incredible taste."

Avery tilted her hand to study the ring and her eyes fixed on it. Yesterday, I walked in on her in her office, admiring it.

She shook her head and glanced at me out of the corner of her eye. "I don't know how he found it."

I smiled, and satisfaction spread throughout my chest. "I have my ways."

Seeing Avery admire that ring made me a happy guy. The day I got her greenlight on the engagement plan, I paid a visit to Hannah. In the musty little bookstore, Hannah flipped through the pages of a book on vintage jewelry, pointing out the shape and style Avery was drawn to. I drove to Victoria three hours away and scoured jewelry stores for something vintage, something people would believe Avery would want. Did I drop a bit of money on the ring? Sure I did, but the second her eyes lit up, that didn't matter as much.

Miri looked between the two of us. "Have you picked a date yet?"

"We're still thinking about it." Avery shrugged. "Probably next year or the year after."

I had the urge to put my arm around her again but stopped myself.

Something weird had been happening lately—I'd been thinking about Avery more and more.

First, it was that awkward kiss for the photo Miri took. I thought about how my mouth brushed her cheek and the mouthful of hair I got. I had desperately wanted a do-over, because I was Emmett Rhodes, and I didn't do bad kisses.

I got the do-over when I proposed to Avery in the restaurant. The way her soft mouth felt under mine, fucking hell. She was so soft and sweet, and her hair was like silk around my fingers, and it still wasn't enough. That kiss was too chaste. I was Emmett Rhodes, and I didn't do chaste kisses.

So, I needed one more do-over, and it was going to be a good one. I didn't know when it would happen but I was sure we'd have an opportunity at some point. As soon as we had our do-over kiss, I could stop wondering and thinking about her and her body and what her tits looked like, and I could focus on the election.

"Can I interest anyone in some snacks before we begin the tour?" Miri asked, pulling out a tray of tarts from behind the desk. "Scott helped me make them last night."

Rule number one of running for mayor: if someone offers you food, you accept. Allergy? Don't care. Picky eater? Shut up. Full off the smoothie, three eggs, and avocado toast you ate an hour before? Choke it down, buddy.

"Absolutely." I accepted a tart and took a bite. I didn't recognize the texture of the filling.

"These look great," Avery told her. *Perfect, Avery. Exactly like that.* "What are they?"

"These are the turtles that didn't make it," Miri replied, and I choked and spat half the tart out into my napkin.

Avery put her hand over her mouth, either in shock or laughter or both.

"I'm kidding!" Miri trilled, laughing. "They're mincemeat."

Avery and Don began laughing at me and my face went red.

"You got me," I told Miri, grinning at her. It felt more like baring my teeth at her, and her eyes widened. "Shall we begin the tour?"

"Great idea," Miri concurred, and we entered the facility. Miri led us past the reception area and further into the building, chatting about the rescue organization as Don took notes, Avery asked polite questions, and I tried not to look too hard through any of the windows we passed.

"How do the turtles find their way here?" Avery asked.

Miri nodded with enthusiasm. "Some are injured by boat propellers in the harbor, some are hit by cars, some are attacked by animals or sharks, and people call us and we send someone out to scoop the little guy up. Some are cold-stunned by sudden drops of temperature." She stopped at the door and gestured for us to go inside. "And sometimes, people just can't give their pet turtle the love and affection it needs. We take pet turtles as well as sea turtles. Let's go say hello to some now."

Eugh. My stomach turned.

"I'm just going to go make a quick call—" I started, but Avery's arm looped through mine.

"He can make the call later." She looked up at me. Her eyes sparkled with mischief and revenge under the fluorescent lights. "Come on, Emmett, let's go touch the turtles."

I stared down at her with an expression I hoped conveyed how much trouble she was in, but the expression she wore conveyed how much fun she was having with this. This was a game to her. Me being grossed out by turtles was a goddamn game to her.

Miri opened the door, and we stepped into a room filled with large tanks. My gaze darted to Miri, the floor, the ceiling, Avery, to Don's camera as he snapped pictures, anywhere but those slow-moving slimy things behind the glass. Avery's arm was still entwined in mine, and her other hand rested on my bicep. I could feel the warmth of her hand through my shirt. Maybe she thought I'd make a run for it. Or maybe she wanted to find an excuse to touch me.

The thought sent a little spark down my spine.

She was just trying to sell it, this fake relationship of ours. She wasn't doing this because she wanted to.

I glanced at her delicate hand and the ring I bought her. I didn't mind this part, the touching. Not one bit.

"—doesn't have a generator so during the last outage, all the tank-heating equipment lost power," Miri was explaining, "and the turtles were so cold."

"Did you hear that, Emmett?" Avery glanced up at me with an overly sympathetic expression. "The turtles were *cold*. Isn't that awful?"

I nodded. "Yep. That really sucks. Isn't the ocean pretty cold?"

Miri laughed and slapped my shoulder again. "Oh, you."

I shot Avery a confused expression and she bit back a laugh. "*Oh, you,*" she mouthed when Miri and Don weren't looking, and I suppressed a laugh. She tried to unlink her arm, but I put my hand on it to hold her there.

"You becoming mayor would save the turtles, Emmett," Don noted, writing. "I'm going to put that in the article."

Avery beamed. "Please do."

"Yes," Miri gasped, slapping her forehead. "I didn't even think of that. How could I not think of that?"

"Emmett," Avery said, in a tone that told me she was up to something. "Does your campaign have a mascot?"

"Oh. My. God," Miri's mouth dropped open. "Avery, are you thinking what I'm thinking?"

I breathed through my nose. The election. Being mayor. Will and his family returning to Queen's Cove.

Avery nodded. "Turtle mascot?"

"Turtle mascot!" Miri cried, clapping her hands. She turned to a tank and unlatched the lid.

My heart dropped through my stomach. On instinct, I took a step back, but Avery held my arm. She was stronger than she looked. I bet that woman hit the gym regularly. A flicker of wonder at what she looked like naked flashed into my mind, but Miri turned around with a disgusting turtle, and I forgot all about naked Avery.

"Look," Miri gazed at the wrinkled creature with adoration.

"Uh…" I winced. "Wow. And he is… something." My stomach turned again, and I regretted eating breakfast. The turtle's arms were splayed out like it was skydiving, and its weird eyes stared into my soul.

"Her name is Elizabeth, after your mother. She made a

donation a couple months ago. We name a turtle after everyone who donates."

Don gasped. "I have an incredible idea."

"What?" Avery asked, and her eyes flashed with entertainment. I flexed my arm under her hand in warning, and her nails dug into me, but instead of hurting me like she intended, I found it strangely hot. The hair on the nape of my neck stood up.

"I can see it in my head—mayoral candidate Emmett Rhodes vows to keep turtles warm," Don revealed. "With a picture of Emmett holding the turtle. Front page!"

"Yes!" Miri nodded and stepped toward me with the creature.

"No," I blurted out.

Miri and Don gave me a funny look. Avery raised her eyebrows at me, that playful smile still on her lips.

"I mean," I began, "Avery should be in the photo with me, being my fiancée and all." Yes. Right. If I was going down, she was coming down with me. "Holding a turtle of her own."

Avery shrugged. "Sure. Sounds great."

Damn it.

"Look at us, putting our heads together," Miri beamed. She took another step toward me, holding the turtle out like she was handing me my newborn baby. "Don't make any sudden movements or she'll bite you."

"What?" I said in a higher pitch and Avery shook with laughter, but it was too late. Miri practically threw the thing at me, my hands came up, and I was holding it.

In my hands.

A gag rose up in my throat.

It was so cold and wet.

The underside of its shell was like a wet balloon.

My stomach lurched. I hated this. This was hell.

Miri unlatched another tank and I looked down at Avery, barely containing herself. "You will pay for this," I breathed.

She winked at me and my mouth gaped open. Winking was *my* move. Not hers. Mine. I didn't like this.

"Here you go." Miri held another turtle out, which Avery accepted from her.

Don held up his camera and snapped a picture. "Say cheese."

"I think you're supposed to say that before the picture," I told him.

"Let's do one where we're kissing the turtles," Avery suggested, and everything I ate that morning thrashed in my stomach.

"Great idea." Don lifted his camera up again. "Emmett, lift your turtle up to your lips like Avery is."

I closed my eyes and inhaled before lifting the awful thing up to my face. I made direct eye contact with it, staring into its beady little eyes. I felt bad for the turtle. She didn't want to be doing this, either. This was humiliating for both of us.

"Purse your lips, Emmett," Miri instructed, nodding. "Like you're kissing her."

Avery nudged me. She could hardly contain her grin. "Yeah, Emmett, give Elizabeth a kiss."

"I'm going to be sick," I whispered.

I didn't actually kiss it. Neither did Avery, I was pretty sure. We just held them close to our lips and pretended. The second the camera flash went off, I put that thing back in Miri's hands and rushed over to the sink to wash my hands. I probably had salmonella poisoning from holding it. Cold shivers ran up and down my spine, and every few seconds, a gag rose in my throat.

A few minutes later, the tour was over, and Avery and I waved goodbye to Don and Miri as we left.

"Come back soon," Miri called after us.

"Not fucking likely," I said under my breath.

The second Miri went back inside I wiped my hands on

Avery. "That was disgusting. I can't believe you made me do it. I can still feel it on my hands."

She was howling with laughter. "I can't believe you did everything we suggested. I didn't actually expect you to kiss the turtle."

"What?" My face crumpled into horror. "Are you kidding?"

Avery couldn't breathe, she was laughing so hard. She was doubled over, leaning on my car. "Oh my god." She straightened up with tears in her eyes. "This has been the best day ever, and it isn't even lunchtime." She grinned at me. "Speaking of lunch, how about you come by the restaurant, and we'll make you some mincemeat pies?"

"I'm never eating again," I told her, and she dissolved into a new round of laughter. "You're still coming to the engagement party tomorrow, right?"

Her laughter subsided, and she nodded. "Of course. Six?"

"Five or five-thirty. It would be better if you were there when people started arriving."

She nodded again. Her deep blue eyes were so bright out in the sunlight. "Alright." She checked the time on her phone. "I have to go, see you later."

"See you."

"This was fun." She leaned forward and gave me a quick kiss on the cheek before turning, walking to her car, and driving away. I stood there the whole time, watching with a dumb, confused look on my face.

I glanced around the empty parking lot. There was no one around to convince of our relationship in that moment. Avery did that because she wanted to. I narrowed my eyes, the feel of her soft lips on my jaw replaying again and again in my head. An image of Avery in my bed, naked, flashed through my head, and my cock ached.

Shit.

I had a thing for Avery Adams.

11

Emmett

A KNOCK on the front door woke me up from my afternoon nap. What time was it? I fumbled for my phone, eyes bleary and head foggy with sleep.

Five o'clock. I overslept, and the caterers were here.

I pulled pants on, not bothering with a shirt, rushed downstairs, and opened the door, squinting in the light. "Hey, come on in—oh. Hi."

Avery stood on my front doorstep in a short dress that came to mid-thigh. It was black with flowers on it, short-sleeved, very demure except for the neckline. My gaze snagged on her necklace, a silver locket resting on a hint of her cleavage.

Soft. Smooth. My fingers twitched with the urge to graze her neckline, skim over the smooth skin and trace down further.

Blood raced to my cock before I could tear my focus up to her face. I inhaled sharply. I was standing at my front door, hard and wearing sweatpants, an unfortunate combination.

"Hi," I repeated, gaze returning to her cleavage. She always wore higher necklines, I thought. Had I noticed her tits before? Standing there, they were all I *could* notice. "The caterers aren't even here yet." I tensed my thighs, something I had read once helped pull blood away from an inconvenient erection.

I tore my gaze up to her face, only to find her staring at my bare chest with a look I could only describe as hungry.

My cock was hard again.

"Um." She blinked and glanced up at me. Her lids were heavy. "Did you just wake up?"

"I was having a nap." I opened the door and gestured for her to come in, tensing my thighs like crazy to dispel the boner which was visible through these sweatpants.

She walked past me into the foyer, and I was gifted with a view of her incredible legs, long and toned. I bet her skin was soft. I bet it would feel amazing to run my mouth up her thighs right before I—

"Make yourself at home," I told her, halfway up the stairs. "I'm going to have a quick shower."

Jesus Christ, Rhodes, get your shit together.

Twenty seconds later, I stood in my shower, shivering under the icy water.

I am not going to beat off in the shower thinking about Avery.

I will not think about how her tits look incredible.

I will not think about running my mouth down the hem of her neckline.

The doorbell rang again. That would be the caterer. I reached for the faucet to turn the water off before I caught myself. Avery would let the caterer in. She wasn't the kind of person to sit around and watch, she'd jump in wherever she was needed. I liked that about her, I realized. She was a team player.

She'd probably try to help *too much* tonight. Not that I didn't want her helping, but I wanted her to relax, have fun, and put work mode aside for a night. I made a mental note to mention this to Div in case he saw her loading the dishwasher or plating appetizers.

Tonight was important. I had invited a lot of people from town—my family, my friends, Avery's friends, anyone influential. It was important they saw us together in my home, and more importantly, that they saw me as a stable, dependable guy who had his life together. Not a horndog who couldn't keep his boner down like some teenager.

Did I have a thing for Avery? Sure. Of course. Who wouldn't? I had always thought she was cute and fun to spar with, but I had never been turned on by her like this.

I gave myself a break, though. We were pretending to be a couple, this kind of confusion came with the territory. It didn't mean anything.

Besides, to Avery, this was just a deal.

I climbed out of the shower. The kiss we shared at the restaurant flashed into my head. I groaned and rubbed a towel over my wet hair. I was going to get one more do-over kiss to get it out of my system and then focus on the campaign. That was the reason we were doing this, after all.

After I was dressed and threw a bit of product in my hair, I headed back downstairs. Avery chatted with the caterer while making room in my fridge for the hors d'oeuvres. The bartender was setting up on the patio. Shortly after, people began to arrive. Music was playing. The doorbell rang.

"Hannah, hey," I greeted, opening the door. She blushed and handed me a wine bottle. "Happy engagement. I don't know anything about wine," she admitted with obvious discomfort, wincing at the bottle.

"Well, it's your lucky day because I love this one," I said, reaching out to hug her. She seemed surprised and blinked a few times. "Come on in."

"Your house is beautiful." She stepped into the foyer and glanced past me with a little wave and smile to Avery. "Hey."

Avery wrapped her in a big hug. "You came."

"Of course I'm here. It's your engagement party."

Behind her, Wyatt and Holden climbed the steps. "Who

invited the riff-raff?" I asked. Wyatt gave me a friendly shove and walked past me into the house.

"You guys know Hannah, right?"

Hannah was frozen. "I have to use the bathroom," she excused herself and scurried away.

Odd.

"Avery," Holden said.

"Hey, Holden." She smiled at him. "Thanks for coming."

"I'm not staying long," he told her. "I don't like parties."

She gave him a thumbs up. "Okay then."

Later, everyone had drinks and a server circled with hors d'oeuvres while people made conversation and laughed and made fun of the seventies disco playlist Wyatt had put on. The bartender shook drinks at his makeshift bar on the side of the patio while the sun began to set through the trees.

"How's the campaign going?" my mom asked as we stood on the patio. We were leaning against the railing. I glanced around for Avery but didn't see her. She must be inside.

"Great, I think." I thought back to Div's latest update this morning. "Our polling numbers are up, and we have lots of engagement, lots of questions from the locals."

The second Avery and I got fake-engaged, my polling numbers jumped. I still wasn't at Isaac-level approvals, which bothered me, but Div and I had spent hours on the campaign last night, and there wasn't much more I could do except keep myself seen in Queen's Cove and prove I was a responsible guy.

My dad tilted his beer at me. "Div seems like a great assistant."

"He is. He's holding the campaign together." I had mentioned to Div privately that after the election, he could have his choice of either joining me at town hall as my assistant or getting a promotion at Rhodes Construction.

"And things with Avery seem to be going very well." My mom gave me a confidential smile.

"They are." My chest tightened a little, and I glanced around again but didn't see her.

"Excuse me a moment," my dad told us. "Elizabeth, would you like another drink?"

"That would be lovely." She gave him a warm smile and brushed his arm before turning to me. "I was surprised when you proposed, but I should have known you always have something up your sleeve. She'll be a lovely addition to our family and I'm looking forward to spending more time with her." She beamed. "I can't tell you how happy I am you chose her."

A pang of guilt stabbed me in the stomach. All my mother ever wanted was for her kids to be happy, and I knew she liked Avery. I wouldn't be able to keep her from getting attached to Avery, that was just the way my mother was, warm and kind and welcoming. I swallowed, thinking of how hard she'd take it when Avery and I called it quits. She wouldn't say anything because she never wanted to put her worries on us, but I knew it would make her sad.

My dad returned with a fresh drink for my mom. "Elizabeth, I brought you something weird I think you'll like. It's called a French 75."

My mom took a sip of the champagne flute, and her eyebrows rose with delight. "Mmmm. Something bubbly, something a little sour?"

"Lemon, champagne, and gin. Careful," I told her. "They're strong."

"Yeah, you don't want to see us get wild or we might make another Rhodes son." My dad squeezed my mom around the shoulders, and she shook her head and rolled her eyes.

I winced. "Alright, keep it PG."

"Let's set up a dinner with Avery soon," my dad suggested to me and my mom.

"Emmett." Div appeared at my side, gently pushing a guilty-looking Avery toward me. "I found her behind the bar."

Her cheeks were pink. "I'm just making sure he has what he needs."

"Thanks," I said to Div and wrapped my arm around Avery's shoulders, pulling her to me.

"Avery, congratulations on buying the restaurant," my dad told her.

"Thank you, but it's not a done deal yet." Her gaze cut to mine.

I gave her shoulder a light squeeze and glanced down at her, into her dark blue eyes. "It'll happen." I gave her a little wink, and she smiled.

"Have you set a date yet?" My mom's eyes glowed with excitement, but she was trying to keep it subdued so as to not scare us.

Avery waved a hand. "In a few years. We haven't thought too much about it. We're not in a rush."

"Oh. Well." Disappointment flashed over my mom's face. "That's fine, too. Just don't get married while we're in Europe!" She laughed.

"Right, your trip. When do you two leave?" I asked them. I looked down at Avery. "They rented a place in the south of France for six months starting in July."

Avery's eyes lit up. "Amazing. You're going to eat like royalty."

Sam gestured at us. "You two should come stay with us. It's a big house, lots of room."

"Maybe," Avery mused with a lopsided grin. "I'm not sure if I can leave the restaurant while we're transferring ownership." She gave them a pressed smile and shrugged.

"Maybe you can do some location scouting," Elizabeth suggested, wiggling her eyebrows at us. "A summer wedding in the south of France? What could be more romantic?"

A thought struck me.

"Excuse us for a second," I told my parents. "We need to

check on the food." I pulled Avery into the house and through the party.

"Why are you being so weird?" she asked as we stepped into the quiet kitchen.

"I have a great idea. I don't know if you knew this about me but I'm a genius."

She stared at me.

"It's fine to be intimidated by my intellectual prowess." I shot her a charming grin.

Her nostrils flickered with rage, and happy feelings floated in my chest.

"Did you pull me in here to brag about yourself?"

"No." I braced my hands on her arms. "We should get married."

She froze. "What? For real? No way."

I shook my head. "We wouldn't *actually* get married, fuck no. We could sign a fake document or something. But we should have a wedding. Adams, you saw how my mom went ape shit in there for a wedding. Think of how the town would react." I sighed. "My polls would shoot through the roof."

"Elizabeth did not go 'ape shit' in there, she was politely asking questions."

"This is the boost I need to crush Isaac," I told her. "I have a good feeling about this."

She shook her head. "Emmett, no. We're already in too deep. I'm not planning a stupid wedding I don't want."

I leaned down, closer to her. "Adams, you wouldn't have to lift a finger. It would all be taken care of."

She shook her head again. "No. I'm not doing it."

I paused, thinking, ignoring how warm her skin was through the sleeves of her dress. Avery wanted the restaurant. I was already cosigning on her loan, we'd agreed to it. I was already giving her double-paned energy-efficient windows because she agreed to the engagement.

When I was at the restaurant a few weeks ago, I noticed water damage to part of the deck.

That was it. That was the bargaining tool I needed.

"Deck repairs," I told her. "Rhodes Construction will replace those rotting planks so you can open up the rest of the patio." I wiggled my eyebrows at her. "More patio space means more income throughout the summer."

She narrowed her eyes at me. "New deck."

I scoffed. "Hell, no."

She crossed her arms over her chest. "The new planks won't match the old planks. It'll look cheaply done."

I narrowed my eyes back at her. "Our work never looks cheaply done."

"New deck." Our faces were inches apart.

I leaned in further. "No. Repaired deck."

We stared at each other a moment and a spark passed between our gazes. Were we going to kiss again?

Was this my do-over opportunity?

"No deal." She shrugged and moved to walk out of the kitchen, but I held her in place.

"Okay, okay. New deck. Jesus Christ, Adams, you are a tough negotiator."

She gave me a wicked smile I felt all the way down to my cock before leaning in and rising up on her toes until her mouth was close to my ear. "That's because I have all the power," she whispered, and I shivered both from her words and from her breath tickling my ear.

She broke out of my grasp and walked out of the kitchen, and I stood there, thinking about what it would feel like if she pulled my earlobe into her mouth. I shivered again, and my cock ached. Jesus.

I had a thing for Avery Adams, and I had to get it out of my system.

Tonight. I'd make a move on her tonight.

"Great news," I said to my parents as I walked back onto

the patio. Avery stood next to them, and I pulled her tight to me. "Since you'll be in France for so long, we're going to get married before you leave."

Their mouths fell open.

"Honey, that's great," my mom said. "You know we leave in a month, right?" She glanced between Avery and me. "And you really aren't pregnant?"

Avery snorted. "I really am not pregnant."

The image of Avery and me, naked in my bed, me thrusting into her and spilling into her, flashed into my head. Putting a baby in her.

I never cared to have kids before.

The idea of Avery carrying our kid? Why was that so appealing to me?

I cleared my throat. "We just don't want to drag this out forever. We don't want it looming over us for a couple years."

"Looming?" my mom repeated.

They frowned at us, and I glanced at Avery, who shot me an incredulous look. It was as if she was trying not to roll her eyes.

"I mean," I started, smiling at her, "we're just so in love, we don't want to wait."

"Aw, that's nice." My dad looked wistful.

"Do you have a dress picked out?" Elizabeth asked.

"Oh. A dress. Right." Avery frowned. "I guess I'm going to need one of those."

Elizabeth laughed. "If I didn't know you two better, I'd think you weren't interested in the wedding at all."

Beneath my arm, Avery tensed. I glanced down at her, and something passed between our gazes. I squeezed her tighter, and she looked back to Elizabeth with a smile.

"I've never been good at wedding stuff," she said.

Elizabeth pulled out her phone. "Let's go to Wedding Bells in Victoria next weekend."

"Sorry?" Avery blinked.

"Wedding dress shopping. I'm coming with you." She looked up. "I assume your mom will be there, too? It'll be nice to meet her."

Avery tensed again. Instinctively, my hand moved from her arm to the top of her shoulder and my thumb brushed the skin just above her collar, where her neck met her shoulder. Why was she getting worked up about her mom going shopping with her? It didn't seem like a big deal.

"I don't think she can make it, it's pretty short notice," she said.

My dad, always the astute one, picked up on Avery's discomfort. "I heard you two paid a visit to our local turtle emporium today."

"Gross," I told them, and my mom grinned.

Avery's eyes lit up. "Oh my god, I forgot. One second." She pulled away from me and I let her, but she returned a second later with a stack of photographs. She held one up. "Elizabeth, it's you."

My mom took one look at the photo and started howling. Sam took another photograph from Avery and threw his head back, laughing.

"What?" I asked.

Holden walked out onto the patio, looked over Elizabeth's shoulder, then at me, then back at the picture, and grinned.

"What?" I demanded.

"I stopped by Don's place on my way here," Avery told me. "He printed out the pictures for me." She closed her eyes and shook her head in satisfaction. "And they are *good*."

"What's going on?" Wyatt asked, taking the photo from my dad. "Oh, dude," he said, laughing and looking at me with pity. "You'll do anything to win, huh?"

"I didn't have a choice," I told them, speaking above their laughter. "Avery set me up." I cringed down at the picture of Avery and me, turtles held up to our faces. The camera had captured Avery's pure mirth and my cold fear.

The caterer signaled that dinner was ready. I exhaled in relief and led Avery inside.

"We haven't talked about the wedding," Avery murmured to me just before the patio door. My arm was still firmly around her shoulders. I didn't think she'd keep trying to help during dinner, but I couldn't be sure, and besides, we looked like a great couple with my arm around her. Picture-perfect. She was wearing perfume tonight, something light and citrusy, oranges maybe, with a spicy note I couldn't identify.

"Div will hire a planner to put it together," I promised. "We don't have to worry about a thing."

"Okay," she yielded, frowning. "But what about the money part?"

I should have known she would ask about this. "What about it?"

"We haven't discussed the budget."

"That's because it's none of your business."

She snorted. "Um, it kind of *is* my business since I'm involved. How much do I owe you?"

I shook my head. "Don't worry about it."

She made a face. "Emmett."

"Adams. You're not paying for it."

"Yes, I am."

"No." I gave her a firm look. My firmest, sternest look. "You aren't. Look, Adams, I don't know if you've figured this out, but I have lots of money. Who am I going to spend it on, my brothers? My parents? I already do that. My mom has all the damn antique teapots she likes. No one could drink that much tea. I have a nice house, I have a nice car, I have everything I need. I'm set. The wedding money is going straight back into the local vendors of the town. Besides," I said, swallowing. "It's for the election, so it's money well spent."

She stared into my eyes. Our faces were only a foot apart. "I don't like this."

"Tough shit, baby. Come on, let's eat." I ignored the way

her mouth fell open and pulled her inside. I guess Avery didn't get a lot of *tough shit, baby*s, and that made me grin. We took a seat at the table.

The caterer had added a few tables to mine so the group of thirty could sit comfortably, and my home was filled with lively conversation as the food was served. Those stupid pictures from the turtle jail circulated, and laughter rippled through the room as people saw them. At least my guests were having a good time. Avery was chatting with Hannah and a friend of mine from the town council, engrossed in a conversation about rare books. It was nice to see her relax like this.

I caught the server's attention. "Could she please have another?" I asked, handing him Avery's empty drink. A few minutes later, a replacement drink arrived, and Avery reached out and took a sip.

"Thanks," she whispered to me, hand coming to my arm.

Something pinged in my chest, like a guitar string. I liked when she touched me like that, something small, not sexual but just affectionate. I could feel a little hit of pleasure in my bloodstream when her skin made contact with mine. I wasn't usually like this with women. I didn't *like* women like this. But I was beginning to like Avery, which was a good thing, because we were stuck in this thing for another month at least.

"No problem," I replied under my breath, and she smiled and pulled her hand back to her lap.

When everyone was finished eating and the plates were cleared, my dad raised his glass.

"I'd like to make a toast," he said. The table quieted down and everyone turned to Sam. "Avery," he began, smiling warmly at her, the only way he knew how, "we hardly know you, but damn, we sure like you."

There was a rush of *awww*s. Avery grinned into her lap beside me and on its own, my arm came up around her shoulders again.

"You make Emmett a happy, happy man." Sam lifted his glass. "Welcome to the family. To Avery and Emmett."

"To Avery and Emmett," everyone chorused, and around the table, glasses clinked.

Avery and I locked gazes as we clinked our glasses together. There was something in our gaze—camaraderie. We had set our weapons aside for a brief moment and we were in this together, this huge lie for the greater good. My gaze skimmed over her pretty face, her big blue eyes, and the freckles sprinkled over her nose.

"Now kiss," Wyatt called.

"Kiss, kiss!" others echoed.

Avery's eyes widened and the corners of her mouth hitched. My gaze fell to her lips and then to the dip of her neckline and that soft cleavage before I ripped my gaze back up to her mouth. A flash of what I had felt when I opened the door that afternoon rocked through me. I frowned.

This was my chance. My do-over. Third time's the charm.

My hand came to the back of her head, I pulled her toward me, and I kissed her.

Soft. That was the first thing I noticed. Her mouth, her hair, her hands on the front of my shirt, soft. Light. Delicate and gentle, all of it. My other hand came to the part where her neck met her shoulder and brushed the skin. She shivered beneath my hands and mouth. My fingers tangled into her hair, grabbed a fistful, and gently tilted her head back, giving me better access to that sweet, pliant mouth. I slid my tongue into her, tasted her, and need rolled through me.

Jesus *Christ*. This was so, so much better than that chaste kiss at our proposal. It should have been like this. My tongue swept over hers and a tiny noise escaped her throat. That noise sent every blood cell straight to my cock and I was a teenager again, popping boners over a kiss. One of her hands came to my thigh, her nails digging into me, making me harder. I groaned into her mouth. I was enveloped in her scent, a mix of shampoo and that spicy orange perfume of hers.

Someone cleared their throat, and we froze.

Everyone stared at us with various degrees of wide-eyed shock.

She let go of my shirt, her mouth detached from mine, and I pulled my hands from her hair and neck. She shifted back into her chair, face reddening. I was more concerned with hiding the rock-hard display of affection in my lap.

Wyatt raised his eyebrows at me, grinning. "Nice," he said, and Holden elbowed him.

"Okaaaay, guess we don't have to worry too much about not being grandparents," my dad joked, and the guests laughed.

The caterers brought out the cake. It said *Congratulations, Avery and Emmett!* on it.

"You've been practicing without me, Adams," I murmured in her ear.

She cleared her throat, and I took a long slug of my beer. My skin was on fire. I was still hard, sitting here in a room with my closest friends and family. I couldn't stop replaying that little moan of hers, the way it felt under my hands as it hummed through her, the way it felt in my mouth.

I originally wanted a do-over because our first couple of kisses were so terrible. Chaste and quick and bland. But that kiss tonight? It wasn't chaste and it wasn't bland. It was too quick, though, and I wanted more. I wanted another try. I craved her mouth on mine again, as if I'd had one bite of something and wanted the entire plate.

I had to hear that little moan again.

12

Avery

DINNER AND DESSERT WERE FINISHED, most of the guests had gone home, and there were a handful of us sitting in the living room, drinking and chatting when Wyatt pulled the lacy black underwear out of the couch. A few people turned to me with *busted!* expressions.

My stomach dropped through the floor.

"What's this?" Wyatt asked, swinging the black scrap of lace around in the air.

Holden choked on his beer and started laughing. Emmett gave Wyatt a lazy, smug grin. "What do you think it is, genius?"

Everyone looked at me with big grins. My face was on fire and I shot Emmett a look I hoped conveyed *you will pay for this.*

"Somebody was getting busy on the couch," someone sang.

I stood up. "Ha, ha, yes, oops. That's where those went. I'm going to get another drink."

Emmett stood and reached to grab the underwear out of Wyatt's grasp, and I practically sprinted into the kitchen.

I leaned my butt against the counter and closed my eyes, exhaling. This thing with Emmett was getting out of control.

His mom was coming wedding dress shopping with me. My gut twisted, thinking of how her eyes lit up. She was so excited. She didn't have a daughter of her own, all she had was boys. Holden was a grump who couldn't stand people, Wyatt only cared about surfing, and Finn didn't stay in one place long enough to meet anyone, let alone get married, so I was her only shot at all the fun mother-in-law wedding stuff.

Mother-in-law.

I was such an asshole, leading Elizabeth and Sam on like this. They thought it was real. We'd done too good of a job convincing them, and now they were hooked.

Shit.

And that kiss.

Double shit.

I kept getting flashes of electricity down my spine. There'd been a pressure low in my belly since he grabbed me and kissed me. That kiss. I'd *never* had a kiss like that in my life. I'd seen kisses like that on the big screen and read about them in books but never even dreamed it could be like that.

I wanted to do it again.

I shivered and wrapped my arms around myself. This was getting out of control. *I* was getting out of control.

"Hey," Emmett's voice greeted me, and I opened my eyes.

"You rat," I chided him, and he gave me a guilty grin and took the spot at the counter beside me. I ripped the underwear out of his hands.

"You know I'll do what it takes to win. The look on your face when Wyatt pulled them out, it was worth that stupid turtle rescue," he told me.

I couldn't help myself, I laughed. "The look on your face in those pictures was worth my pretend underwear being whipped around the living room."

He looked down at me and his gaze dropped to my mouth. "We're even, for now."

"I'm keeping them, you know," I vowed with defiance.

"Oh, really?" His gaze lingered on my face, and there it was again, that zing down my spine. I took a steadying breath, but it didn't do a thing to slow my accelerating pulse. "I bought those myself. You're going to wear them?"

I didn't answer. The conversation had slipped into dangerous territory, fast. This was all supposed to be fake, but this zingy, electric feeling didn't feel pretend.

"What was that, earlier?" he asked in a low voice, still gazing at me. His eyes were darkening.

"What do you mean?" I was breathless. My chest was tight, like I was on the top of a roller coaster about to drop.

"That kiss. Why'd you kiss me like that?" He glanced down to my mouth and then back up to my eyes.

I gave a little laugh of disbelief. "You're the one who kissed *me*."

His gaze dropped again to my mouth and lingered there. He turned so he was leaning his side against the counter, facing me head-on. I looked away but he reached up and tilted my chin back to him. I couldn't breathe, my body was so wound up and tense. When his fingers made contact with my jaw, I felt it right down between my legs.

"It was different," he said.

All I could do was nod.

"You want to do it again?" he asked in a low voice. "For practice."

Before I could finish nodding, his hands came to my hips and I gasped when he hoisted me onto the counter, facing him. He pushed my knees apart and my eyes widened at the expression on his face.

Motivated. His eyes were dark but focused. His gaze skimmed over me, not sure whether to look in my eyes or at my lips or along the neckline of my dress. His hands rested on the bare skin of my knees, and I could feel my underwear getting wet.

Holy shit, what was happening?

And *why* was I enjoying this so much?

His hands came back to my hips, he pulled me toward him, put his mouth on mine, and I melted.

Half of the tension inside me settled, and half only wound tighter. This was what I wanted, but I always wanted *more*. Making out on the kitchen counter like teenagers was all I needed, but the next second, I wanted more, faster, harder, less clothing, more skin. One of my hands fisted into his hair and he groaned and slid his tongue over mine. My other hand pulled his shirt tails out so I could skim my hand up what I thought might be—*yes it was!*—a ridged six-pack.

He pulled me to him harder, flush against him, and his hard length pushed against me.

"Oh my god," I breathed into his mouth, and his erection pulsed against me.

He let out another groan. "Jesus Christ, Avery."

There was something about how his hand was firmly in my hair, holding my mouth to his with no chance of escape, that made me very, very wet. His other hand came back to my knee, sliding up my inner thigh, closer to my center. I gasped. My body was on fire. I was about to explode.

"They're in here, making a baby on the counter," one of Emmett's friends called at the doorway, and I jerked away from Emmett.

Emmett walked a few steps away and leaned over the counter. His back rose and fell with his heavy breathing. I slid off the counter to standing, opened the fridge, and for some reason, grabbed a bottle of hot sauce.

"I'm going to…" I trailed off. "Yeah."

"I need a minute," Emmett murmured into the counter with a strained voice.

I nodded. Yep. The memory of what he needed a minute for, pressed into me, was seared into my brain.

Back out in the living room, I placed the hot sauce on the table as everyone began clapping. "Found it."

The party continued, and I spent the next few hours trying to act normal around Emmett. Once in a while, our gazes would meet and I'd feel another pulse between my legs, but I ignored it. This was an agreement. It wasn't real, and I wasn't supposed to be turned on like this. I tried to push the feelings aside, but when Emmett's hand eventually rested on my ankle, I stood.

"I'm going to head home," I told the group, not looking at him.

Emmett frowned and jumped up. "You're leaving?"

I nodded. "I'm tired. Bye, everyone."

I wasn't tired. I worked in the restaurant industry, I was awake past midnight regularly, but I couldn't sit here, remembering his mouth on mine and his hands in my hair. It was driving me nuts.

A round of goodbyes followed me from the living room to the kitchen, where I placed my glass in the dishwasher. Emmett was on my heels.

"I can't believe you're tired. What about all those late nights at the restaurant?"

Shit. Busted. I gave him a lopsided smile. "I've had enough socializing and *lying*"—I whispered the word—"for one night."

Also, I was pretty sure if Emmett kissed me one more time tonight, I wouldn't leave until morning. The thought was simultaneously thrilling and terrifying.

He moved in front of me as I tried to exit the kitchen. "Why don't you stay in the guest bedroom?"

"Because I don't have all my stuff. This may come as a shock to you but I don't wake up like this." I gestured at my face and hair.

"I bet you're cute when you wake up." His tone was teasing and persuasive.

I narrowed my eyes at him. That kiss, and now this? "What's gotten into you?"

The corners of his mouth rose in a wicked smile and he shrugged. "Just wondering."

"Just wondering what?" I gave him a light push to move past him. He caught my hand and spun me around so I faced him.

"What it would be like."

Another zing of electricity shot down my spine, and the pressure between my legs increased. Emmett looked down at me with that dark gaze I saw in the kitchen.

I wondered what it would be like, too. What his skin would feel like if I stripped his shirt off and ran my mouth down his flat stomach. What his tongue would feel like on my nipples. What it would feel like to stroke the hard length that pressed against me in the kitchen and feel him shudder.

I didn't like this out-of-control, overwhelming urge. I'd never felt like this before. Sex was always just an itch to scratch but with Emmett, it was more. It felt like something I needed.

It felt dangerous.

I shivered and shook the thoughts out of my head. I was here for one reason—to fulfill my end of the bargain so I could get my restaurant. I wasn't here to play house with the most attractive guy in town.

"I'm going home," I told him firmly.

"Are you walking?" He frowned. "It isn't safe."

"It's safe, I walk home from the restaurant all the time in the middle of the night."

"There are cougars."

I laughed and sighed. "I'll call a cab."

"No need," Hannah cut in behind me. "I'll drive you. I only had a glass of wine with dinner, I'm okay to drive."

"Great. Thanks, Hannah." I looked back at Emmett with raised eyebrows. "Happy?"

He nodded, but he was still frowning. "Next time, you stay in the guest bedroom."

"Why would she stay in the guest bedroom?" Hannah asked, slipping her cream-colored Converse sneakers on.

My mouth fell open and Emmett and I exchanged an *oops* look.

"He meant his bedroom," I told her.

He nodded. "Yeah. That's what I call it. The guest bedroom."

Hannah frowned in confusion, and when she stooped to put the other shoe on, I gave Emmett a *what the hell?* look.

"Emmett's drunk," I told Hannah, and it was his turn to shoot me that look. "Goodnight, Emmett."

"Goodnight, Emmett." She glanced over her shoulder at him. "Maybe have some water."

He gave me an unimpressed look. "I will. Thanks for coming, Hannah."

I followed Hannah out the door. "We have that meeting at the bank tomorrow," I reminded him.

"Yep, I know." He leaned on the door frame, watching me. "Goodnight."

"Goodnight, Adams. Text me when you get home."

He stayed at the door until we got in the car and drove away.

I glanced over at Hannah while she made her way toward my place. "Did you have a good time tonight?"

The corners of her lips tugged in a small smile, and she nodded at me. "I did. I was nervous about going but I'm happy I went."

Hannah was the kind of person who was anxious to enter social situations but often had fun once she was there. She just needed a push. That's where I usually came in. Sometimes I worried if it weren't for me, Hannah wouldn't leave her bookstore. She often joked she felt more comfortable around fictional men than real ones.

"I'm happy you showed up, too." I squeezed her shoulder.

She bit her lip, and her expression shuttered while she watched the road. She swallowed.

"What's up?"

She shook her head. "Nothing." Her voice was light.

"No, it's something. What is it?"

Her gaze cut to me and then back to the road. "I guess I'm surprised you didn't tell me about Emmett. He said you were unsure about the two of you and that's why you didn't want to tell anyone but..." She winced. "I thought we were better friends than that. I wouldn't have told anyone."

My heart sank in my chest. Fuck. I was such an asshole.

"I asked you a couple months ago if you were interested in dating anyone in town," she continued, worry written on her face. "And you said no."

The biggest asshole in the world. Hannah was so sweet, so kind, so selfless, and so thoughtful. She was my closest friend in this town and here I was, making her feel like total crap.

"It's all fake," I blurted out.

Shit. My head fell back on the head rest, and I sent her a tentative glance.

She gave me a strange look. "Huh?"

"The whole thing with Emmett, it's all a big lie. We aren't engaged, we aren't even dating." My words tumbled out. "I don't even like the guy."

She blinked at the road, lips parted. We were on my street, so she pulled into the driveway of my place. She parked the car without a word and sat staring up at the old house. I could hear music playing and people talking in the backyard.

Hannah glanced at me. "Um. Can you explain, please?"

I started talking and couldn't stop. I told her everything. How he approached me and told me about his low poll numbers, how he wanted to win the election but being single was hurting him, how he agreed to cosign on my loan if I'd pretend to be his girlfriend, how he convinced me to get fake-engaged and then fake-married, all of it.

To Hannah's credit, she listened and didn't say a word, she just let me blab all my secrets to her while she wore a curious expression. When I was finished, I slumped back in my seat.

"Well?" I lifted my eyebrows. "Am I destined for the lowest level of hell for lying to an entire town?"

She tapped her chin with narrowed eyes. "Maybe not the lowest level."

I snorted, and she grinned at me.

"A new deck and new windows is a pretty good deal," she mused.

I winced. "Elizabeth is so excited."

"And you really don't like him? Like not even a little bit?"

I hesitated. I didn't. I knew I didn't. But those kisses, they were so good. I felt them down to my toes, to the ends of my hair, to the tips of my fingernails. I swallowed, thinking about his fingers against my scalp and his tongue slicking against mine. A shiver ran down my neck.

I didn't want to lie to Hannah again.

"It's Emmett Rhodes. Of course, I have a little crush on him." I shrugged. "But it's nothing serious. Really. It's all fake, it's all for show."

She looked dubious.

"It's all fake," I emphasized. "And I'm sorry to do this to you but you can't tell a soul."

She rolled her eyes. "Who am I going to tell? I spend my days with Oliver Twist, Harry Potter, and Daisy Buchanan. My second-best friend, besides you, is Jane Austen. Your secret is safe."

Relief settled in my chest. It was Hannah, and I knew I could trust her. I felt lighter, like my heavy backpack of fake-relationship bullshit had been set down for a few minutes.

"Thank you. Oh," I remembered, "wedding dress shopping. Can you please come with me? It's next weekend."

Her face lit up. "Sure, I'd love to."

"Okay, good." I leaned over and gave her a quick hug. "Thanks, Han. You're the best, you know that?"

We said our goodbyes and I went inside. Moments after I stepped in the door, my phone buzzed. It was a text from Emmett.

???

Yes? I responded.

Just making sure you got home okay.

I stared at the messages with curiosity. Emmett cared about one thing—the election—so him being so concerned about me getting home okay struck me as odd.

My heart beat faster at the thought of him caring about me.

But when I thought about what I had told Hannah in the car—*it's all fake, it's all for show*—I sobered. Besides, Emmett was the kind of person who asked how everyone was doing, asked about their family members, asked how their work was going. Schmoozey, I reminded myself. Emmett was all up in everyone's business, and Elizabeth had raised him to be endlessly polite. That's what he was doing. He was just being polite.

Home safe. Thanks. See you tomorrow, I texted.

Goodnight, Adams.

My mouth twisted with rueful pleasure at the sight of my nickname. His nickname for me. In my bedroom, I plugged my phone in and got undressed for bed. As I undressed, the underwear fell out of my pocket and onto the floor.

The decoy underwear. I snorted and picked them up, inspecting them. The fabric was soft silk. The lace was high quality. They looked like my size.

I raised an eyebrow. Emmett had put effort into buying these. The image of him shopping for underwear online, or explaining to a sales associate in a store what he wanted, flashed into my head and the pressure and heaviness between my legs was back.

I dropped the underwear like they were on fire.

I spent about half an hour lying in bed in my dark bedroom, trying to fall asleep and failing. Despite pushing all thoughts of Emmett out of my head, the pressure between my legs lingered. Thoughts of Emmett's warm mouth, the scrape of his stubble, the firm touch of his fingers lingered. The tension within me lingered, and I groaned in frustration.

I needed to fall asleep, I told myself as my hands slipped into my underwear. Sleep was important, and when I didn't sleep enough, I was grouchy, I thought as my fingers made contact with my center. I sighed as my fingers slid over my wetness. No one would know I was thinking about Emmett when I did this. I was alone, and no one would know. This was normal. He probably thought about me while he did this.

The image of Emmett alone in his bed, stroking his cock while thinking about me, sent a fresh flood of wetness to my folds and I sighed again.

My fingers made quick circles, and within moments, I tipped over the edge with pleasure, eyes wrenched closed and mouth open. I shuddered and whimpered, remembering the way his length pressed into me in the kitchen earlier tonight, the way his mouth scraped my neck, and how the electricity sparked within me. My fingers moved fast, and every ounce of tension was wrung from my body as I came.

When I was done, I sank into the pillows, catching my breath.

I didn't feel better. I felt empty, and the needy twitchiness in my limbs lingered. I still wanted more. My mind protested but my body needed Emmett's mouth, his hands, his length.

We had been spending too much time together. That's why I was feeling like this. I'd tell Emmett we needed to walk it back. We'd convinced everyone we were a perfect, happy, devoted couple with our excessive PDA, so we didn't need to kiss anymore.

Tomorrow. I'd tell Emmett tomorrow.

13

Avery

"WHAT ARE YOU DOING?" Emmett murmured over my shoulder the next morning as I hammered a nail into the campaign sign in front of the restaurant. When I arrived ten minutes prior, one of the wooden stakes had split.

He wore a white t-shirt that looked great against his tan, but he knew that, and *knowing* he knew that annoyed me. My gaze flicked over the hem of his sleeve, fitted but not too tight. I caught a glimpse of his forearms.

I woke up horny this morning, and that made me grumpy.

Focus, I reminded myself.

We had a meeting with the bank in an hour, during which Emmett would sign on the dotted line and the restaurant would be all mine.

Well, not quite. This was just the business loan portion. Keiko and I would meet in a few weeks to sign the paperwork. Today was a big deal, though. After today, I'd be in the home stretch. All I had to do was hold up my end of the bargain with Emmett and play his adoring fiancée.

I wasn't sure where staring at his forearms fit into that.

Focus, I reminded myself again.

"Your sign is falling apart." I hammered another nail in

and jiggled the post to make sure it was secure. "You should take better care of these."

He stooped down to inspect my work. "Where'd you get that hammer?"

"I borrowed it from Jim at the hardware store." I stood and brushed my hands off.

Emmett shot me a curious expression before a smile grew on his face. "Thanks."

I shrugged. "I didn't do it for you." My tone sounded sharper than I intended.

"Oh, yeah?" His eyebrow rose. He didn't believe me. "Why are you so grouchy today?" A devilish grin came over his features. "Miss me last night?" He winked and bit his lip.

Irritation spiked in my shoulders. "If you're going to block my restaurant with this monstrosity, at least keep it in good condition."

"It's not your restaurant yet," he reminded me with a grin, and I frowned at him.

His smile brightened. "Relax, Adams, everything will go smoothly today at the bank." He reached for the hammer. "I'll take that back to Jim. Thanks for helping out on the Emmett Rhodes campaign." He leaned down and, fast as lightning, tilted my chin up and gave me a quick kiss before striding away, crossing the street, and disappearing into the hardware store.

From that instant of contact, my pulse had picked up. My body had tasted Emmett's mouth, and my body wanted more.

My grouchiness kicked up one notch.

I glanced around at the empty street. There were a few tourists out but no locals that I could spot, and the sign had hid us from diners inside the restaurant.

I narrowed my eyes at the hardware store. What was Emmett up to? There was no one around to keep the charade up for.

The pressure I tried to relieve last night? It was still there. I stared at the door of the hardware store Emmett had disappeared through. I was still wound tight, thinking about his mouth on my neck, his teeth scraping my skin, his hands all over me, his fingers where mine were last night.

Shit. I think I have to sleep with Emmett Rhodes.

I barked a laugh and climbed the steps to the restaurant. One hundred percent no. Never, ever.

"What's so funny?" Max asked when I stepped inside.

I shook my head. "Nothing."

———

"CAN you not do that here, please?" I asked Emmett later as he returned to his stool at the bar after greeting a family who had just been seated. "This is a family place. They don't want to see you schmoozing all over the place."

"I'm just saying hello to some friends." He took a sip of water. "Friends are people you talk to on a regular basis and spend time with," he explained slowly.

I gave him a blank stare, which only made him grin harder as I wiped the counter.

"Wow, you are just a wealth of knowledge. Thank you so much for sharing it with me."

"For you, Adams? Anytime." He turned as Holden took the seat next to him. "There he is."

Holden nodded once at me in greeting. "Avery."

"Hi, Holden. Can I get you anything?"

Emmett glanced around. "Don't you have staff who can take our orders? This doesn't seem like an effective use of your time."

"Relax," I scolded him. "I like talking to customers. It's called customer service."

Emmett gestured at himself. "I'm a customer, and I want you to take a break, sit down, and eat lunch with us."

Holden nodded. "Join us, Avery. I haven't had a chance to

congratulate you yet." He paused, thinking. "Congratulations."

I smiled at him. "Thanks, Holden." A man of few words and no pretense. If only Emmett could be more like him. I would never, *ever* admit this out loud, but Emmett was a bit better-looking than Holden. Holden was a big guy, tall and broad. Emmett was a bit slimmer, still tall, but he had a swimmer's body, all long, lean muscle. Long, lean muscle that looked pretty good in a white t-shirt. Too bad his insides didn't match his outsides. Holden had him there.

"Why can't you be more like Holden?" I asked Emmett, gesturing to his brother. "Men should be seen and not heard." My gaze snagged on where his t-shirt stretched across his shoulders.

The corner of Holden's mouth kicked up. Emmett stretched out in his chair, taking up as much space as he could. He cocked an eyebrow at me with a little smile on his face. "Yeah? And do you like what you see, Adams?"

My face heated. I did, and he knew I did, and somehow, that made it worse.

Something in my expression made Emmett laugh, and he dropped the teasing tone. "Sit with us and have lunch."

"Avery, take a break," Max urged behind me. "I can take the bar."

It was three against one, and my stomach was rumbling with hunger, so I dropped the notepad and pen on the counter and walked around the other side.

Max pulled a pen and paper out of his apron. "Alright, lunch orders."

"Go ahead." Emmett placed his hand on my arm and I ignored the spike of awareness at the contact.

"Salmon burger, please." My voice was tight.

"Holden?" Emmett asked.

"Roast beef sandwich." He nodded once at Max. "Thank you."

Max looked up with his pen poised. "Fries on the side?"

"Yes—"

"He'll have a salad on the side." Emmett glanced at Holden with a raised eyebrow. "You don't eat enough vegetables, and the salads are good here."

Max looked to Holden, who rolled his eyes and grunted an acknowledgment.

"And I'll have the salmon burger with a side salad," Emmett told Max with a smile. "Thanks, Max."

"Thanks, Max," I called after him as he dropped the orders off with the kitchen. "Do you always order for your brother?" I asked Emmett.

Holden stood suddenly, his phone buzzing. "Be right back."

Emmett watched Holden walk out the front door with his phone to his ear. "I didn't order for him, I made an adjustment." He turned toward me, letting his gaze rake over my face.

My mouth hitched up. "Right. Adjustment."

"The guy barely cooks for himself, and when he does, it's something sad like Mr. Noodle."

My mouth fell open. "Hey, what's wrong with Mr. Noodle?"

He gave me a look. "Do not tell anyone you eat Mr. Noodle or our whole cover will be blown. No one would believe I'd marry a woman who ate Mr. Noodle."

A laugh bubbled out of me just as the door opened and a familiar nasally voice cut through my thoughts.

"Max," Chuck called, snapping his fingers to get Max's attention, who was in the middle of taking a customer's order at another table. "Get me a club sandwich to go, extra mayo."

Max grimaced and held up a finger to Chuck to signal he'd be there in a moment.

Chuck looked over to me and raised his hands. "Hello?

Can I get some service over here? Jeez." He shook his head and rolled his eyes.

Emmett set his napkin down, stood up, and walked over to Chuck. I inhaled sharply.

What was happening?

"No, Emmett, don't—"

Emmett stepped up to Chuck, leaned down, and said something quietly to him. He wore a pleasant, friendly smile but his gaze was hard. He leaned one hand on the wall and the other clenched into a fist at his side. Chuck's expression changed from exasperated to defensive. Chuck spat something back at Emmett. I could only see Emmett's profile, but his jaw hardened, his hand flexed, and whatever he said to Chuck caused the guy to look terrified.

My gaze flicked back to Emmett's expression. My lips parted, studying his set jaw and clenched hand, and again, my mind was flooded with images of last night in his kitchen, his mouth furious against mine and his hands all over me.

I shivered.

"What's happening over there?" Max asked at my side. "Are they going to fight?" He lowered his voice. "That would be so hot."

"I know," I murmured before catching myself. "I mean, no, we don't want a fight here."

Chuck said something to his wife and the two turned and left. Emmett watched them leave before returning to his seat like nothing happened.

"God, I can't stand that guy," Emmett muttered, reading through his menu. "I always take clients out to restaurants because seeing how someone treats serving staff tells me what they're like as a person. If they're assholes, we don't work with them." He glanced at me. "What? You don't agree?"

I frowned. "No, I do. You're right."

Holden returned. "I gotta go." He slipped his phone back

into his pocket. "McKinley site," he said to Emmett by way of explanation. "A water line broke."

Emmett waved his hand. "Go, go. I'll bring your lunch to the office."

I said a quick goodbye to Holden, and he left.

Emmett and I ate our food and a funny peace settled over us. Perhaps it was only funny because it was brand-new to us. People stopped by to say hello, to say congratulations, and Emmett made brief small talk with them while I listened. I watched how people interacted with him, how they wanted to share with him, and how he remembered small details about their lives. If he was schmoozing, he was damn good at it. I suspected he wasn't schmoozing, though. This was just Emmett.

I couldn't stop picturing the way his jaw tensed and his fist clenched, how *hot* Emmett looked when he was mad. Hot enough to threaten this whole plan we had concocted. I would have to be very, very careful from here on out.

"You're interested in people." I tilted my head at him after someone from his company left. "You care about these people. It's not an act."

He gave me an amused look. "Of course it's not an act." He checked the time. "We should go."

I nodded and moved to clear our plates, but Emmett put his hand on mine to stop me.

"It's fine," I told him. "Max is busy."

Max appeared at my side. "I've got it."

"Thanks, Max, I appreciate it." Emmett wrapped his hand around mine and pulled me toward the door. "Come on, Adams, let's go get you a restaurant."

14

Avery

"EVERYTHING SEEMS TO BE IN ORDER," Harold, the loan specialist, told us in his monotone voice before he cleared his throat. "Ms. Adams, if you'll please sign there," he said, pointing to the line for my signature on the paperwork.

I leaned forward and scrawled my name. Harold nodded with satisfaction.

"And Mr. Rhodes, if you'll please sign there," Harold said, pointing to the line beside my name.

Emmett leaned forward and paused.

This was it. This was the moment everything went wrong. I had been waiting for this moment all day. The floor was about to fall through or there'd be an earthquake or the pen would explode in his hand. Something would get in the way of Emmett cosigning on my loan.

He gave me a quick, cheeky grin and signed his name in scratchy loops before setting the pen down.

"Very good." Harold collected the papers. "Thank you for your business."

I waited. "That's it?"

Harold blinked. "Were you expecting something else?"

Emmett raised an eyebrow at me, amused.

"No, I guess not." I shrugged.

It wasn't supposed to be this easy. I didn't even have to work for it. Yes, I had to endure Emmett and play pretend with him, but let's be real, it wasn't *that* difficult.

And now I had the loan, so I could buy the restaurant as soon as Keiko returned from her most recent trip to Vancouver.

Harold wove his fingers together and shifted while Emmett stood up.

"We'll get out of your hair. Thanks, Harold." Emmett reached for my hand. "Come on, darling."

I stared at where our hands were joined as I let him lead me out of the bank, but just before the doors, someone called his name.

"Emmett," a woman about his mom's age said, walking up to us. "Do you have a moment to sign the Backpack Buddies paperwork?"

"Sure." He turned to me. "I'll just be a second." His fingers brushed my arm before he headed over.

I waited outside and a few minutes later, he joined me. "Sorry about that."

I shook my head. "No problem. What's Backpack Buddies?"

"It's nothing. I'm hungry again." He nodded his chin toward the main street, where tents and booths had been set up with local food and crafts. "Let's wander through the farmer's market."

Something in his expression caught my attention though. Embarrassment? He wouldn't meet my gaze. He was very focused.

"What is it?" I pressed.

He shook his head again and grabbed my hand. "Nothing. Do you think they have those waffles again?"

With my other hand, I slipped my phone out of my back pocket and googled 'Backpack Buddies.'

"Backpack Buddies is a school program on Vancouver Island that provides backpacks of food for low-income school children so they may have nutritious meals for evenings and weekends," I read as we walked toward the market, hand in hand. My insides melted like ice cream on a hot day.

Emmett groaned and rolled his eyes. "You're nosy, you know that?"

"Emmett," I said in a teasing tone.

He ignored me.

"Emmett," I dropped his hand and tucked myself under his arm. "Are you secretly a good guy?"

His brow furrowed. "It's for the tax write-off."

I shook my head. "No, it isn't."

He looked at me and my stomach did a slow, delicious roll. His gaze settled on me, so comfortably warm. "Please don't tell anyone."

"Why not?"

He shrugged and looked away. "It's sleazy, using that for the campaign. I want to focus on things I can do for the town."

I couldn't help the smile that crept onto my face. "Alright. I won't say a word."

He sent a quick glance to me. "Thanks." His thumb absent-mindedly stroked my shoulder.

"Emmett?"

He glanced down at me. The side of his mouth hitched, tilting the little white scar, and my finger twitched. I wanted to trace that scar with my fingertip.

"Thanks for cosigning on my loan." My throat tightened and I had the urge to shut my mouth but I knew I needed to say this. If it wasn't for Emmett, Chuck would be swapping out Table Three for a stripper pole and installing neon lights behind the bar. I could go the route of kicking myself for every time I bought name-brand cookies instead of the cheap ones, every useless dollar spent on jewelry, but instead, I just felt grateful to Emmett for trusting me with the loan.

"I know I give you a lot of crap but…" I bit my lip and gave him a rueful smile. "I'd be screwed without you, so thanks. I promise to do what I can so you're elected." I swallowed. "I do think you'd do a better job than Isaac."

He watched me with a little knowing smile on his face, like he knew a secret. His thumb still brushed my skin and I found it difficult to focus on anything else. "Thanks, Adams. I appreciate that. I know you'll hold up your end of the bargain." He chewed on his lip. "I trust you."

My face was warm. This was a lot of seriousness for us.

I swallowed and my gaze dropped to his mouth again. "How'd you get that scar?"

"This?" He pointed to his lip.

I nodded.

"Wyatt and I were horsing around as kids in the living room and I slipped and hit my face on the coffee table." His mouth tilted again. "I wish it was from something cooler, like skateboarding."

I snorted, letting my gaze linger once more on the scar before grabbing his arm. "Come on, let's go get you some green juice, or whatever."

He laughed and let me pull him into the farmer's market.

We wandered through the booths, saying hello to the vendors and buying veggies from local farms. The restaurant purchased from many of the vendors but they were usually so busy during deliveries that we didn't have much time to chat, so it was nice to have a few moments to catch up. Emmett shook hands and held babies that were pushed into his arms and tasted the samples that were thrust into his mouth.

"Do you want to buy a raffle ticket?" a teenage girl asked, holding a string of them. "We're raising money for our prom."

"Sure." I fished out my wallet.

"I'll buy some, too," Emmett told her. "When's the prom?"

She accepted our money and handed the tickets over. "It's tomorrow night."

We thanked her and wandered on to the next booth.

"I wore a floor-length ice-blue dress to my prom," I told Emmett. "My friends and I couldn't get a limo because they were all booked up so we rented a horse and carriage."

He nodded a quick hello to the booth owner and grinned at me. "That sounds fun."

"It was. What about you, what was your prom like?"

He shrugged. "I didn't go to mine."

I reared back, touching his arm. "I'm sorry, what? *You* didn't go to your prom? Were you in the hospital or something?"

The side of his mouth hitched up as he glanced over the little jars of honey on the table. "Nope. It just didn't work out."

I followed him to the fruit stand. "What does that mean?"

"My girlfriend in high school broke up with me the day before," he said with a rueful smile while he placed apples in a bag, "and I didn't want to go to prom and watch her make out with another guy."

I frowned. Inside my chest, my heart twisted for him. "That's terrible. What a shitty thing to do."

He shrugged. "It's fine, it was for the best. They're happily married now so I can't blame them. And I think he had a crush on her for a while and I didn't know it."

"I can't believe *you* had a girlfriend." I gave him a little teasing grin. "Thought you weren't that kind of guy."

He laughed. "Yeah, well, Nat helped me figure that out fast."

Record scratch. I paused, narrowing my eyes.

"Nat? Will's Nat?"

He nodded. "Yep. Will's Nat."

"Wow." So Emmett dated a girl and then she dumped him for his best friend. "What do you mean, she helped you figure it out?"

My head raced with ideas. Pregnancy scare? Did Emmett get Nat pregnant, she wanted to keep it and he didn't? The idea of Emmett getting anyone else pregnant sent jealous rage through my veins.

He sucked in a breath and inspected the apple in his hand before tucking it in the bag. "She had a plan, she wanted a family one day and didn't see me as the kind of guy who could provide that. I didn't care about that stuff."

My heart split in half, thinking of a teenage version of Emmett, gangly and young, sitting home alone on his prom night, thinking about how he wasn't good enough for Nat's life plan.

He saw my sad expression and laughed. "Adams, it's fine. Really. She apologized years later for dumping me the night before prom. Besides, I like being an uncle. Will's a much better dad and husband than I'd ever be."

My hand came to my chest, hearing those words. Is that why Emmett didn't want a relationship? Because someone didn't want him, she wanted his best friend instead?

I knew they were just teenagers when this happened. I knew this. I also knew Nat was a lovely person. She and Will had been into the restaurant for date night, and she was friendly, polite, and patient. People made mistakes. I had done things I wasn't proud of.

But she had also made Emmett feel pain. She'd made him feel like he wasn't worthy.

In an ugly place in the back of my mind, I wondered if he still had a thing for her. They were both in their mid-thirties and from what I had seen, Will and Nat were happily married. I had never seen Emmett and Nat together, though. Maybe he still carried a torch for her.

An idea struck me and I brightened up. "What are you doing tomorrow night?" I asked him.

"We have dinner with my family, remember?"

"Right." Elizabeth had called and invited us to dinner at their place tomorrow. The whole family would be there. This might still work. "I'll be right back."

He gave me a curious look but nodded, and I walked away and pulled my phone out. After a quick call to Miri, during which she asked many questions about the upcoming wedding I wasn't able to answer and I asked her my own questions, before I returned to Emmett, who was paying the fruit vendor.

"I have a proposition for you," I told him as we wandered to the next stand.

"Okay." He raised an eyebrow at me.

"Let's go to prom tomorrow night." I wiggled my eyebrows at him. "We can get all dressed up, rent a limo, awkwardly slow dance amidst the scent of teen lust, it'll be so fun."

He looked uncertain. "I don't know."

"Come on," I pleaded. I looped my arm through his as we walked. "I promise it'll be fun. And a great campaign opportunity. Isaac never volunteers around town. Also, it'll make Miri so happy."

His gaze lingered on me and he smiled. "Well, if it'll make Miri happy."

I nodded, flushed and excited. "It will, it really will. This is going to be great."

15

Emmett

I PARKED outside Avery's place just before eight. Dinner with my family had been moved to another night after my mom found out about Avery and me going to prom, and after Div informed me the only limo in town was booked by a group of teenagers, my dad had insisted I pick Avery up in his Porsche.

It was an emerald-green 1989 Porsche 911, and my dad's pride and joy. He was a simple guy, not materialistic at all, often wore t-shirts with small holes in them. All his clothes were purchased by my mother, and growing up, he had taught us to fix things instead of buying something new.

But this car, he loved this car. He normally kept it in the garage under a cover and only drove it out when there was zero chance of rain.

I had begged him to take the car to pick Nat up for prom seventeen years ago, and finally, he relented.

My shoulders tensed, thinking about that day, and I shook my head to myself as I made my way up the gravel path beside Avery's house. It was seventeen years ago. It wasn't a big deal.

Something crunched under my foot as I turned the corner

into the backyard—a beer can. There were a lot of them, strewn around the yard.

"Hey, bud." A guy in his twenties with shoulder-length blond hair and an unbuttoned Hawaiian shirt perched on the wall bordering a small patio. A few other guys sat on lawn chairs held together with duct tape. I recognized the Hawaiian shirt guy, he worked for Wyatt at the surf shop in the summers. The rank smell of weed hung in the air.

Summer workers. They flocked to Queen's Cove for the waves, babes, and parties. I'd have bet this house was subdivided into at least four rental units, and none of it was done to code.

I tilted my chin at him. "Hey."

"Nice suit. You here to pick up Laser?" he asked with a smirk.

I raised an eyebrow. "Laser?"

He pointed upstairs at Avery's apartment. "The chick's a natural at beer pong." He mimed the throwing motion and made a *pew* noise. "Like a laser."

Something possessive and grumpy flared in my chest.

Normally, I'd stop to chat with these guys. Ask them where they're from, how long they're in town, how are they liking it here, yada yada. I liked chatting with people. I liked getting to know people.

There was something about this guy I didn't like, though. I didn't like that he had a nickname for Adams. I didn't like how much I didn't like him. I wasn't like this. This wasn't who I was.

"Who are you, her accountant?" one of his friends asked and they dissolved into laughter.

The guy stopped laughing when he realized I was giving him my most intimidating glare. The one I used when clients tried to swindle Rhodes Construction out of payment. My *no fucking way* look.

"I'm her fiancé." My voice was gritty.

Hawaiian shirt guy's eyebrows rose. "For real, bro?"

"For real." I climbed the stairs without another word and opened Avery's front door.

"Honey, I'm home," I called as I stepped inside. My pulse picked up as I climbed the stairs. I was nervous about prom, which was stupid because it was a dance for teenagers, what did I have to be nervous about?

"I'm almost ready, be out in a second." Her voice came from another room.

I wandered further into the little apartment and searched for a glass. The first cabinet was filled with instant noodle packages. I shook my head with disappointment. Sad. So sad. The drawer below was stuffed with takeout menus, chopsticks, and soy sauce packages.

Her fridge was even more barren. Mustard, oat milk, and a carton of eggs.

"You eat like a frat boy."

"Stop snooping!" she called back.

I found a glass, poured myself some water, then wandered into the living room and took a seat on the couch. Where was her TV? A laptop lay on the floor beside the couch, plugged in and charging, and a big book on vintage fashion sat on the scratched wooden coffee table. The walls were barren. This place looked like college housing, temporary and bland and expressionless.

"Thanks for waiting." She breezed past me into the living room, and I caught the scent of her spicy citrus perfume.

My head whipped in her direction. She wore a floor-length emerald-green velvet dress with tiny little straps. Her hair was loose and wavy around her shoulders and my fingers twitched with the urge to touch her. She turned and looked at me, sitting on the couch, and my gaze dropped to where her neckline plunged.

She gave me an appreciative eyebrow wiggle. "You look good." She winked.

Lust rattled through me like a freight train, and I clenched my hands at my sides. My cock ached with the need to haul her into her bedroom and sink deep into her. I couldn't tell what she had done with her makeup, but she was gorgeous. Natural and sweet and pretty. A delicate silver chain hung around her neck, and my gaze slid down to the slight cleavage above her neckline. Was she wearing a bra? I couldn't tell.

I frowned. Where had *that* come from? Jesus Christ, Rhodes. I cleared my throat and dragged my gaze away from her. Anywhere but her.

The wall. The wall was a good place to look.

My gaze was back to her tits. Jesus Christ, Adams was hot. She always wore those blazers over t-shirts, so I couldn't see anything. I bet her tits were incredible. I bet they felt incredible.

Wait, she said something.

"What?" I asked her, swallowing and trying to ignore how hard I was.

She gave me a funny look. "I said you look good. That suit looks great on you."

"Thanks." My voice sounded hoarse.

Think about turtles. Turtles are gross. They're slimy.

Good. This was helping.

I cleared my throat. "That suit looks great on you, too." What? "I mean, you do, too. Look good. You look good, too."

She snorted. "Are you okay?"

"Yes." My cock throbbed and I tried not to picture her in the decoy underwear I had bought. I shouldn't have bought those. What a mistake. The image of her wearing them had been sneaking into my head at the most inconvenient times.

Avery wandered over to me and placed her hand on my shoulder. Her perfume wafted into my periphery again and I had the overwhelming urge to bury my face in her neck and huff her into my soul.

She leaned down to look at me, giving me a front-row seat to her goddamn incredible tits, right in my face.

"You look weird."

"I'm fine," I rasped as I held on for dear life to my control. "Can I have some water?"

I just needed to get her tits out of my face before I said or did something very stupid.

"You have some right there." She picked up my glass and handed it to me.

Right. Shit.

I rubbed my hand over my face and inhaled, trying to calm myself. My cock throbbed with need. I should have jerked off in the shower before tonight. I had been putting that off lately because I had a sneaking suspicion the second my hand wrapped around myself, I wouldn't be able to get Avery out of my head.

"Right. Thanks." I took it from her and downed the glass while she watched with a small grin. "Where's your TV?" I was desperate to change the subject.

She leaned down to slip her heels on and again, I couldn't tear my gaze from her perfect tits. An image of me yanking the dress down and running my tongue over her pinched nipples played in my head. Fuck.

She shrugged. "Don't have one."

Turtles. Slimy turtles staring at you. Turtle crawling on your bed. Avery crawling on your bed. Shit. No.

"Hannah said you love old movies." My voice sounded far away. Hannah had told me this when I asked her about engagement rings.

"I watch them on my laptop."

"Your laptop is a thousand years old. They found it in an Egyptian tomb."

She grinned at me and stood. "Are you ready, or do you want to continue staring at my tits all night?"

Our eyes locked and a laugh burst out of my chest. Busted. "Why not both?" A sly smile grew on my face.

Avery locked up and my hand came to her elbow as we descended the stairs.

"Uh oh, Laser's on the loose!" that fucking Hawaiian shirt guy called from the patio. He wiggled his eyebrows at her and his gaze also snagged on her neckline.

Any grin on my face dropped when he looked at her like that. My hand slipped around her waist and I locked her to my side.

Hawaiian Shirt Fuckface leaned in further to her chest. "Is that the vintage moonstone pendant you got a couple weeks ago?"

She nodded with enthusiasm and her hand brushed the necklace. "It sure is."

He leaned in further to study the necklace and white rage flooded my veins. "What a piece." He grinned lazily up at her. My teeth gritted and my jaw was tense. I was staring a hole through this guy's skull.

A thought struck me like a punch in the gut. Avery only hooked up with summer workers. I didn't know if it was a rule, but it was a general guideline. I thought back to our conversation about discreetly dating on the side.

What if, at one point, she had something going with *this guy*? What if she wanted to continue dating this guy? What if she was just waiting until we were done to hook up with him again?

My jaw clenched. This asshole had to be twenty-three or twenty-four. She didn't have to date the guy, maybe she just used him for sex. He was just downstairs, what could be more convenient than that?

Rage rocketed through my veins and my arm tightened around her waist. God, he had a stupid face. A punchable face, that's what Holden called faces like his, all mashed around and stupid-looking. He couldn't even grow a proper beard.

Another feeling rattled through me—possessiveness. One word came to mind and my hand tensed over Avery's waist.

Mine.

"We're going to be late," I said, steering her away to the side of the yard, away from them. I glanced over my shoulder with my best *don't fucking dare* expression. "Don't wait up for Mommy."

"Bye, guys," Avery called back.

I kept my hand firmly on her waist while we walked to the car. When we approached, she whistled with approval.

"Cool car."

I winked at her, still feeling possessive. "Only the best for you, *darling*."

"You know how to make a girl feel special." She turned to me and gestured at her dress. "What do you think of the dress? Do I look good enough to be seen with Emmett Rhodes tonight?"

She put her hand on her waist and wiggled a little.

My control snapped like a rubber band. *Fuck it.*

I grabbed her waist and hauled her against me. Her eyes flared with surprise, and I leaned down to kiss her.

She gasped into my mouth, and I used the opportunity to taste her. I put all my confusing possessive feelings into kissing her, wrapping my arms around her to pull her close to me, tasting her. She relaxed against me.

Mine.

A little moan escaped her lips, and it went straight to my cock. Her mouth was so soft and sweet and pliant and welcoming and *fucking hell,* this felt incredible. My fingers tangled into her silky hair, and I grabbed a handful, pulling and giving myself more access to her mouth. I groaned into her and pressed her against the car. My erection pressed into her stomach and she pressed right back.

My head spun. Kissing Avery was like a drug I couldn't have just a taste of, I always needed more. I could already see myself in the shower, stroking my cock and thinking about this moment with her sweet little ass in my hand while she moaned into my mouth.

My hand slipped up the soft fabric of her dress and covered one of those perfect tits. I groaned low into her mouth and the second my thumb found that pinched little peak, she whimpered and thrust against me. Desire wrenched through me. I nearly came right there.

I pushed myself off her and took a deep breath, walking a few steps away to collect myself. My cock strained in my pants, desperate to fuck her. Desperate to know what she felt like. Desperate to make her feel good.

Fuck.

I took a step toward her and looked down at her. Her chest rose and fell, and my gaze snagged on her cleavage again before dragging back up to her eyes, which were drowsy and heavy. My cock pulsed again.

"You look goddamn gorgeous tonight, Adams."

"Thanks." She sounded breathless.

"I don't want you seeing other guys while we're together." My voice was gravelly and hard. I swallowed but maintained eye contact.

She nodded, dazed. "I know. We talked about this."

We talked about it but I needed to make sure she was a hundred percent clear. I took another step closer and my mouth hovered inches from hers. Her dark blue eyes widened. "I'm the only one who touches you. Do you understand?"

She nodded again and her gaze slid to my mouth. She wanted more of me. She wanted my mouth back on her. If I lingered too long on that realization, she'd be over my shoulder as I hauled her back to her apartment so I could tear this dress off and show her what I could really do with my mouth.

Instead, I reached past her to open her door. Once she was inside, I stalked around to the other side, got in, and started the car. We drove for two minutes in silence before she turned to me.

"Did you think…" She narrowed her eyes at me and a little grin appeared on her lips. "…that Carter and I…" She gave me a funny look.

I swallowed again. That fucking guy.

"Emmett," she said in a low voice, and my cock pulsed again.

Her saying my name these days did funny things to me. I heard it in my head, in different tones. I heard her gasping it, moaning it, crying it out.

"I'm not hooking up with anyone. Especially not Carter."

"Good."

"He's twenty-two. And too frat-boy for my taste."

Even the thought of her with someone else made me white-knuckle the steering wheel. "I don't know your type. Maybe you wanted an outlet."

She laughed. "An outlet for what?"

I swallowed again. An outlet for what we were doing against the car before. An outlet for what was making me hard more and more often these days. "Maybe you just needed someone to have sex with."

"Oh." She watched me and I watched the road. "And you thought some young guy who smokes pot for breakfast was who I would choose?" I could hear the grin in her voice.

"He was looking at you like he wanted that."

She laughed. "Yeah, he's got a little crush on me." She shrugged. "So what?" Her mouth dropped open. "Emmett, are you *jealous*?"

"I don't like it." Especially not with him living below her, always there. Looking… with his stupid eyes. My gaze slid over to Avery, sitting there with her legs crossed and her arm draped over the door. She had rolled the window down and her hair fluttered in the wind around her shoulders. Her skin looked so soft.

"You are. You're jealous." Her grin was back and her gaze raked over my form with appreciation.

I didn't answer her. I *was* jealous. She knew I was fucking jealous. I reached out and rested my hand on her thigh. Her breath caught in her throat and her muscles tensed under my hand for a brief moment before relaxing. Fucking hell, I was so hard. I could just turn the car around and go straight to my place.

No. Shit. What was I thinking? It wasn't like that with us. Fucking hell. I had never been so horny and angry at the same time.

"You don't have anything to worry about." Her voice was soft.

"Good." I glanced at her and then back to the road. "If you need an outlet, you call me. I'll make you come harder than he ever could."

A shiver rolled through her. Her thighs tensed and pressed together under my hand, and we locked eyes. Her mouth parted. "Noted."

I turned back to the road. What was I doing? What Avery and I were doing, it was a contract, and now I was getting jealous and telling her not to see other guys? Telling her I'd make her come hard? I removed my hand from Avery's thigh and immediately wanted to put it back, but this wasn't what she signed up for. Guilt and frustration hit me deep in my gut and I frowned as I drove.

Avery flicked the radio on and we arrived at the school a few minutes later. I kept my hand on her back as we walked inside.

The prom would be held inside the school gymnasium and only a few teachers had arrived. The lights had been dimmed, a few disco balls had been strung up, and gold and black balloons floated in the air. A song I recognized from the radio played. Avery squeezed my arm and a thrill sparked in my chest.

"Oh my god. This is so cool." She grinned at me, and her eyes sparkled. "Thank you so much for agreeing to this."

I could have laughed. I was the lucky one. I couldn't even remember why I hesitated before saying yes to this.

Right. Because Nat had dumped me the day before my prom and went with my best friend.

I waited for the pang in my chest at the memory, but it didn't show up. Avery shifted toward me, and the plush velvet of her dress brushed my palm.

I watched her and smiled. "No problem." It felt like an understatement.

"Don't you two look gorgeous." Miri approached with her eyes lit up. "You look like movie stars. I'm going to stick you two at the drinks table."

The teenagers began to pour in and the energy in the gym buzzed. Avery and I were occupied for the next hour at the drinks table, pouring punch and handing out napkins. It was fun, surprisingly. The kids were excited and Avery was enjoying herself, chatting with everyone and admiring the girls' dresses and hairstyles. Scott dropped by to say hello.

"Take a break," Miri told us. "I'll take over from here."

Avery handed off another glass of punch. "Are you sure?"

"Thanks, Miri." I didn't wait for her answer and pulled Avery toward the dance floor. "Come on, let's show these teens how awkward we can be."

She laughed and let me lead her out there. I grabbed her hand and spun her around, and when she smiled at me, my heart flipped in my chest. Goddamn, she was gorgeous.

We danced a few songs before a slow song came on and my hands came to her waist.

"Adams, will you slow dance with me?" I asked her in a low voice, pulling her closer.

She nodded and placed her hands behind my neck. "I

haven't slow danced like this since high school."

I pulled her flush against me so we were essentially hugging.

"Pretty sure we need to leave room for Jesus," she murmured below my ear.

"This isn't a Catholic school." One hand was on her lower back, the other was between her shoulders, running my fingers over her smooth skin. She sighed and relaxed against me.

"This is nice." Her head came to my shoulder.

My heart twisted again in the best way. I was floating, standing here in a school gym that smelled like sweat and Axe body spray, with the most beautiful, funny, infuriating woman I had ever met tucked against me. I wracked my brain for when I had ever felt like this before and came up with nothing.

I pressed my mouth onto the top of her head, and the realization hit me.

After the election was over, my agreement with Avery would finish, and whatever this was that we were doing, it would end.

No more making out in the kitchen or against the car. No more dinners. No more of her teasing me with pictures of the turtle rescue.

My arms gripped her tighter and she made a little noise of contentment against my chest.

I didn't want this to end. The thought shocked me as it rippled through my head, but it was the truth. I enjoyed spending time with Avery, even when she was pissing me off or pushing my buttons. I couldn't wait to see her. My pulse picked up whenever we touched. I thought about her constantly, not just thoughts about sinking my cock into her and making her writhe with an orgasm; I thought about her at her restaurant, how cute she looked when she was focused on something, how pretty her hair was, and how much I liked it when she made fun of me.

Shit.

My fingers paused in her hair and my throat tightened.

This wasn't supposed to happen. I didn't do this kind of thing. I wasn't this kind of guy. This was a Will thing to do. I was Emmett Rhodes, unattached, bachelor for life.

After the election, my life with Avery was a big blank. One big wash of unknown. Would we stay together? Would we break up and only see each other once in a while around town? My chest tightened at the idea of not seeing her almost every day, but the idea of staying married, being married *for real*, sent a streak of panic through me.

I didn't know what I wanted.

When Will and Nat got together, he knew exactly what he wanted. He had everything planned out, even from eighteen years old. They'd finish college, they'd get married, they'd save for a few years, and then they'd start a family.

I had no plan. I had no clue what I wanted. All I knew was I wanted Avery.

There was a flash and Avery lifted her head. Miri inspected the photo on her camera with a smile. "Just perfect."

"Do you need help?" Avery asked and I pulled her closer. I didn't want to help. I just wanted to sway here with her pressed up against me until the early hours of the morning.

Miri waved a hand. "We're fine for now. Come find me once we start cleaning up."

Avery's head returned to my chest and the song played on. When it ended and an upbeat tune began, she lifted her head and gave me a huge smile. "I love this song."

I shrugged my jacket off and tossed it onto a nearby chair. "Show me your moves, Adams."

We danced for an hour, but it seemed like ten minutes. Song after song, some slow and some fast, we moved around that dance floor, surrounded by awkward teenagers who laughed at us. Avery didn't care, so I didn't care. All that mattered was that she was having fun.

At one point, the photographer's line had disappeared, so I convinced Avery to get our photo taken.

"This is awkward." She shook with laughter as I made her stand behind me and place her hands on my waist.

"It's supposed to be awkward, Adams. I thought you wanted me to have the full prom experience."

The camera flash went off and the photographer laughed. "One more, for the heck of it."

I turned, tilted Avery's chin, and dropped a kiss on her mouth. Another flash went off, and I should have broken off the kiss there, but I didn't. My tongue slid against the seam of her mouth and she opened up so I could taste her. One hand was behind her head as leverage, the other on her ass. I gripped and she exhaled into me. My cock stiffened again.

The photographer cleared her throat. "Next."

Avery broke away first. A blush grew on her cheeks. "Sorry." She wore a dazed expression as she pulled me back to the dance floor.

When the prom was over and the kids had gone home, Avery and I hung back to clean up.

"Emmett, help me lift this table, would you?" Scott asked, and together we carried folding tables into the supplies room. When we were finished, I glanced around the gym for Avery.

Miri appeared at my side. "You two can get out of here." Scott walked by with a punch bowl. "Scott, honey, that goes in the car. Thank you." She turned back to me. "Thank you so much for helping out."

"Miri, the pleasure was all ours."

"It sure was," Avery said at my side. Even in the ugly gym lighting, she was pretty. Her skin glowed from the dancing. She looked up at me, smiling softly. "Hi."

"Hi." My arm came up around her shoulders easily. "Ready to go?"

She nodded.

I shot Miri a grateful smile. "Bye, Miri."

"Bye, Miri," Avery echoed. Her arm slid around my waist as we strolled out the gym doors. "Was prom everything you wanted?"

I thought back to the teenage version of myself, playing video games alone on prom night while my friends got all dressed up, danced, and rode in the limo. What would have happened if Nat hadn't broken up with me? I would have had a decent time, but not like this. Nat and I didn't click the way Avery and I did. Nat and I were never silly and carefree the way Avery and I were. Besides, Will would have been on the sidelines, watching the girl he liked dance with another guy. He had once confessed he felt awful for going to prom with Nat, knowing she had broken up with me the day before, but I was quick to assure him things had worked out as they should have.

They did, I realized as I looked down at the woman tucked under my arm.

"Everything and more."

Avery energized me. I had always been happy being alone. I prided myself in being unattached, but my body wanted to be connected to hers at all times. I had discovered the other side of things. This feeling in my chest was foreign to me, and I didn't have a clue what to do with it.

I knew two conflicting truths: I wanted Avery, and I wasn't the kind of guy who settled down.

I swallowed, studying her eyes, such a deep, dark blue— like the ocean when I was out on my morning run.

She could crush me, I realized. She could snap me in half with a flick of her little finger. My chest tightened. How had I found myself in this situation? I wasn't the kind of guy to fall like this, and yet, here I was.

I told her the truth. "This time, I went to prom with the right girl."

16

Avery

WE WERE JUST ABOUT to exit the school when a thought struck me.

"Your class photo. I want to see it."

He scoffed. "No way. I'm way better looking now."

This time, I went to prom with the right girl, he had said to me moments before. I kept replaying it in my head, ignoring the curls of delight in my stomach.

I gave him a sidelong look, standing there in his suit, dashing and handsome. It had to be custom-made, the way it fit his broad shoulders. When I walked into my living room this evening and saw him sitting there, looking like the lead in one of those old movies I loved, I could barely restrain myself from hopping into his lap and rubbing myself against him like a cat.

"Good god," I snorted. "Your cockiness knows no bounds. I want to see your photo, even if you look like a dork. I want to know you."

I want to know you? Did I just say that? Jeez, that was a bit intimate.

He watched me with a funny look, and I scrambled.

"Tell you what. If we ever go to Vancouver, I'll show you my picture at my high school. I wore glitter eyeliner so you're in for a treat."

The side of his mouth tugged up but he still watched me with a peculiar expression. "Why would we be in Vancouver?"

Fantastic, so I had dug myself further into the hole. *Dig up, Avery*. I made it sound like we would be taking a trip there together. Like we would continue this whatever-we-were-doing longer than the arrangement. My heart twisted.

"I mean, if *you* are ever in Vancouver."

He maintained eye contact and my stomach somersaulted.

When he spoke, his tone was teasing. "I can't just walk into a random high school alone. I'll get arrested. You'd have to come with me."

A grin spread across my face. "Deal."

"Deal." He rolled his eyes and grabbed my hands. "Come on, Adams, let's go look at pictures of teenage dorks."

———

"OF COURSE YOU WERE CLASS PRESIDENT." I ran my finger along the cold glass in front of his senior year photo—a younger version of him with the same confident, smug smile. "You look like the kind of guy I'd have a crush on."

Earlier, when I rested my head on his chest and we swayed with the music amid dozens of horny teenagers, I melted into him. He was so warm and his fingers in my hair made me so deliriously comfortable, I could have stayed put the entire night.

I sighed, staring at the teenage photo of him. And that kiss against the car. *That kiss*. The way he grabbed me so assertively and pressed me up against the window.

I'd remember that kiss. I'd remember it so hard my ghost would be sighing thinking about it. I'd remember the way my body clenched with pleasure when he ran his thumb over my nipple. All night since that kiss, I'd been wound tight and tense.

The angel in my head sweetly reminded me I was going to speak to Emmett about pulling back on the PDA.

The devil in my head didn't want to pull back, though. She wanted more. She wanted Emmett's hot mouth all over her skin, everywhere. A shiver rolled through me and the hairs on my arms stood up.

Tonight, I'd invite Emmett in, and we'd see where things went. I saw him in my mind, stretched out in my bed, naked, sheets rumpled and messy like his hair. A little thrill ran up and down the back of my legs. All that smooth skin and ridges. The abs I knew he worked hard to maintain.

It took all my control not to drag him out of here this instant.

I turned back to his photo. "I would have had the biggest crush on you."

"Oh, yeah?" He raised an eyebrow with the same smug grin as in the photo.

I nodded. "Oh, yeah." I scanned through the other photos until I found one with the name Will Henry below. "Aw, and there's Will."

He peered over my shoulder, and I could feel his warmth against my back. "Yep, that's Will. He's got a few more wrinkles now, though."

I snorted. "So do you."

"Yeah, but I look handsome with a few wrinkles." He winked at me.

"I hate to admit it but you're right." I turned back to the photos and found the one with the pretty young woman with chestnut hair. "And there's Nat."

He nodded. "That's Nat."

My ears worked hard to pick up anything in his voice, any

affection or wistfulness that indicated Nat was the one that got away, but I came up short. I swallowed and stared at her picture. "Do you still have a thing for her?" It came out more tentative than I wanted. I was supposed to make it sound like I didn't care.

He scoffed. "No." From behind, he wrapped his arm around me. "I'm glad she dumped me." He planted a kiss on my cheek. His stubble scraped my skin.

I was glad she dumped him, too, as I leaned back against him.

"Do you still talk to him often?"

"Every couple days."

"You miss him." I could hear it in his voice.

"Of course. We've been friends since we were kids. He's like my brother. That's why I'm running for mayor. So he and his family can move back here."

My mind paused. "I thought you were running so you could fix the electrical grid."

He nodded. "So they don't have to deal with the power outages. It's a lot for them to handle. Kara shouldn't have to grow up away from her community."

I vaguely remembered thinking Emmett was like my dad, all schmoozey and charming. My dad never would have done something like this, though. He only thought about himself.

Emmett was doing all this so his best friend's family could have a better life. So they could return home. That never would have occurred to my dad.

"I'm getting tired," I told him with a small smile, holding eye contact with his light gray eyes.

"Oh, yeah?" His voice was soft as he leaned down to graze his mouth on my ear.

My breath caught and my eyes fluttered closed. "Yep. Exhausted."

"We should get you home, then."

I bit my lip with excitement.

He grabbed my hand and pulled me down the dim hallway, past the lockers and display cases with trophies and pictures, past the empty administrative office, and out the front doors. In the parking lot, I struggled to keep up with his long strides in my heels, so he stopped, bent over, and hoisted me over his shoulder.

"Put me down, you caveman!" I yelled, laughing.

"You're too slow." I could hear the laugh in his voice as well.

He pushed me into the car. I couldn't stop laughing, but the pressure that had been building in me for weeks had settled between my legs. I was breathless and antsy at the thought of what might happen in my apartment in about twenty minutes.

Emmett and I were totally going to have sex.

I had to give the guy credit—he drove the speed limit the entire way to my house.

I turned to him. "Miri's turtles move faster than you. Now who's too slow?"

He shot me a cheeky grin. "Adams, I'm a law-abiding citizen, and you're a bad influence on me."

"You have no idea." I gave him my most devious smile.

His gaze darkened, and I inhaled sharply, squeezing my thighs together. My center pulsed and I bit my lip, staring out the window. This was so on. The tension had been building between Emmett and me, and now we were going to let it free and have the best sex ever. He was going to tear my dress off the second we got inside my apartment before I even closed the door.

He parked the car in front of my place, and I was halfway up the path around the side of the house before he turned the engine off. He jogged to catch up with me.

"I hope your little friend wears earplugs," he said to me under his breath as we turned the corner.

I snorted but stopped abruptly when we came face to face

with all the guys who lived downstairs, standing in the back-yard in the dark, hauling their belongings out of the house and into plastic bags.

"What's going on? Did you get evicted?" It wouldn't be the first time someone downstairs had been kicked out.

Carter stepped forward, and Emmett straightened before his arm locked around my waist. I bit back a grin—I kind of loved how jealous he was. I had zero plans to do anything with Carter, but I didn't mind seeing Emmett lose his mind over me.

"Bad news, Laser," Carter told us. "We have bedbugs."

Emmett and I froze, looking at all the bags of stuff, and Emmett pulled me back a step from Carter. I could feel the expression of horror and hesitation on my face.

"Um. Gross." I glanced upstairs at my front door. "Do you think they're—"

"Don't even think about it, Adams. There's no way in hell either of us is going inside your apartment."

Carter waved his hand. "Bro, I'm sure her place is fine."

Emmett gave him the coldest expression I'd ever seen. "Actually, *bro*, bedbugs can crawl into other units through light sockets."

I winced at him. "Really?"

He nodded with an equally grossed-out expression, and I shuddered. I pictured lifting up my bedsheets and seeing the little dark dots moving around. I shuddered again.

"I don't want to go in there," I told Emmett. "Don't make me."

"Like hell you are. Come on." He pulled me toward the car.

"Where are we going?"

"You're staying at my place."

We drove home in near silence, only punctuated by one of us shivering or gagging in disgust. So much for getting laid tonight—any desire or lust I felt back at the prom had disappeared the second I heard the word *bedbugs*, and I suspected the same for Emmett.

"I feel like they're on me." My hands raked over my scalp. "Are they in my hair?"

"Adams, I can't look because if I see one, I'll drive this car right off the road."

I burst out laughing. "This was the worst prom ever."

He started laughing too. "The prom was great, but the afterparty is worse than the time I got dumped."

That made me laugh harder. I knew he was kidding but our terrible luck kept me giggling. When we pulled up to his garage, I was still laughing.

We made our way from the garage to the front door before Emmett paused, took his jacket off, and placed it on the railing.

"Leave your dress out here, it doesn't seem like it's going to rain," he told me, undoing his tie, and I frowned.

"What are you talking about? What are you doing?"

He gave me an *are you crazy* look. "We were inside your apartment earlier. We could be carriers."

"Ewwwww. You think there's a bedbug hitchhiker on us right now?"

"I have no idea, but there is no way I'm letting either of us inside with these clothes."

A jolt of excitement sparked through me. "I'm not getting naked in front of you!" *At least not without a little warm-up*, I thought.

He took his shirt off and I had a front-row view to every ridge and muscle down his torso. My mouth parted.

"I won't look. I'm going to go inside and get you something to wear," he told me. He snorted as my gaze raked down his abs. "See something you like, Adams?"

My face burned. His hands came to his belt, and I whirled

around, facing the other way. This was *not* what I had in mind when I wanted Emmett naked. Stupid bedbugs. Stupid Carter and his stupid gross friends, ruining my night that was supposed to be filled with orgasms. I crossed my arms over my chest.

"I'll be right back." He stepped inside. Moments later, he returned, still shirtless but wearing sweatpants and holding a t-shirt.

"That's it? Don't you have a bathrobe or something? One of those flannel ones?"

He laughed. "What? No. I'm not seventy-five. Come on, Adams, it's cold."

"I know it's cold." All the hairs on my arms stood on end, but I wasn't sure if it was from the chill or the ridges down Emmett's stomach. I wanted to scrape my teeth over them and feel them jump.

He hung the shirt on the doorknob and stepped back inside.

"No looking," I told him.

"I won't, I promise. I'll make us some tea."

Tea. If I wasn't sure sex was off the table at the threat of bedbugs, now I knew for sure. No one had sex after drinking tea. Tea was the least horny drink.

I sighed and undid the zipper of my dress. Thank god Emmett lived in the forest, surrounded by dense fir trees. The last thing I needed was some creepy neighbor spotting me naked at his front door. I slipped the dress off and draped it over the railing beside his suit. I glanced down at myself—underwear and bra too?

I didn't want to go commando in Emmett's home (or did I?), but I also didn't want to bring any bedbugs with me. I gagged again at the thought that there could be one hiding in my bra or underwear and whipped them off lightning-fast before slipping Emmett's t-shirt over my head.

THAT KIND OF GUY

It smelled like him. Woodsy, musky, and masculine. Desire curled low in my stomach.

The horny devil on my shoulder opened one eye, awakening a little.

17

Avery

"PEPPERMINT?" he called from the kitchen when I closed the door.

"Sure." *We can do our taxes and meal planning while we're at it*, I thought with disappointment. Sex was off the table. So much for that dress I had picked out because of the cleavage it gave me.

He had his back to me in the kitchen, pouring hot water into mugs, but when he turned, his gaze snagged on my bare legs. His t-shirt was big on me but still only came to my thighs.

His gaze darkened before he blinked it away and placed a mug in front of me.

"Thanks."

"Anytime."

I stood there, biting my lip, debating whether I should ask. Cold air was brushing against my lady parts. I wasn't used to going commando.

"What?" He raised an eyebrow. "What is it?"

"Do you—" My words broke off. I didn't want to ask. I could feel my face heating.

"What?"

"Do you have any more decoy underwear?"

A little grin twisted onto his mouth. "Decoy underwear? You going commando right now, Adams?"

My face burned. "I can go get my underwear if you don't mind Carter's bedbugs." I whirled around, and he caught my arm with his hand.

"Don't you dare," he said with a husky laugh. "No, I don't have any more decoy underwear. You'll have to do without." His hand rested on my arm, and he stared down at me with an intense expression. His chest was rising and falling, and my pulse beat in my ears.

Why was this a bad idea again?

"You should go to bed." He continued watching me with a darkened gaze.

I nodded and put my hands on his chest and ran my fingers over the smooth muscle. Jesus Christ, he was ripped. "I should."

"You're exhausted." His fingers tilted my jaw and his mouth came to the sensitive skin on my neck. His teeth nipped it and my breath caught.

The pressure between my legs was back.

"Mhm." I gently scraped my nails down his abs and the muscles jumped beneath my fingers.

Below the waistband of his sweatpants, his erection was obvious, jutting out. My lips parted and a shiver ran through me.

Fucking hell, I was so, so turned on. There was no way I could sleep, now or maybe ever. I'd lie there in bed, staring at the ceiling and trying not to think about what it would feel like for his thick length to slide into me. Even thinking about it now had wetness pooling between my legs.

I swallowed. "Remember when we talked about having an outlet?"

His gaze darkened even further, and he nodded. He leaned down and his hand came to the back of my thigh, brushing up higher, higher, higher over the sensitive skin below my ass before his large palm grasped the flesh.

He breathed out hard. "You have a magnificent ass."

"An outlet." My voice sounded huskier than usual. "I need one."

He brushed his mouth against my neck again and a little whimper escaped my mouth. "It might make things complicated."

His breath tickled my ear and neck and I shivered again. He smelled incredible, like cedar and deodorant and soap. Masculine, clean, and strong. I could feel the heat from his skin radiating off him. His neck was so close to my mouth, mere inches away, and it would be almost no effort to just—

He groaned as I pressed my lips against his neck. His Adam's apple bobbed, and his head fell back slightly.

I knew this was a bad idea, but I didn't care. I wanted it. I wanted *him*. My entire body hummed for him, a low vibration that sent shivers to my core and made me do things I normally wouldn't. The pressure built low in my belly, and we hadn't even *done anything* yet. I had never been this turned on before. No one had made me feel like this. I had to relieve the pressure, or I'd explode.

My teeth scraped his skin and he turned and captured my mouth with his. A moan traveled from my throat into his and my hands raked his hair as his tongue slid against mine, tasting me. One of his hands was wrapped in my hair and the other grasped my ass and lifted me onto the counter. He stood between my knees. I only wore a t-shirt and was hyper-aware of the wetness between my legs exposed to the air, exposed to Emmett, but he ignored me there, making me want him even more. His mouth was needy, demanding, and assertive, and it sent heat to my center. Wetness and warmth flooded me.

"I need you," he rasped into my ear, breaking the kiss and pressing a series of them down my neck. "I need you so fucking badly, Avery. I've been thinking about this constantly. You have no idea how badly I need this."

He covered my mouth with his and slicked his tongue against mine. His hands were all over me—in my hair, on my breasts, pinching my nipples. I sighed my response, tilted my head back with closed eyes.

My hands slid into the waistband of his sweatpants and around his cock. It was hot in my hand, heavy and thick, and he shuddered as I stroked his shaft.

He broke our kiss and leaned down to scrape his teeth over my nipple over the t-shirt. I gasped.

"I need to see you," he rasped out in a low voice, gazing at me with dark eyes, heavy with lust and need.

All I could do was nod. Yes, fucking hell, yes, I needed him to see me, too.

He yanked the t-shirt over my head, exposing my breasts. My nipples were pinched and desperate to be touched. I sat on the counter, naked and open to him, but before I could freak out about that, he tilted my chin up and our gazes locked.

My breath caught. The way he looked at me—I had *never* been looked at like that in my life. I would have felt it burning me up the way it was now.

Both our chests were rising and falling. His eyes were dark and hot, and he looked drugged. "You are so fucking beautiful."

My lips parted, watching how he had transformed, and before I could say a word, he lowered his mouth to one of the pinched peaks and my head fell back. He pulled me toward him, the other hand came to my other breast, and I let out a small cry in his kitchen at the pure pleasure of it. I was delirious with need, but this was too good. I couldn't move while he had his mouth on my breast.

His hand stroked my back and I arched against him, writhing with tension and pressure. My nails scraped the skin of his abs and he shivered under my touch, groaning and gripping me harder, sucking on my nipple and pulling another strangled whimper from me.

My hand slid down again into his waistband and wrapped around his thick length, rock hard and pressing urgently against the front of his pants, and his nails dug into my back. He pulsed in my hand.

"Jesus Christ," he groaned. "Careful."

I slid my hand up and down the entire length of his cock, heavy in my hand, and his breath was ragged as he leaned his forehead against my chest. "Or what?"

"Fuck, Avery. Fuck," he groaned again, his fingers tensing on my back.

I continued to explore his cock and listen to the desperate noises coming out of his throat. He was hard, and every movement looked like it caused him pain. His gaze begged me to put him out of his misery.

God, he was so fucking beautiful like this.

"I promise I will be very, very careful," I said, stroking him with a firmer grasp, and his lips parted.

"That's it." His voice was a low growl.

He pulled himself from my grasp. I reached for him, but he slid his hands up my thighs, and his fingers came to my core.

My mind went blank.

I couldn't move, it felt so good.

"Fuck, Avery, you're so wet." His mouth was on my ear as his fingers worked tight, soft circles on my clit. I whimpered, biting my lip and gripping his shoulders while he worked at my core, building the tension within me.

"Oh my god," I managed, writhing against him. "Oh my god, Emmett, that feels fucking incredible."

"I love it when you say my name," he said into my neck, his teeth scraping me. Liquid rushed to my center, and he made a noise of appreciation. "Say it again. I want to hear you say my name when I make you come."

I didn't even have the energy to protest. "Emmett," I moaned, and his fingers plunged inside me. I let out a small cry. "Oh my god. Emmett."

His fingers plunged in again, locating the button that would undo me, rewarding me.

"Emmett, don't stop," I begged, reaching for his cock. "Do not fucking stop." I grasped his hard length and stroked.

"I won't," he rasped. "I'm going to make you come so hard." His fingers continued to pulse against my front wall, making me light-headed with pleasure, and his other hand returned to my slick clit. Short, sharp whimpers were spilling out of my mouth. The pressure in my core was so strong, I could barely stand it. All-consuming. I couldn't think, I didn't know what month it was, I was only focused on how incredible his hands felt and how I'd do anything to come right now.

"I can't handle this, it's too good." I leaned my head against his chest. My hand moved faster on his cock, but he pulled it away.

"Not yet," he growled. "You first."

I reached for him again and his fingers moved faster and more urgently over my slick center. I moaned as the tension built and wrapped my hand around him once again. He increased the pressure both on my center and with his fingers inside me, pushing against my G-spot urgently. I stroked him hard, and he pulsed in my hand.

He glared at me. "Don't you dare fucking make me come first."

I liked this side of Emmett, this angry, furious version of him. I knew I'd replay this moment again and again.

"I'm barely touching you." My voice was breathless and ragged.

"I'm going to make you come so hard you forget your own name," he gritted out.

I could feel myself tipping.

He leaned his forehead against mine. His eyes were black. "I'm going to make you come so hard that from now on, you think about me when you do." His fingers worked faster, sliding across my folds and stroking the button inside me. I could barely breathe, it felt so good. I was wound so tight.

I gasped for air. His fingers were so intense. My hand stroked his throbbing cock, and I couldn't wait to have it inside me. But for now, I just wanted him to relieve the pressure coiling around my spine. My skin prickled and was on fire at the same time. Electricity shot up and down my limbs, and my legs started to shake.

"Emmett," I whispered. I could feel myself tipping. I wrapped my legs around him.

"Louder," he demanded. His cock strained in my hand.

I moaned in response, my forehead falling against his chest. "Please."

"Say it." His fingers eased up and I whimpered in protest. "You know what to do."

I needed to come. I needed it so badly. Humans weren't meant to be on the precipice of extreme pleasure for so long. I hated him for dangling it in front of me like this.

"Emmett." His name rang out of my mouth in desperation.

He responded by increasing the pressure and speed of his fingers and I fell over the edge. I was frozen, my mouth open in a silent scream and my limbs paralyzed. I fell back, and one of his arms wrapped around to catch me while the other stayed buried within me. I pulsed around his fingers, clenching him and moaning against his chest as I came.

My hand stayed wrapped around his thick length the entire time and as the waves of intense orgasm began to subside, I stroked him hard and fast. He clutched me harder to him.

He groaned against me, and his head fell to my shoulder

as hot liquid spilled over my hand. He shuddered and a smug grin spread across my face. He lifted his head to look at me. We were both breathing heavy, trying to catch our breath.

Making Emmett come was my new addiction. The way he lost control under my hand, the way he shuddered against me, the way his perfect exterior cracked and he let the primal need shine through—I needed more.

"That was fun." My voice shook, just like my legs.

He sagged against me, his mouth against my neck. "Nice work, Adams."

We caught our breath for a few moments before he lifted me up off the counter, pressing soft, sweet kisses up and down my neck while carrying me upstairs. Our tea sat on the counter in the kitchen, cold and forgotten.

We crawled into Emmett's bed, and he flicked the light off. He pulled me against his chest, and I listened to his heartbeat, the slow thumping lulling me to sleep. I refused to worry about what this meant for us, where we were going, or what would happen. All I could think about was how content I was, and how I couldn't wait to do it again.

18

Avery

"LET'S JUST TIGHTEN THIS UP," the sales associate, Geraldine, said before clamping metal clips up the back of my dress to make it fit and I stared at my reflection.

I hated this.

"How does it look?" Elizabeth called. She was sitting outside the dressing room, drinking champagne with Hannah, Max, and Div. Div had stopped in for breakfast at the restaurant yesterday morning and I'd extended the invitation to him. He seemed like someone who would tell me the truth about dresses.

"She's breathtaking," Geraldine called back as she tightened the bodice.

"Too tight," I gasped.

The dress had so much volume I could barely fit in the dressing room. Geraldine was pressed up against the walls.

I didn't have an idea of the dress I wanted because I had never thought about it. I figured, if I were to ever get married, it would be a simple, private ceremony, and I'd wear a dress I could wear again and again. Something practical, like a wrap dress I could wear to work. Nothing against big weddings, I loved attending them, but all eyes on me? Not my bag.

I remembered standing in front of the store with the others. This was just another thing to cross off the list, and the restaurant would be mine. Geraldine had insisted this one looked better on than hanging up, so I'd shrugged my shoulders and gave it a whirl. Besides, this experience was just as much for Elizabeth, Hannah, Max, and Div as it was for me. The rest of the dresses hanging outside the dressing room were chosen by them. I'd said yes to every suggestion. I didn't know anything about wedding dresses, and I trusted my people who were here today would never let me wear something hideous.

One dress had caught my eye while we browsed the store, sipping champagne and running our fingers over the fabrics. It was soft cream silk, with capped sleeves that draped slightly, and delicate beadwork on the bodice. It looked like something out of the twenties, and I couldn't take my eyes off it.

"Oooh, vintage," Hannah said at my side before grabbing it. "Add it to the pile."

"No," I said, putting it back on the rack. "I don't think it's quite my style."

I don't know why I did that. The dress was so delicate and interesting and unique, and I wanted it but something in me hesitated and turned away. This wedding was fake, I reminded myself. A dress like that would make it feel too real, and that felt risky, like putting my fingers too close to the candle flame.

In the dressing room, through the blur of the veil Geraldine had popped on my head, I stared at my reflection. Oh, how the mighty have fallen. Carted around and dressed up like a doll, but it was to get what I wanted.

The money had arrived in my bank account a few days ago and Keiko and I had a meeting scheduled at the bank a couple days after the wedding.

Part of me couldn't believe it had happened. Emmett had signed a paper and a bank had given me a mountain of money to buy a restaurant. It was a dream. This kind of thing didn't happen to people like me. I didn't know what *people like me* meant, but I knew I was very, very lucky.

"Alright, princess, go on out," Geraldine said, opening the dressing room door and shoving me out. The skirt was wider than the door, so she had to push with both hands on my back.

I stumbled out and my entourage gasped. They couldn't see my face through the veil and I couldn't see theirs.

"What do you think?" I asked, squinting at them.

"What do *you* think?" Elizabeth asked, her voice deliberately light.

"Isn't it divine?" Geraldine asked beside me. "So modern, so elegant, like a Disney princess."

I lifted the veil up. "I don't know if this is the dress for me."

Everyone except Geraldine sagged with relief. Elizabeth and Hannah winced at each other.

"Thank god," Max said, shaking his head.

"You cannot marry Emmett in that dress," Div told me. "You look like one of those dolls they sell on QVC after two in the morning that lonely Boomers buy."

"And add to the creepy collection they display in their dining room," Max added, and they dissolved into laughter.

"My daughter wore this dress at her wedding," Geraldine told us with wide eyes.

Elizabeth stood and put her hand on Geraldine's shoulder. "I'm sure it was lovely on her. Avery, honey, why don't you try on another."

Over and over, Geraldine pulled the dresses over my shoulders and shoved me out into the viewing area like a show dog. Over and over again, Geraldine saw my bare boobs. I didn't have a choice in either, and after the third dress, I stopped caring.

"This one is nice," Hannah said, raising her eyebrows, watching my reaction as I stepped out.

I nodded with a pleasant smile, staring at the satin bodice with clamshell cups. "It is."

"Your boobs look great," Div added.

"They do," I agreed, glancing at the ample cleavage the structured bodice provided. "They sure do."

The memory of Emmett staring hungrily at my boobs the other night before prom flashed into my head and I bit back a grin.

Emmett. Even the guy's name sent a little shiver of excitement and horniness through me.

The other night was... incredible. It was the best sex I'd ever had and we didn't even have sex. Not that I'd ever admit that to Emmett, the guy had an oversized ego as it was. But the way his fingers slicked over me, the way he located the button inside me and undid me, the way he groaned and collapsed against me as he came in my hand.

Jesus.

"Are you okay?" Hannah asked with concern. "You're flushed."

I snapped to attention. No horny thoughts about Emmett, not while his mother was sitting in front of me. I swallowed and smiled at Hannah. "Just a little hungry, I think."

Hungry for more sexy times with Emmett, maybe.

Elizabeth gestured at my dress. "This isn't the one."

I glanced at the dress over her shoulder again, the vintage one, and turned back to them. "Well, gang, which one do you think it is? The second?" The second was a simple, slinky satin dress with a low back. It was pretty, and I looked pretty in it.

Hannah got up and walked around the couch. My stomach flopped. She reached for the dress, *the dress*, picked it up, and brought it to Geraldine. "One more."

"No," I said shaking my head. "I think the second one is better."

"Just humor us," Hannah said. "Please? Then we'll get lunch."

There was a flicker of challenge on her normally shy face. My stomach dropped. She knew. She knew there was something about this dress.

Geraldine took the dress from her and guided me back to the dressing room. I stared at the wall without a mirror while she helped me into it. The lining was satin and smooth. Goddammit. The weight of the dress felt perfect, luxurious, and heavy. It made me want to run my hands over myself again and again.

I could feel the worry on my face as I stepped out.

Hannah's eyes lit up. Elizabeth gasped. Max and Div didn't say a word.

"What?" I asked. "Bad?"

"See for yourself," Elizabeth said.

I looked in the mirror and my heart flipped upside down in my chest. I bit my lip.

And then I started crying.

Elizabeth jumped up. "This is the one! We found it."

"I knew it," Hannah whispered to herself.

Geraldine sprinted to the front desk. "I'll ring it up."

"Wha—" I started. "Hold on." I wiped at my eyes.

I studied my reflection again. The dress fit me perfectly, with a few cinches and clips here and there by Geraldine, and it was gorgeous. So gorgeous. Like, spend months hunting on eBay and vintage websites, kind of gorgeous. I swallowed again. My throat was tight but my heart flip-flopped. I wanted this dress, I could admit, I wanted it so badly, but could I marry Emmett in this dress? This was a real wedding dress, not just in the way it looked but how it felt. Could I fake-marry Emmett in a real wedding dress?

"You look beautiful," Hannah told me with a soft smile, and I gave her one back.

I was going to be brave, and I was going to buy the gorgeous dress that made me feel like a million bucks.

Max and Div were sifting through the veils, discussing which one fit my head better.

"No veils," I told them. I tilted my chin at the sparkly comb clips on the table near them. "But you can pick a hairpin."

Their eyes lit up and they hurried over to find something.

I glanced at my reflection again and shoved away the thoughts of hesitation. It was fine.

"Alterations will take three to four months," Geraldine called over, and my stomach tensed. The wedding was next week. I'd have to choose a different dress, something that didn't need alterations.

Elizabeth smiled and put her hand on my shoulder. "I'll be doing the alterations."

I gave her a grateful look.

"Don't you even dare," Div told me when I slipped my wallet out of my purse. "Emmett said to watch you like a hawk because you might try to pay."

"Come on," Max said, pulling me out of the shop.

"I don't even know how much it costs," I protested.

"Doesn't matter," Max ignored my objections.

Within minutes, we all reconvened outside. Div held the box, and I couldn't take my eyes off it.

The group of us headed to a nearby restaurant for lunch, talking and laughing and in high spirits. This morning, in anticipation of dress shopping, I was filled with dread, but now I felt lighter, happier, and optimistic.

This was all going to be just fine.

"What a lovely day," Elizabeth said once we were seated, "with my future daughter-in-law." She smiled warmly at me, and I felt it all the way down to my toes.

And then a pang of cold guilt hit me in the stomach. I couldn't get too used to this. I cleared my throat. "The ahi tuna looks good."

"I can't wait to meet your parents," she told me, reading her own menu. "They must be so excited that their baby is getting married."

A rock dropped in my stomach.

I had spoken with my mom on the phone yesterday. I had called her with the intention of telling her about the restaurant and getting married and then I just... froze. The words wouldn't come out of my mouth. I had listened while my mom told me about the book she was reading and then we said goodbye and hung up. After I failed to tell her, calling my dad wasn't even an option. I hadn't spoken to the guy in close to two years.

I shifted in my seat, picturing him pulling Emmett aside and asking to borrow money. Shame unfurled in me and made its way up into my throat.

"Mhm." I swallowed the shame down and stared at my menu. "I wonder if the tuna is fresh or frozen."

"Are they spending a few days in town?" She turned to me. "I'd love to have them over for dinner."

"Um, I'm not sure," I said, eyes glued to my menu. "They're pretty busy with stuff."

I pictured my mom meeting Emmett, and him turning on the politician's charm with her. Would she think he was too much like my dad? Would she disapprove? Would she fall in love with him like everyone else?

The knots in my stomach turned over. Why did it matter? Emmett and I weren't getting married for real. I knew this, and yet somehow, I had to keep reminding myself.

"Do you smell smoke?" Max asked, staring straight at me with a knowing look.

I narrowed my eyes at him.

"No?" Hannah said, sniffing the air.

Max continued to look at me. *"Liar, liar, pants on fire,"* he mouthed.

I stared at my menu. I'd call them today. I'd call them individually and tell them I was getting married and ask them to come.

A shudder of anxiety rolled through me.

Tomorrow. I'd call them tomorrow.

19

Emmett

"I THOUGHT we were going to the beach," Avery said as we drove down the highway.

I had been thinking about Avery all day. During my morning run along the beach, I thought about her pretty blue eyes. While I showered, I replayed her sitting on the kitchen counter, crying out my name with my fingers deep inside her. How sexy she had looked, stepping into the kitchen in only my t-shirt, and then pulling it off to expose her perfect tits. They fit perfectly into my hands, and the way her head fell back when I slid my tongue over her nipple—fucking hell.

I couldn't stop thinking about last night, and it wasn't even sex. It was hand stuff. That was it. She got me off with her hand like I was a horny teenager.

I thought about what it would feel like to put my mouth on her, and how incredible she must taste. I should have done that last night, but I was greedy and wanted to feel her squeeze around my fingers.

"We're going to a different beach." I shot her a sly look. "It's a secret beach."

I thought about her sleepy sigh of contentment in bed while I read Div's email with poll results that showed me neck-

and-neck with Isaac. I thought about the way her smile lit up the room when she made fun of me for being grossed out by turtles.

All day, I looked forward to coming home to Avery.

I never, ever thought I'd say this, but thank god for bedbugs.

I could do without washing machines, though. Washing machines had ruined my plan of having Avery either wearing only my t-shirts or nothing at all.

Her lips parted in surprise and her eyes lit up. "Oh, really?"

I nodded. "It's a Rhodes family secret, though. You can't tell a soul or you'll be excommunicated."

She laughed. "You're telling me right now."

Castle Beach was a secret, I wasn't lying about that. It wasn't on Google Maps or in any tourism brochures. Some locals knew about it, we'd seen them there, but the unspoken rule was we didn't post about it on social media and didn't direct tourists here. There were no repercussions, though.

Bringing Avery here felt right. She was the closest to a wife I'd ever get. She knew my parents, she was close with my mom, and she should know about the beach. I wanted to share it with her.

I grinned at her. "We're getting married so it's fine."

We shared a glance, the *we've got a secret* look. My heart squeezed.

When I turned off the highway onto a dirt road, she wrenched around in her seat to look behind us. "I didn't even know this road was here. I'm not sure I can find it again on my own."

"I'll have to bring you back." I reached over and placed my hand on her thigh and she grinned out the window.

We bumped along the road and parked in a small clearing. Takeout and beach blanket in hand, I led her down a trail to the beach, holding her hand at the steep parts, even though she was wearing sneakers and capable of climbing down herself. My body craved her touch. Any excuse to put my hands on her, and I did it without hesitation. Even better, her mouth twitched up every time we made contact, which warmed my chest.

The path ended and turned to sand, and we stepped out onto the beach.

"Oh, wow." Avery paused where the sand started and looked out at the sparkling water.

Castle Beach was in a small, protected cove. Across the water, the forest rose out of the sea. We had the beach to ourselves. A light breeze carried off the ocean, and it smelled fresh and clean. This was so much better than the popular beach in Queen's Cove, which would be packed tonight.

"The sky looks so beautiful." She sighed and shook her head with a wistful expression on her face. "We live in the most beautiful place on the planet."

The blue sky stretched out endlessly, the thick green forest was lush as ever, and the sea sparkled. "We sure do."

I kicked my shoes off and led us to a log down the beach we could sit against. She shook out the blanket and I unpacked the takeout as she took a seat and watched. I grinned at how her eyes lit up at the bottle of wine I pulled out.

"I grabbed it before we left," I told her before pouring it into a couple travel mugs.

Her smile was shy. "Thanks for bringing me here."

"Anytime. I like to run here in the mornings."

She shook her head and gave me a teasing look. "Early bird."

"You should try it. It's nice waking up before everyone else. The water's calm, it's just you and the birds and the waves. It's very serene."

She started opening the takeout boxes with our sushi. "That's what I like about being up late, after everyone has gone to bed. It feels like I'm the only person awake in the whole town, when it's silent and all the lights are out. Sometimes I stay at the restaurant long past when everyone has gone home just to get work done. It's peaceful." She smiled softly at me and my chest panged.

We sat there, eating and talking and laughing and listening to the waves wash up against the shore, and the sun dipped lower in the sky. I enjoyed watching her eat. Something about procuring her food and seeing her enjoy it gave me satisfaction. The urge to feed and provide for my woman.

My woman? I sounded like a caveman.

I glanced at her again.

Mine.

The idea of anyone else putting their hands on Avery, even smiling at her like that fucking Carter guy, sent hot rage through my veins and made me furious.

Avery was mine. There was no doubt about that. I just didn't know what to do about it. I was out of my depth here.

A giggle bubbled out of her and I gave her a curious look.

She grinned wider. "Remember when you thought I was gay because I didn't like you?" She laughed again and her eyes glittered.

I snorted. "I also thought you'd be dutiful."

"The joke was on you." She ate another piece of salmon nigiri.

"It sure was."

I had entered this arrangement thinking it would be so simple. We'd take a few photos for social media, I'd sign on the dotted line of her loan, and we'd part ways. Easy. Straightforward. Emotionless.

I swallowed. This thing I was doing with Avery, it was easy, but it was anything but straightforward or emotionless. I couldn't imagine not spending time with her after this. I couldn't imagine her moving out of my home or my life, which she fit so perfectly into. I wanted to drop by The

Arbutus every day to chat with her over lunch until I was a hundred years old.

You don't understand, Will had joked once when I made fun of him for not wanting to take a trip with me. *You're not the family kind of guy.*

My chest tightened, and I brushed the confusing thoughts aside, bringing my attention back to the present. There were only two pieces of nigiri left.

"I can see why you like running a restaurant, if everyone eats like you," I told Avery as she ate another piece.

She narrowed her eyes and chewed. "Is that a compliment? I can't tell."

"Of course it's a compliment. You enjoy food. I bet it's rewarding to watch people go home happy after eating at The Arbutus."

A wistful look came over her face. "It is. I like standing near the bar and watching everyone talking and laughing. There were these two older women who came in the other day for lunch, and they stayed for three hours, drinking wine and laughing so hard they were crying, and I just knew they had been friends for twenty or thirty years." She swallowed and smiled, remembering. "It was like I got a flash of who they were when they were young." She shook her head. "I don't know what it is. There's something about the restaurant that's special. Keiko and her family put so much into it and made it this important part of our community." Her expression shuttered, just a moment, and she blinked. "I want to keep that going."

I nodded. "You will. Everything worked out okay with the money?"

"Yes." She glanced down at her hands and then back up at me. "Thank you for that."

"Don't mention it. Seriously."

She gave me a grateful smile. Golden hour was starting, the hour before sunset when the last rays of sun cast a warm orange glow on everything, and her eyes glittered in the light. Behind us in the trees, hundreds of birds were chirping. "It's like the birds are all saying goodnight to each other," she observed, grinning.

I smiled at her and remembered something. "Wedding dress shopping must have gone well today."

She narrowed her eyes. "Did someone show you a picture?"

I shook my head. "Saw a charge on my credit card."

She sagged with relief. "Okay, good." A smile grew on her face. "I don't want you to see my dress until the wedding. It's bad luck."

"Are you happy with it?"

She couldn't contain her grin and gave a little wiggle of excitement. "Yes. I am. It's gorgeous. Oh, and I'll pay you back for it. You shouldn't have to pay for it, I'm sure you're already paying enough for the wedding."

"Absolutely not." I was already shaking my head. Something that made her this excited, this happy? I'd pay for it a thousand times.

"Come on." She gave me a flat look. "Emmett."

"No." My voice was stern. "I'm going to be blunt here." I turned to her. "Remember what I told you before. I have lots of money and no one to spend it on. Myself? I have everything I need. My mom? I spoil her rotten. Let me buy you a pretty dress."

She looked away but I could see her beaming from the way the apples of her cheeks rose. "Fine."

"Fine," I repeated, satisfied. "Also, Div asked me about your parents, and I wasn't sure."

She turned back to me. "What do you mean?" A little crease formed between her eyebrows.

"He wants to know if they're coming. Something about a seating chart."

The crease deepened and she pressed her mouth into a tight line.

Something was wrong. "Adams? What's going on?"

"My dad is a dick," she blurted out.

I blinked at her.

She wrung her hands. "Okay, maybe not a dick. He doesn't mean to be, but he just kind of... sucks." She winced. "That sounds bad. I'm a bad person. He's just slippery, and I've been putting off inviting him. I know I have to," she told me. "And I will. I've just been procrastinating." She frowned and studied her hands, twirling my ring around her finger.

Watching the anxiety on her face, the way her mouth pressed into an unhappy line, it broke my goddamn heart.

"You don't have to invite him. It's our wedding. We can do whatever we want."

She winced. "What if he finds out? He'd be crushed."

Uncertainty crossed her face and she looked so different from the confident and self-assured Avery I knew. I opened my arms. "Come here." I gestured for her to slide closer.

A moment of hesitation crossed her face before she scooted over, and I pulled her against me so her back rested against my chest, her head tucked under my chin, and we both watched the ocean. Comfort hummed in my chest, and she relaxed against me. This was better, much better.

"If you don't want him there, you're allowed to say no." My voice was a murmur into her hair as my arms pulled over her chest, locking her against me. Her hair smelled incredible, and it took everything I had not to bury my face in her neck. "What do you think he'll do?"

She sighed, and I rubbed my hand up and down her arm. I hated seeing her like this, anxious and uncertain.

"I don't even know how to describe him."

"Try."

"He's the most charming, friendly, funny guy you've ever met." Her tone was contemplative, and I wished I could see her face. "He's everyone's best friend and so passionate about life. Everything is more fun with him around. He's the life of the party." Her voice changed to a more hesitant tone. "And he has all these big ideas."

She paused.

Oh. It hit me. He was like me.

"Did I tell you my parents had a restaurant when I was a kid?"

"No," I murmured into her hair. "You didn't."

She nodded. "They did. My mom always wanted to have a restaurant, my grandparents had one for a bit and she loved it. She saved all her money, worked two jobs when I was young, and when I was twelve, they bought a place." She tensed beneath me, and I rubbed her arm again. "My dad was so excited, and he has the kind of personality where he kind of takes over things." She shrugged. "He took over her dream. He had all these grand ideas and he totally changed the place." A low noise of irritation came out of her throat. "He spent all their money on his grand ideas."

She exhaled slowly.

This was starting to make sense. *Avery* was starting to make more sense. Anger seeped into my bloodstream at this guy who had failed to take care of his family, failed to create the best life possible for them, and instead dragged them down with his impulses and poor business choices.

I worked to keep my voice neutral. "What happened to the restaurant?"

"It went out of business, of course, because he didn't know what the fuck he was doing, but by the time my mom figured that out, he was gone."

My eyebrows rose in alarm. "Gone? He left?"

She shrugged. "Yep. He said it wasn't his dream, it was my mom's dream, and he had to pursue his own passions."

Rage. White-hot rage. Furious, unbridled rage rattled through my body.

What kind of person did that? What kind of father and husband left his family, especially after he had dug their grave of debt?

"He's not coming to the wedding," I growled.

"I can't *not* invite him." She didn't sound like she believed that.

I shook my head. "He's not coming."

She was quiet a moment before she nodded and relaxed against me. "Okay. He's not coming."

We were quiet again, staring at the setting sun, the splashes of color across the sky.

A thought struck me and I frowned. "You know I'd never do that to you, right? Not that you need me for anything. You're so fiercely independent and I can see why now." I swallowed. "But you need to know I would never do something like that."

She nodded. "I know," she whispered. She turned her head and caught my gaze before nodding again. "I know."

"Good."

We sat there for a long time, listening to the waves and watching the water crash against the shore, watching the sun fall lower and lower. Something had changed between us with that conversation. All the cards were out on the table. This was why Avery didn't like me for so long. It was because I reminded her of her dad.

Rage spiked my bloodstream again. That fucking asshole. I'd never met the guy but I hated him for what he did to Avery, how he made her feel uncertain and confused. Fathers should be like Will, devoted and consistent and adoring.

I would never let Avery down like her dad had. I wasn't like Will—I didn't know what kind of guy I was anymore— but I sure as hell was going to live up to Avery's expectations.

20

Emmett

WE STAYED AT THE BEACH, Avery sitting between my legs, locked against me until the sun set and the sky darkened and she shivered against my chest. We made our way back to the car by the light of our phone flashlights and drove home in content silence with my hand resting on her leg. After a few moments, her hand settled over mine, and she shot me a soft smile.

My heart flipped over in my chest. "You're beautiful."

She gave me a rueful smile and looked out the window.

"You don't believe me?" I glanced between her and the road. "I'm going to keep saying it until you do. You're beautiful."

She rolled her eyes with a grin. "Okay, okay. I believe you."

I squeezed her leg. "Good."

We got home, and when she paused in front of the door, waiting for me to unlock it, I tilted my chin at her. "Use the keys I gave you."

I watched as she fished her keyring out of her bag and unlocked the door. It was so satisfying to see her do that, but I couldn't figure out why.

It's because she's mine. It's because her living here feels right.

Desire unfurled in me, desire I had kept in check all night. I didn't want to contain it anymore, though. I wanted to show Avery how fucking flawless she was. I was going to show her she was mine.

We stepped into the dark house, and the moment she set her bag down, my hands were on her shoulders, turning her to me. I tilted her chin up, and she let out a soft gasp a split second before my mouth covered hers.

She relaxed against me, her perfect tits pressing into my chest as my arms wrapped around her, and my mouth brushed her soft, full lips.

"Hi," she breathed against my mouth.

"Hi," I murmured back.

I could get used to this.

I kicked the front door closed behind us and pulled Avery with me toward the stairs, kissing her and moving my hands over her. I needed to touch all of her, I needed to make her moan the way she did the other night with my fingers in her tight wetness. I reached up and brushed her nipple, and she jerked with a small cry against my mouth.

My cock was uncomfortably hard. We needed to get upstairs faster. My tongue slicked against hers before I tugged her hair back, opening her deeper to me. She nipped my bottom lip with her teeth. My cock ached and I groaned.

I stooped down, grabbed her ass, and hauled her up. Her legs looped around my waist and I carried her up the stairs.

"I want you," she murmured against my mouth, and my cock strained again. "I need you to make me come again."

"You haven't seen anything yet." I broke our kiss to press my mouth along her neck. She gasped. "I can't wait for you to come on my face."

She moaned and rubbed against me. I stepped inside my bedroom before gently lowering her to the bed. I whipped her top off and she laughed in surprise.

"Eager." Her voice was low.

My mouth came to her cleavage and her head fell back.

"You have no fucking clue how eager. I've been thinking about this since you came around my fingers."

I pressed kisses along the soft, supple flesh above her bra, and her breath came out in little gasps. Her hands fisted my hair, pulling and making me groan against her skin. I could barely handle it, this delicate game of indulging my need to claim her and drawing it out to torture her with pleasure. I was grinding myself against the bed like a teenager. I flipped the clasp of her bra and her delectable tits popped out. One of the tight peaks pinched when I slid my tongue over it, and she cried out in the dark bedroom.

A low chuckle rumbled out of my throat. Fucking hell, I loved this. I loved making her breathless and hungry. Every cell in my body, every drop of blood craved this like water, like air.

When my mouth left her nipple, she groaned with protest.

"Pants off." I worked at her fly. "Now."

She laughed, low and husky. "Demanding." She moved to slip them off.

In the dim moonlight, I could barely see her, so I reached across the bed and flicked the light on. The room illuminated with warm lighting, and I gazed upon her face, flushed with parted lips and heavy-lidded eyes.

"Fucking gorgeous."

She gave me a heated look and her hands came to my belt, undoing the buckle while holding eye contact. My cock pulsed and I yanked my shirt over my head.

"Your body is amazing," she sighed, sitting up and pressing kisses over my abs. My hands came back to her breasts, and I rolled her tight little nipples in my fingers, pulling gasps from her mouth before I pushed her shoulders back so she was lying down again.

My gaze snagged on her black lace underwear.

"Adams." My voice caught. "Are these the decoy underwear?"

She gave me a wicked smile. "Yes."

Lust roared through me and my eyelids fell closed. The thought of my sweet, sexy little Avery wearing underwear I bought for her—my control nearly broke. I swallowed and mentally moved half my net worth to an account reserved for buying Avery lingerie. Why hadn't I thought of this before?

Her hands slid over my chest and her mouth covered mine again. "I can't stop kissing you."

I grinned against her mouth before breaking our kiss. I needed to give her more than just kisses. I kneeled on the floor and looped my hands behind her knees before dragging her to the edge of the bed. Her breathing was shallow.

Avery was always so in control. She was so independent and never let anyone help her. I suspected from the way her head fell back, she enjoyed me being in control.

So did I.

I slid my fingers up her thigh and her breath caught. I skimmed the black lace and found her hot, damp center. Her mouth made an O and she inhaled sharply.

"You're wet. Your underwear is soaked." I ran my finger over the damp fabric, and she moaned and nodded. My voice was low and teasing. "Adams, are you turned on or something?"

"Or something. Stop teasing me," she bit out as my fingers drew circles over the fabric.

My own control teetered on the edge, and my body longed to sink into her and thrust until she filled the bedroom with cries, but I needed to draw this out. Seeing Avery's desire was a drug to me, and I needed to toy with her until she was in a frenzy. I needed her control to snap first.

"Is something wrong?" I asked with innocence, slipping my arm beneath her back to pull her toward me. My mouth came to her nipple again and she cried.

"Emmett," she growled.

"What do you want, Adams?" My tongue worked fast against her nipple and her breath came out in shudders.

I'd give her what she wanted, but I was going make her beg for it.

"More," she groaned and thrust against my fingers. I pulled my hand back and she fell back against the bed in anguish. "Emmett!" She was pissed now, and I grinned big at her.

"Tell me what you want, and I'll give it to you."

"I want you to lick me until I scream."

Her underwear was off before she realized it and the whimpery moan that came out of her throat when my mouth met her slick pussy? I'd remember that sound until the day I died.

My tongue worked fast over her folds, dragging her wetness up and down over her clit as she wrenched underneath me, gasping. One hand rolled her nipple and the other slid between her legs. I slipped a finger into her core. She arched and gasped.

"Is this what you wanted?"

She moaned. I removed my finger from her.

"Emmett." Her voice was hard and furious. She lifted her head to glare at me and I gave her the slyest, most wicked smile.

"Is this what you wanted?" I repeated slowly, sliding the finger back inside her, locating her G-spot and pressing.

Her eyes closed and she collapsed back onto the bed. "Yes." Her back arched and her tits were thrust toward heaven. "Emmett, don't stop."

I wouldn't. Nothing could drag me away from between Avery's legs. Her pussy was the sweetest thing I'd ever tasted, and I ate her up. Her moans filled my ears and she raked my hair, making me shudder. I was so turned on it was almost blinding, but I worked to make Avery come like it was my life's purpose. I pressed harder inside her, adding a second finger, and her wet cunt clenched me like a vise. My tongue swiped circles in her liquid, dragging across her silk, and her thighs tightened around my head.

I sucked on her clit, and she jerked in response, fluttering around my fingers.

"I'm coming, Emmett, I'm coming." She gasped for air. "Emmett, Emmett, Emmett." She wove a spell around me with her words as her core gripped me and she shuddered. Her legs clamped around my head, and I let her ride out the orgasm, only removing my mouth when her gasps stopped and she relaxed against the bed.

The content sigh she made as her eyes fluttered closed, chest still heaving for air? I heard that sigh in my soul. That sound was my doing.

My cock ached with the need to fill her core. I needed to feel her clench my cock the way she had clenched my fingers.

"All done?" I stood and lowered myself over her on the bed, then pressed a soft kiss on her collarbone.

Her eyes opened and she gave me a heated look before she wrapped her hand around my cock and stroked. "Not even close."

She stroked again, hard, and my breath exploded out of me. I was closer than I realized. Going down on Avery had pushed me to the brink and pleasure coiled around the base of my spine. "Avery, no. I'm not going to last."

She lifted her chin to me in challenge, stroking again. "So don't."

I grabbed her wrists and pinned them above her head. She pushed her hips up and I felt her wet center drag against my length. My head fell forward beside hers.

"Don't tease me like that." My eyes were wrenched closed. My control hung on by a thread.

Her gaze was full of fire as she slid herself against me again. "Do you want to fuck me?"

My hips jerked. "More than anything."

Her legs parted further beneath me. "So do it."

"Condom?" I rasped. Fucking hell, I could barely hold on. Her pussy was so hot and slick against my cock, and I could barely breathe with the need to bury myself within her.

She gave a jerky nod and I yanked the bedside drawer open, ripped the foil open, and rolled it over myself.

"Hurry up," she urged, her lids heavy.

She didn't need to tell me twice. I positioned myself at her center and slowly pushed into her tight wetness.

"Yes," she breathed, adjusting her hips to accommodate me. "Fucking yes."

"Tight." I rasped. "Fuck, Avery, you're so tight and wet."

I slid out and back in and she arched with a little cry. My soul left my body as pleasure rattled through my veins. I couldn't think, I could barely breathe, all I could do was slide in and out of her tight core as she clenched me. Her hand came to her clit and I pushed it away.

"Mine." I swirled my fingers over her clit.

She cried out and I plunged into her again. Pressure grew around the base of my spine and every nerve ending in my body lit up. I could feel it happening, growing within me, but I couldn't. Not until Avery came again. She had to come again. I had to see that sweet little mouth part as she fell over the edge again.

I paused, pulling her knees up beside me so I could sink deeper and when I thrust again, she gave a sharp cry of delight.

"Right there."

My fingers worked faster, and her whimpers made my cock even harder. I was so fucking close, but I held on as hard as I could, waiting for her as I filled her again and again. She jerked against me, mouth parted and eyes closed tight. She jerked again, and her eyes opened, gazing up at me through a haze. She was so fucking beautiful. She was everything to me, she was all I thought about, and now I had tasted her and sunk deep inside her, I had changed. I needed this every day, forever. Everything would be second to this.

Her orgasm racked through her, and she clenched me hard, crying out my name into the bedroom. I let myself lose control, thrusting into her. My pleasure followed right behind, rippling through me as I shuddered my release into her. Stars burst behind my eyes, rendering me unable to speak, think, and do anything but push into her and spill into her core.

When the waves subsided, my head fell forward onto the bed. We both strained to catch our breaths. Something had happened. Something was different with us and deep inside me. My DNA had rearranged the second I slid into her, and we were connected. I was different. I wasn't the pre-Avery Emmett, and I hadn't been for a long time.

She sighed with satisfaction, and I grinned against her ear.

"Great work," I told her, and she laughed.

"You did all the work."

I lifted my head to look down into her eyes. She beamed at me with flushed cheeks and drowsy eyes.

Cold fear bit at the edges of my consciousness.

I didn't want this to end. I wanted to do this every day with Avery, forever.

This feeling, there was only one name for it. I swallowed.

The cold spread in my chest as I looked into her eyes. I was in love with her, and I wanted to marry her for real.

Shit.

"You should stay here for a bit," I spoke without thinking. "For a few weeks after the wedding."

She watched me with a thoughtful expression.

"To sell it," I lied.

She gave me a soft smile and nodded. "Okay."

I relaxed and dropped a gentle kiss on her mouth. "Okay."

She fell asleep wrapped around me, her steady breaths

slowing, and I lay there staring at the ceiling, thinking. This was still a deal to Avery, so I couldn't tell her the truth. I glanced down at her and brushed a lock of hair behind her ear. In her sleep, she made a quiet *mmm* of satisfaction, and my chest panged.

I couldn't tell her the truth, but I could enjoy every second I had with her.

21

Avery

I WOKE that morning with my back arching off the bed and Emmett's tongue on my clit.

"Good morning," he murmured against my thigh after making me come. He pressed light kisses across my skin as I sunk back into the pillows, eyes closed and breathing hard.

"It sure is." I glanced down at him with a grin. Was this real? Never in a million years would I have predicted I'd be so lucky as to wake up like this. "Thank you."

"You are very, very welcome." He moved to lay down beside me, propping himself up on his side, watching me with a satisfied smile on his face. He was shirtless, only wearing running shorts, and his cheeks were tinged with pink and bronze. His hair was damp with sweat.

Goddamn, he was good-looking.

I bit my lip. "If I knew you could do that with your mouth, I would have said yes to this a lot faster."

He laughed. I loved the way the skin around his eyes crinkled when he laughed like that.

"What time is it?"

"A little after nine." He leaned down to place a soft kiss on my arm.

"Did you go for a run already?"

He nodded.

"Early bird," I whispered and turned on my side, facing him. My body was languid, relaxed, and worn out in the best way. My fingers brushed over his chest and shoulders, tracing the defined muscles. "Why didn't you wake me?"

"You needed your rest after last night." His gaze flickered with heat, and a wicked smile grew on his features.

I sighed with contentment. "Last night felt like a dream."

His smile grew. "A good dream, I hope."

"The best dream."

His hand came to my arm, and he brushed his fingers across my skin. He watched his hand closely. "The wedding is tomorrow."

I nodded. "Mhm."

His eyes met mine, so beautiful in the morning light. "We still on, Adams?"

There was something about the way he looked at me with that soft, affectionate gaze tinged with uncertainty that made my heart expand in my chest. I was marrying this guy tomorrow, and I didn't feel a lick of hesitation. I probably should have, because who would do what we were doing? No one. It was crazy. I knew that, and yet, lying in his bed, sated and boneless and comfortable, gazing upon his freaking gorgeous face, running my hands over his incredible body, I couldn't think of any reasons why we *shouldn't* get married tomorrow.

"I'll be there. I'll be the one in the white dress."

He grinned and pulled me against him. "Come here." His mouth covered mine.

"I have morning breath," I protested.

"Don't care," he mumbled against me.

Our kisses started slow, but apparently, the sex marathon from the last twelve hours hadn't wrung us out yet because after a few minutes, we became more frantic, and our hands explored. His length pressed against me, and I slipped my hand into his running shorts.

"Wait, I'm sweaty."

I shook my head at him. "Don't care."

But he slid out from under me and jogged over to the bathroom.

"Get back here!"

"I'll be fast, I promise."

A second later, I heard the shower turn on. I slipped out of bed and paused at the door of the bathroom, watching my Greek god stand under the water, head tilted back to wet his hair, eyes closed. His erection jutted out and a flush of pleasure and excitement bloomed low in my belly.

"Hi," I said, stepping into the shower.

His eyes opened and flared with heat as he pulled me closer. "Hi."

———

"CAN I make you some breakfast before I leave, *sweetheart*?" Emmett asked downstairs as he moved around the kitchen.

I poured a coffee and shook my head. "No, thank you, *darling*. I'll have something at the restaurant. I don't like to eat right away in the mornings."

"Noted." He pressed a kiss against my temple, making me grin into my coffee.

Last night was... sigh. And then again last night was... sigh. And this morning? Sigh. And then again in the shower? Siiiiigh.

I took a sip of coffee, surveying him over the mug. "If this is life being married to Emmett Rhodes, I could get used to it."

He chuckled and wrapped his arms around me from behind. I settled into his warm embrace, leaning back into him.

"Let me make you dinner tonight. We can have a quiet night before tomorrow's chaos."

And he even cooked. What wormhole had I tripped and fell through? "That sounds perfect."

His mouth came to my neck, and I shivered. What was it about his touch that elicited such a reaction from me? It was like I was magnetized to him, drawn to him, and responsive to any touch or brush of his fingers. Even after two orgasms this morning, I craved his touch.

"Do we have time?" My voice was soft, my desire growing. "Don't you have to get to work?"

"Don't care." His voice was low. He kissed the corner of my mouth and my eyes fell closed.

On the counter, a phone buzzed.

"Is that me or you?" I mumbled against his mouth.

"Don't care," he said again. He turned my chair so I faced him before gripping my hair, tilting my head back, and kissing me deep. I moaned into his mouth.

The buzzing stopped and the kitchen was quiet except for the rustle of our hands on each other's clothing and the little gasps coming from me as Emmett ran his mouth down my neck.

The buzzing started again.

He groaned in irritation and raised his head to look over my shoulder. "It's your phone."

"I'll turn it off." I reached for it. Max's name flashed across the screen. I frowned at Emmett. "I should get this."

"No." He took it from my hand and placed it on the counter before pulling me back to him.

I laughed and melted into him.

The buzzing began again, and Emmett groaned.

"Let me just see what he wants, and we can go back to fooling around like teenagers," I told him, and he sighed, keeping his arms locked around me. I answered the call. "Hi, Max."

"This better be good," Emmett growled beside me, loud enough for Max to hear.

"Finally." Max's voice was tense and urgent. "Did you see my texts?"

"No, I've been away from my phone." My gaze flicked to Emmett. He watched me with dark eyes and began to unzip my hoodie. I grinned and slapped his hand away. "What's up?"

"Three servers are sick, the supplier's truck was in an accident so we don't have any eggs, a busload of hungry tourists just walked in the door, and we never have enough forks! Where do all the forks go? Are the dishwashers just throwing them in the garbage?" His voice wavered. "We can't be the kind of place to use plastic forks, Avery. We just can't. Why are Friday mornings always like this?"

"Okay, okay. Take a deep breath." I adopted the voice of a calm woman, like on commercials. Emmett's hands roamed my torso and I bit back a grin and leaned into his warmth. "Who was driving? Was it John? Is he okay?"

"Yes, and he's fine. It was just a fender bender but I think he popped a tire."

"I'm going to call the grocery store and call in a favor. You'll have eggs in ten minutes. I'll find the forks. It's going to be okay. I'm on my way."

Emmett's mouth was on my ear, making me shiver. "She's sick. She can't work."

"Are you sick too!?" Max squeaked.

"No, Max, I'm fine," I laughed. "Emmett's just joking."

"Not joking," Emmett murmured against the crook of my neck. "Think you have a fever."

Max huffed a breath. "Also, I saw Chuck talking to Keiko."

I froze. "About what?" Emmett lifted his head to listen.

"I don't know, but she looked uncomfortable."

I chewed my lip. "Okay. Hold down the fort until I get there. I'll be there in a few minutes."

We hung up and Emmett and I looked at each other.

"He's up to something." Emmett's hands came to my shoulders and a crease formed between his eyebrows. "I don't like how he's been hanging around so much lately."

"I don't like it either, but I can't stop him. I'll check in with Keiko today to make sure we're all good." We had a bank appointment on Tuesday to sign the paperwork and transfer the business over to me. I knew the next few days would be a blur, with the wedding and all, but four days seemed like forever.

I rose up on my toes to give Emmett a quick kiss. "I should go."

"I'll drive you."

The morning flew by as Max, myself, and one other server managed to keep a full restaurant happy. The busload of tourists turned out to be in great spirits, and very understanding of our staff shortage. The dishwasher had *not* been tossing the forks in the garbage, but placing them in a spot four feet away from where Max thought they were, so that issue was sorted. John, the delivery driver, showed up after lunch with a new tire and all the food we had been running out of.

During the lull between lunch and dinner, Max and I stood at the bar, catching our breaths. There were a few lingering tables but the rush was over and everything was under control.

"We haven't had a day like that in a while." I sounded dazed.

Max leaned against the bar, staring at nothing in front of him. "I can't feel my feet."

"Go home." I nudged him with my elbow. "You've been here since opening. I'm supposed to be the workaholic, not you."

"I'll wait until Rachel gets here,"

The front door opened and Rachel breezed in. "Hey," she said with a cheerful smile.

I turned to Max. "Go home."

Max relented and left. Two more servers arrived and we prepared for dinner service. It was Friday night so the restaurant was full of tourists, and I stepped in at the bar to help mix drinks. At one point, I went to my office and shot Emmett a quick text.

We're slammed tonight, is it okay if I raincheck on our dinner? I'm so sorry.

He responded immediately.

Absolutely. I'll be here when you get home.

Home. My chest felt the downward tug of disappointment, though. Did I *miss* Emmett? I'd only seen him that morning, but I had thought about him throughout the day, felt his fingers in my hair and his arms around me and his lips on mine. A fraction of me pulled away, telling me this was too delicious, too indulgent and it wouldn't last. The rest of me wanted more. The rest of me wanted as much Emmett as I could get.

Come by the restaurant around eight, I texted. I hesitated but my fingers texted the words before I could hold them back. I miss you.

I miss you, too, Adams. See you around eight.

My heart swooped and dipped and I bit back a smile before slipping the phone into my pocket and opening the door to my office.

Elizabeth stood in the doorway with her hand poised, about to knock.

A big grin stretched over my face. "Hello, there."

Her face lit up when she saw me. "Just the person I was looking for. How are you doing, honey?"

I nodded. "Good, good. Come in." I stepped back and she followed me into my small office, taking a seat. "The chaos of this morning is over and now we're back to regular chaotic levels around here."

She raised an eyebrow, the same way Emmett did sometimes. "I meant about tomorrow."

The wedding. Right. I glanced down at the sparkly ring on my finger, the one I had gotten so used to wearing I wasn't sure how I'd ever take it off. I was getting married tomorrow. Fake married, but still, married. An image of Emmett in his suit popped into my head and a little thrill rolled through me. I took a deep breath and nodded. "I'm good."

Elizabeth watched with a concerned expression. "It's okay to be nervous. I was."

I glanced up at her. "You were?"

"Oh, yes. Terrified. It's a big day! All those people, watching, staring, waiting for me to trip on my dress or say the wrong man's name or bolt before I got down the aisle."

I stared at her in horror. I hadn't been thinking about any of those things, but I sure as hell was now.

She threw her hands up. "Not that you're going to do any of that! And if you do, everyone will just laugh it off."

"Okay." I felt dazed and unsure.

She put her hands over mine. "Sweetheart. It's going to be great. I know it."

I looked at where her hands covered mine and smiled again. "I know." I glanced up at her. "I'm lucky to have you."

She melted. "Honey, no. I'm the lucky one." She sighed. "I always worried about Emmett. He's the oldest and he's the one who takes care of everyone else. When his brothers get into trouble or need help, it's Emmett stepping in. He's always at the house, doing repairs and making Sam and I dinner and buying us things. He's so independent and I always worried he'd never have someone in his corner, taking care of him." She swallowed. "Until you, honey. I'm so happy he has you. I can see how much he loves you."

My heart thrashed in my chest, desperate to get out. This

sweet, kind, sincere woman had been nothing but welcoming to me since the day she met me, and here I was, lying to her. My throat squeezed. I *did* love Emmett, though, I just couldn't tell him. The only person I was lying to these days was him.

I nodded at her. I wanted to be that person for Emmett, the person in his corner, looking out for him.

"I love him, too," I admitted, and the tension in my chest eased a fraction. It felt good to say out loud to someone.

Her eyes crinkled. "I know." She gave my hand another warm squeeze, as if she could see my anguish. "Tomorrow's going to be a great day, and we're going to celebrate as a family." She gave me a meaningful look. "That includes you now."

Growing up, it was always just my mom and I. Even when my parents were still together, my dad wasn't *there*. Sure, he lived in the house, but he'd be out late with friends, claiming he was networking or making business deals or whatever. I didn't know his side of the family, and my mom was an only child, so I didn't grow up with cousins and aunts and uncles like other kids did.

So stepping into the Rhodes family like this, with them ushering me in with a red carpet, open arms and all, it was like sinking into bed after a long day at the restaurant. It was everything I didn't realize I wanted. Family. For now, at least.

Heart, meet wrecking ball. Prepare to get smashed into a thousand pieces when this is all over.

"Alright." Elizabeth smiled at me a moment before standing. "I'm excited about tomorrow. It's going to be a great day and we're all going to have a lot of fun. Now, give me a hug."

I stood and let her pull me into an embrace. She smelled like lavender and I mentally catalogued this moment so I'd have it forever.

After Elizabeth left, I returned to the bar to help. Dinner service flew by, and the last diners were finishing their meals when Keiko took a seat at the bar.

I greeted her with a big grin. "Well, hello, stranger. I was wondering if you'd drop by today."

She leaned on the bar and watched as I wiped it down. "Why are you working today? You should be relaxing at home."

"We had a couple staff call in sick. I don't mind. I love it here."

She smiled. "I know you do."

"Would you like a glass of wine?"

She nodded.

"Cab sav or merlot?"

"Cab sav, please." She shifted on her chair and watched my hands as I selected the right glass. She cleared her throat and I shot her a curious glance.

I saw Chuck talking to Keiko. Max's words rang in my head from this morning. *She looked uncomfortable.*

We were so busy today that I had forgotten. I wasn't sure how to bring that up with Keiko without sounding nosy, though. It wasn't my business who she spoke to.

"I wanted to talk to you about something." Her gaze flicked between the bottle I poured from and my eyes.

"Okay." My tone was hesitant.

"It's nothing, but I'd rather you heard it from me and not someone in town. Queen's Cove residents love to gossip."

I remembered how fast news of Emmett and me spread. "Do they ever."

She toyed with the stem of her wine glass. "Chuck approached me today with an offer to buy the restaurant."

My mouth dropped.

Keiko looked up. "I'm not going to sell to him, of course, but I wanted to keep you in the loop. This doesn't change anything."

My mind was going a mile a minute but no coherent thoughts formed. "How did—" I shook my head. "Why does he think—" I broke off again. My throat closed up. That fucking *rat*. He was always sneaking around, just waiting for me to turn my back so he could shove me out of the way. Fury rattled my rib cage. "Fuck."

"Fuck, indeed."

A surprised, humorless laugh fell out of my mouth. It was the first time I had heard Keiko swear. I blinked rapidly. "How much did he offer you?"

She glanced up at me, then back down at her wine. "It's not important."

I narrowed my eyes. "Yes, it is. How much?"

She sighed. "Ten percent more."

"*Ten percent more?*" I gaped at her.

"Avery." Her tone was stern and she pinned me with her gaze. "I am not interested in Chuck owning The Arbutus, and I told him that. My decision is final."

I crossed my arms and leaned against the bar. I hated that Chuck put her in this position, that she was turning down more money because of me. And yet, I'd do anything to buy this place. I uncrossed my arms and twisted my ring around my finger. "Keiko, I don't know what to say. I'm sorry this happened."

"It's okay." She gave me a little smile and took a sip of wine. "Chuck won't get in the way of your dream. Tuesday, it's all yours."

I pulled a deep breath into my lungs and nodded. Tuesday couldn't come soon enough. One wrong move and Chuck was waiting in the wings, ready to scoop this place up.

The front door opened and Emmett walked into the restaurant holding a bouquet. My heart lifted. All the emotions I had been feeling today broke, leaving me exhausted and relieved to see him.

Something in my expression caused Keiko to turn around. "Ah," she said when she saw Emmett. "Avery, go give your fiancé a proper hello. I'm going to enjoy a few moments alone."

I nodded. "Sounds good. Enjoy." I stepped around the bar and wandered over to him. His gaze stayed on me the entire time. "Hi."

"Hi, sweetheart." He dropped a kiss on my cheek. His skin was warm against mine and I felt it down to my toes.

I nodded to the flowers. "Are these for me?" Roses, a deep blood-red, moody and romantic. My heart pinged, and I couldn't hide my smile of delight. I never bought flowers for myself because they'd just die within a few days, and it always seemed like a waste of money. These were beautiful, though. The indulgence of them, that Emmett bought them for *me*, made my stomach flutter.

He nodded. "They are. Is this a good time?"

"You bet. Thank you so much." I stuck my nose into the bouquet and inhaled the fresh floral scent. "What's the occasion?"

"My girl had the day from hell."

My girl. If I had a diary, I'd write those words down so I'd never forget him saying them. I looked around at the restaurant, bathed in soft lighting. "You know, it started great," I gave him a wink, and his gaze heated. "Then it went downhill," I winced, "but it's looking up again. This is just how the restaurant industry is. Stuff happens and we deal with it. Why don't you take a seat, I'll go put these in my office and we can have a drink."

He gave me another quick kiss on my cheek and his stubble brushed my skin. "Sure."

When I returned to the dining room, Emmett was seated at a table near the window with an uncorked bottle of wine.

I slipped into the seat across from him and gave him a soft smile as I leaned my chin on my palm. "I'm happy to see you."

"I'm happy to see you too, Adams. Missed you today." He reached across the table to cover my other hand with his.

I relaxed at the warmth of his hand. If he pulled me out

of here right now and carried me to his bed, I wouldn't mind one bit.

"Tired?"

I wanted to tell him about Chuck making Keiko an offer, but I remembered Elizabeth's words from my office, about how Emmett was always taking care of others. With the campaign, Will's family stuff, and tomorrow's wedding, I didn't want to add yet another problem to his plate. "I'm okay. Tired in a good way."

"What did Chuck want from Keiko this morning?"

So much for not telling him. I guess he did overhear Max telling me that on the phone. I let a long breath out and met his gaze with hesitance. "He made her an offer on The Arbutus."

Emmett's gaze lost all the warmth from moments ago. "What?" His tone was low and cold.

I winced. "He made her an offer ten percent higher than mine." When Emmett glanced over my shoulder at Keiko, I shook my head. "She turned him down. She doesn't want him owning this place either."

Emmett's mouth set in a firm line and his hand made a fist on the table. "Adams, listen to me. That guy will not buy this restaurant."

I nodded, twirling the ring on my ringer. "I know."

"Do you?" His eyebrows went up and he watched my expression. "You're getting your restaurant, Adams." He slipped my left hand into his and moved my ring back and forth. We both studied it as it caught the light and glinted back at us. "We made a deal."

His words comforted something in me, and yet it was another reminder what we were doing was just an agreement.

"I don't want to think about this anymore." I lifted my gaze to meet his as his fingers brushed mine. "I just want to have a nice night with you."

He watched me and I let him. Something about his gaze

made me both energized and at ease. I wanted him to look at me. I enjoyed the way his eyes moved over me, taking in my features.

He pulled his hand back and reached into his jacket pocket. "I have something for you." There was a flare of contained excitement in his eyes.

I tilted my head. "You already gave me flowers."

"I know. I was going to give these to you tomorrow, but you've had a day and I think now's the right time." He placed a little navy-blue velvet box on the table in front of me, and I stared at it.

This looked like the box from the engagement ring on my finger. My heart beat hard and fast in my chest. I glanced up at Emmett and he smiled, waiting and watching. His eyebrows wiggled up and down and my pulse picked up.

Was Emmett proposing...for real?

I cracked the box open.

Earrings.

I nearly laughed at myself. Of course he wasn't proposing for real.

The earrings sparkled, two clusters of diamonds in a similar style to my ring. "Wow," I breathed, glancing up at him.

He beamed back at me. "You like them?"

I nodded. "They're gorgeous."

He seemed pleased. So pleased. "Good. I had the same jeweler who made your ring whip them up."

I snorted. "Whip them up? So casual. Do you have a jeweler on speed dial?"

He raised an eyebrow. "I do now."

A grin grew across my face, and the most delicious warmth spread through my chest.

"You're a good man, you know that?"

Something shuttered behind his eyes. The quickest flicker. Hesitation. It was gone before I could catch it, and he just reached for the bottle of wine to pour me another glass.

I stood. His gaze snagged on me, and he looked like he was going to ask me a question, but I walked around the table, leaned down, and kissed him.

This. It had been ten hours since I had done this last, and yet my entire body felt like I was on the down part of a roller coaster. He groaned into me, and I inhaled him and his fucking incredible scent.

Emmett. *It's Emmett*, I thought to myself. I guess it had always been Emmett.

I didn't know what I was going to do with that thought, so I left it floating in my head while I reminded Emmett of how this kissing thing worked.

"It's not cute anymore," the host, Rachel, called as she passed. "It's getting gross."

We laughed against each other, and I returned to my side of the table. A triumphant, cocky smile spread across my face when I saw Emmett looked a bit dazed. He made a satisfied hum to himself, and heat flared again in his gaze.

"I picked up the marriage certificate today." He watched me closely.

"Okay."

His chest rose and fell as he took a deep breath. He cleared his throat. "We'll sign it at the ceremony, but I won't file it at town hall. The marriage won't be valid unless I file it."

He watched my face as I tried to hold it neutral. Right. Our fake marriage. My heart ached once, sharp and fast, and I swallowed.

The realization hit me. I swatted it away like a wasp at a picnic, but it wouldn't leave.

I didn't want this to be a fake marriage.

I wanted it to be real. I wanted to file that marriage certificate with both our names on it. I wanted to wake up to his mouth on me and his arms around me and us scrambling against each other. I wanted to fall asleep in his bedroom. I wanted it to be my bedroom, too. I wanted to laugh with him at the turtle rescue as he gagged and tried to hand the turtles off. I wanted to go to Rhodes family dinners with him. I wanted more nights at Castle Beach, just the two of us eating sushi and talking.

Hesitation trickled into my mind. Marriage meant we would own everything fifty-fifty. Emmett would co-own The Arbutus.

I lifted my gaze to meet his. Emmett didn't want a real marriage, anyway. He had told me he wasn't a family guy, not a relationship and commitment guy. It wasn't in the cards for him. I had known this from the beginning. We had always been on the same page. This was the deal.

I pushed the thoughts away and nodded. "Okay. We won't file the certificate."

This wasn't an *us* problem, it was a *me* problem. I'd deal with it like I dealt with everything—alone. Besides, it would be easier not to feel these things after our fake marriage was over and I had moved back into my own place and we didn't see each other every day.

I was going to enjoy it while it lasted, though, because I'd never get something like this again.

We sat there for a while, chatting about nothing, just enjoying each other's company until the bottle was empty and Emmett reached for my hand.

"Shall we head home, Adams?" His thumb brushed the back of my hand and I shivered.

I couldn't tell Emmett what he meant to me. I could show him, though. I could pour every ounce of what swirled around inside me, all this affection, longing, and need, into showing him what he meant to me.

Tonight, I'd let myself be a little in love with Emmett Rhodes.

22

Avery

THE ENTIRE DRIVE HOME, we sent secretive little grins across the car at each other. His gaze raked my form with appreciation, and I glanced between his handsome face and his strong hand gripping the steering wheel. His other hand was wrapped around my thigh, anchoring me, reminding me I was his.

I swallowed. If I thought too hard about it, I'd freak out, so I didn't think. I let myself get swallowed up by Emmett and his radiance. I let myself be his.

He parked and caught my hand on the walk up to his front door. Inside, he waited for me to slip my shoes off before he backed me against the front door and placed his hands against the door on either side of my head. I was caged in by him, and I liked it.

His heated gaze met mine as he hovered inches from my mouth. "I've been thinking about you all day."

"Oh, yeah?" I meant to sound confident, but it came out breathless. His proximity was making my pulse race. My hands came to his chest. His warmth radiated through his shirt.

He nodded down at me. "Mhm. And I've been very

patient today."

I shivered at his low tone and nodded back at him.

He glanced at my mouth, and his Adam's apple bobbed.

His mouth was so close, if I just raised myself up on my tiptoes, I could reach him. But I wanted to see what he'd do next. "You don't have to be patient anymore."

Heat flared in his gaze, and he covered my mouth with his. We groaned simultaneously, and his hands came to my ass before he hoisted me against him. My ankles wrapped around his back, my arms looped around his neck, and he carried me up the stairs while we kissed. He tasted like the wine we were drinking and something specifically Emmett.

In the bedroom, we kissed while we shed our clothes, and we kissed while we climbed into his bed, him pulling the fluffy duvet over us. He was so warm. I pressed myself up against him to capture some of his heat, all while my own heat pooled between my legs. His hands roamed my body, not urgently like this morning but slowly, like he was savoring me.

His hard length pushed against my stomach, and I reached for it. He groaned when I stroked him and pulled himself from my grasp.

"I want to touch you." I reached again, but he grabbed my wrists and held firm.

"Not yet." His mouth came to my nipple, and my eyes fell closed. "There's something I need first."

His tongue moved over the pinched peak of my breast while his fingers rolled the other. I made short, sharp whimpers while he worked, and my legs pressed together. His fingers met me there and circled my clit.

"Emmett," I moaned, and he made another noise of appreciation.

"I'll never get sick of you saying my name." His voice was low, and he looked up at me with eyes full of fire. "Never."

Before I could respond, he moved and lowered his mouth to my clit, running his tongue over the sensitive bundle of nerves. My head rolled back. His tongue moved slick circles over me, winding me tighter.

"Fuck, you taste so good. I'm going to do this to you every day. Every day, I'm going to remind you you're mine."

His words only intensified the pleasure. *Mine*, he had said. I liked it. I was Avery Adams, soon-to-be business owner, feminist, and independent person, and I was getting very, very turned on by Emmett laying claim over me.

"I've been thinking about you getting wet all over my face all day." His voice was low as his tongue swirled my clit. He sounded like he was talking to himself, or praying. "I'm addicted to this pussy."

I was charged, full of electricity and ready to snap, when he slid a finger inside me and rubbed my G-spot.

"You're soaking my hand, baby."

Pleasure rattled through me, and when he locked his mouth on my clit and sucked, I came hard around his fingers, my hips jerking against his mouth, crying out his name in the bedroom.

"I wish that was your cock," I rasped, catching my breath. "I wanted to come on you."

He kneeled over me and braced his elbows on either side of my head. He looked down at me with those glittering gray eyes, and I had the most spectacular sensation of seeing my life as it was this very moment. Truly seeing myself, lying here in bed with Emmett, the man I was head-over-heels for, his masculine, clean scent enveloping me, and his body pressed against mine. If I could freeze this moment, keep a little piece of it with me forever, I would.

Emmett's chest thudded against mine.

"I can feel your heartbeat." My voice was barely above a whisper.

His gaze locked on mine. "That's for you, Adams."

My heart overflowed when he said that. I lifted my head to kiss him and moved my hips so his hardness was against my soft center. He wore a pained expression, like I was hurting him.

I waited for him to press into me, and when he didn't, my mouth hitched. "Come on."

A flash of a laugh crossed his face. And was that...nerves? "I don't want this to be over so soon."

Did he mean sex, or did he mean us? Was Emmett feeling the same hesitation to end our agreement that I was?

Was there a chance Emmett was head over heels, undeniably in love with me the way I was with him?

I swallowed and took a shaky breath. "I know. Me neither."

His expression softened, and he dropped another sweet, lingering kiss on my mouth. I shifted again beneath him, reaching down to position him, and he sunk into me, slow and steady.

I moaned against him at the delicious full stretch of his cock inside me. My breaths came out in gasps.

Emmett's forehead dropped to the bed beside my ear, and he groaned as he slowly slid in and out of me. "Avery."

Pleasure coiled around my spine, and my legs tingled as Emmett hit the nerve endings inside me. His fingers came to my clit and again he circled it. My back arched off the bed. I was close again.

"Another?" I sounded incredulous. "Seriously?"

His voice was a growl in my ear. "Let me love you, Avery." His fingers worked fast, and I clenched him hard. He groaned again. "Come for me, baby. I need you to come again."

His words registered—*let me love you*—but I didn't have time to think about them, turn them over, pick through them. The pressure low in my belly expanded and I let out a moan. Emmett looked down into my eyes, and I could feel the silent scream on my face as I came around him, as my orgasm tensed every muscle. Emmett was barely holding on, from his pained expression, but he watched my face with fascination and reverence as the orgasm rolled through me in waves. I was vaguely aware of him saying *good* and *fuck yes* and *that's it* as I arched and gasped.

I nodded at him with my chest heaving, urging him to let himself lose control, and his eyes rolled back into his head as he thrust harder into me. He dropped his forehead to mine. His hips jerked hard.

"Avery." He gritted the words out while gripping me to his chest, and I felt so coveted. Like I belonged to him. "Baby."

We caught our breaths, and as he pressed his mouth to my forehead with a hum of satisfaction, I willed myself to remember every second of this.

I never wanted to forget being in love with Emmett Rhodes.

23

Avery

"I'M SUPPOSED to make sure you've eaten."

Hannah's soft voice yanked me from my daydreams about Emmett and all the delicious things we had done in the past few days.

Naked things. Things that made me gasp and him groan. Things that made my stomach do a delicious roll forward whenever I thought about them.

I stuck my tongue out at her, and she rolled her eyes, smiling before she nudged a granola bar toward me.

We were in the bookstore, getting ready for the wedding. Spice Girls played quietly in the background while we put the finishing touches on our makeup. The side tables beside the squashy blue chairs were cluttered with the contents of our makeup collections. The front door was locked and there was a "Closed for Wedding Day!" sign up I had seen at a few different businesses in town.

Emmett was at Holden's, getting ready with him and Will, who had come into town with his family just for our wedding. Elizabeth had just left after taking a hundred pictures of Hannah and me amongst the books. Div had been ready to hire hair and makeup artists, but I stopped him—I wanted to spend this time alone with Hannah. With everything going on with Emmett and the restaurant, I hadn't spent enough time with her recently.

I glanced at the granola bar. I could already taste the dry, chalky texture in my mouth and I made a face. There was no way I could eat it. My stomach tensed.

I was a bit nervous.

Anxiety rose and dipped in my gut. Despite my protests and grabby hands, Emmett had slid out of bed early this morning. At one point, I heard the shower running, and then after a quick kiss on my forehead, he left, and I'd had the house to myself.

In the bookstore, I smiled at Hannah as I slipped my new earrings, the ones Emmett had given me yesterday, into my ears. "I had lunch. I'm okay." I gestured at her dress. "You look lovely."

She wore an pale blue silk dress with tiny flowers and a cinched waist. She waved a hand, embarrassed at the compliment.

"Thanks." She shrugged. "Just wanted to look great for your big day. Even if the whole wedding is fake." She tilted her head and looked thoughtful. "Emmett might be a genius. As soon as you two started the whole thing, the town went nuts with excitement. And all he had to do was sign on your loan. Who's officiating?"

I selected a lip liner from the table. "Wyatt."

Beside the nearest bookshelf, someone cleared their throat and both our heads snapped in that direction.

It was Cynthia, Chuck's wife, standing there, holding a book about Italy. Her eyes held a funny gleam.

My stomach dropped through the floor. How much did she hear?

Hannah blinked. "Hi, Cynthia, we're closed." She glanced at me and swallowed. "For the wedding."

Cynthia glanced between the two of us, but the expression

gave nothing away. "My mistake. The door was unlocked."

"It's okay." Hannah stood. "I'll ring you up."

Hannah led her to the desk and after a few moments, I heard the front door lock click.

"I thought I locked it," she murmured, sitting down.

I chewed my lip. "Do you think she heard us?"

Hannah shook her head. "I don't know. She didn't say anything." She swallowed. "She creeps me out. Her hair is so spiky."

I stared at the spot on the floor where Cynthia had stood. Even if she had heard, no one would believe her. Right? Emmett and I were too convincing.

"Yeah, she creeps me out, too. Whatever." I rolled my shoulders. "Let's not let her ruin my fake wedding."

That cracked a smile from Hannah. "Agreed. Now, eat that granola bar." She watched me as I unwrapped the bar and took a bite. "Is it, though?"

"Is it what?"

"Fake."

My gaze cut to her, and my stomach dropped.

Guilty.

She knew. She had found me out. I couldn't admit it out loud, though. I wasn't there yet. I rolled my lips between my teeth, choosing my words.

She tilted her head. "It's hard to tell."

The corner of my mouth lifted but I knew the smile didn't reach my eyes. What was I going to say?

Yes, Hannah, I've fallen in love with Emmett Rhodes, the most unavailable guy in town. So unavailable he'd rather have a fake relationship than a real one.

The reality was clear—any real feelings were one-sided, and getting my hopes up was a quick way to be disappointed.

At least I was right, and Emmett and I *were* convincing as a couple.

I swallowed and dipped my brush in powder before fluffing it over my face. "Then we're doing a good job."

Hannah watched me for a moment, and I met her gaze, silently begging her to drop the subject. My heart teetered on the brink of a cliff and if I said the things I was thinking out loud, I'd fall.

She pointed beside me. "Pass me the sharpener, please."

I breathed a sigh of relief, and we put the finishing touches on our hair and makeup before she helped me into my dress in the storeroom.

"Beautiful," she breathed when it was zipped up.

I looked in the mirror. Wearing this dress was like a dream. After a few alterations by Elizabeth, it fit me to the inch. The universe had sent this dress just for me, just to make me feel special and beautiful on my big day.

My big fake day.

There was a knock on the door and we both paused.

"One second," Hannah said before making her way to the front. Murmuring voices carried through the store, and a moment later, my mom appeared at my side.

"I wanted to check on you, see how you were holding up." Her eyes were bright, the same dark blue as my own. She wore a navy-blue tea-length dress embroidered with tiny, delicate white flowers.

My mom had arrived in town first thing this morning, and we'd had breakfast at the restaurant. Her eyes had lit up as she took in the interior with the chandelier and heritage flooring, and again when she looked out the windows along the sparkling water. She was proud of me, I could tell, but there was a tinge of wistfulness in her expression, like she wished she could have a do-over.

When I told her I didn't invite my dad, I waited for her reaction. She simply nodded and patted my hand, and that was that. She understood.

"You look great," I told her. "My mom is such a babe."

She blushed. "Oh, stop it." I could tell she loved it, though. She sighed and stepped back to take me in. "Just beautiful, honey. I'm so proud of you."

My heart ached. I had the urge to tell her it was all real, that I wanted to do this for real, and I was madly in love with Emmett, but she already thought those things. My feelings didn't make sense, so I squeezed them tight to keep them under control.

"Would you like a tea, Rina?" Hannah asked, leaning on a bookshelf.

"That would be lovely, honey, thank you." My mom sent her a grateful smile and when Hannah disappeared into the back, she turned to scan my face. "How are you feeling?"

I couldn't help the grin on my face. "I'm great. I'm excited. It's going to be a fun party."

She pressed her lips together in a line and her hand came to my arm, watching me with pinched eyebrows. "I just want —" She broke off and winced, shaking her head.

"What?"

Her mouth twisted to the side. "I just want to make sure you're making the right decision. Emmett is a very nice man and I can see why you've chosen him, but I wish someone had asked me this question before I got married."

Ah. Of course. I didn't blame my mom for asking this. She barely knew Emmett and she had only heard I was with someone a few weeks ago. Of course it seemed fast. It was fast.

"Emmett isn't Dad."

"I didn't say he was."

I nodded. "I know. I'm saying it. I saw what Dad did, and I won't ever let that happen to me."

Her gaze searched mine. She nodded to herself. "Yes. You're different from me."

I shook my head. "Not so different, no. But you raised me right."

She laughed. "I felt like a failure a lot of times."

"If I could pick, I'd still pick you." I ran my thumb over the fabric of my dress. "I wouldn't do it any other way."

She watched me again, but this time it was with fresh eyes, like she knew I'd be okay. I'd learned from her mistakes. What had happened to her, it wouldn't happen to me.

Hannah breezed into the room with a couple mugs. "Peppermint or Earl Grey?"

My mom smiled. "Peppermint, please."

The three of us sat there, drinking tea and chatting and laughing, until the tea was finished and our makeup was complete.

My mom stood. "May I use the washroom before we head over to town hall?"

Hannah pointed to the back room. "Through there to the left."

My mom stepped into the back, and Hannah and I began to put our shoes on.

"Do you ever want to get married?" I worked the delicate strap through the buckle around my ankle.

"Um." Her fingers fumbled with her own ankle strap and she blinked. "Yes. To the right person, of course." She blinked again, staring at the other shoe in her hand. "We'll see."

I raised an eyebrow at her. "Anyone in mind?"

She snorted and shook her head. "No."

"You know, Emmett has three brothers." My voice was teasing. "I could put in a good word for you."

Hannah's face turned a deep crimson. "Please don't."

My mouth dropped open. "You're blushing."

Her eyes turned into saucers. "No, I'm not."

"You are! Hannah." I leaned in, narrowing my eyes at her, but her gaze was glued to her shoe. "Do you have a crush on one of the Rhodes boys?"

"Nope." Her voice was a high squeak. She looked mortified.

"Liar." I took one look at Hannah's tense shoulders and beet-red face. "I'll drop it for now, but this conversation is not over."

My mom returned and we left the bookstore to walk to town hall. A few people from town spotted us and called over their congratulations, and I waved back and smiled at them. The street was extra quiet, though. More than usual.

"Even the grocery store is closed?" I asked Hannah, pointing over at the darkened building.

"For the wedding."

I didn't expect the grocery store to be closed. A tiny flicker of anxiety lit up my stomach.

This was the whole point of the wedding, to get people in the town invested so they saw Emmett as a stable, responsible guy on the brink of starting a family. I nodded to myself, standing there in front of town hall, about to go inside and get married.

"I'm getting married." I nodded again. "Yep. Getting married in front of a lot of people."

Hannah and my mom exchanged a look before Hannah's concerned gaze roamed my face. "Are you okay? Do you need me to get Emmett?"

Emmett, the guy I was doing this for. The man who I wasn't just having incredible sex with, but who had become a friend. My best friend, except for Hannah. A guy I wanted to help. Right. Emmett. I smiled, thinking of his handsome face with his very straight, strong nose and sharp jaw, and light gray eyes that warmed when he smiled at me.

That tiny little scar on his lip that I loved to brush my fingers over when it was just the two of us in his bed.

Emmett. My heart squeezed.

I shook my head and smiled at Hannah. "No, I'm ready." I faced forward. "Let's do this."

We opened the doors and stepped into the foyer of town

hall. A bored receptionist was on FaceTime and snapping her gum. She glanced up at us.

"Are you getting married?" she asked in a monotone.

I nodded.

The receptionist pointed down a hallway. "That way." She turned back to her phone and continued her conversation.

Div stood at the end of the hallway. "There you are," he said upon seeing us.

Hannah turned to me and blinked a few times. "Well," she started.

I pulled her into a hug. "I know. I love you too."

She laughed against me and when she pulled back, her eyes were wet. She blinked the tears away, disappeared inside the room, and I stood there with my mom.

This was less fake by the minute.

"Shall we do this?" I held my arm out, and my mom looped hers through mine.

"Ready?" Div stood with his hand poised on the door, and we nodded. He opened it a crack, gave someone a thumbs up, and music began before he opened the door.

24

Avery

THE DOOR OPENED and what felt like six thousand people turned to stare at me. My stomach dropped through the floor. My heart began to race in my chest, so hard people could probably see it pounding against my neckline.

My mom took a step forward. I tried to move, but I was frozen in place.

My brain was frozen. Blood rocketed through my veins, but I couldn't think or move. Was the dress always this tight? I could breathe fine during my fitting but right now, I couldn't seem to suck enough air into my lungs.

The music was still playing but every person in the room held their breath in anticipation.

"Honey?" my mom asked out of the corner of her mouth.

I blinked. What was I doing? Why did I say yes to this? This was terrifying. There were so many people, I didn't even know half of them. Emmett's brother Finn had flown back into town just for this. This wasn't fake to them. It was real, and it was a big fucking deal. My eyes darted around like I was a cow en route to the slaughterhouse.

This all hinged on me.

I couldn't do this. I had to leave.

My gaze rose to Emmett, standing at the front of the room, fifty feet away.

He smiled at me.

It wasn't his shiny politician's smile with a hundred teeth. It was the lopsided, amused, affectionate smile he gave me when I said something silly.

Right. Emmett.

My stomach unclenched.

I took a step forward, and my mom stepped with me, letting out a breath of relief. My mouth curved up, and I smiled back at Emmett.

My pulse slowed even more and the banging of my heart in my chest went away. I could do this. I could breathe. I began to walk slowly up the aisle as the music played.

As we approached him, with Wyatt standing behind him, everyone on either side of the aisle disappeared from my vision. I could barely even hear the music. I just watched Emmett, kept my gaze trained on his handsome face, thought about how wonderful he smelled and how nice it was to sit on the beach with him the other night. Maybe we could go back another time just to sit there and watch the waves on the shore and listen to the birds chirp in the trees. This was going to be okay, I just knew it.

When we got to the front, my mom gave me a kiss on the cheek and took a seat, and Emmett held his hand out to me, watching me steadily. His gaze was like a life raft, keeping me afloat, buoyant, and pulling me up to the surface. I took his hand.

This was happening.

Wyatt cleared his throat. His normally shaggy blond hair was tied into a messy bun. A strange giggle bubbled out of my throat, and Emmett gave me a funny look.

"Man bun," I mouthed, and he grinned wider.

Wyatt started speaking. What was he saying? Couldn't tell you. I wasn't even listening. Emmett smiled down at me, running a thumb across the back of my left hand and distracting me.

"You're beautiful," he whispered while Wyatt gave his speech.

My heart flip-flopped in my chest. The way Emmett was looking at me, I *felt* beautiful. I felt like, to him, I was the only person on the planet right now.

He winked at me and squeezed my hand, and I couldn't help but smile wider.

"Emmett, would you like to say your vows?" Wyatt asked and we snapped to attention.

"Right." Emmett reached into his suit jacket and pulled out a piece of paper. "Avery." He paused, looked up at me, and back at his paper. Mischief flashed in his eyes, and I narrowed my eyes.

"According to our records, your copy of Elizabeth Gilbert's *Eat, Pray, Love* is six years overdue."

The guests broke out in laughter. A grin pulled at his features.

"Whoops." He shuffled his papers and mock-winced at the guests. "Wrong paper."

I burst out laughing, and he grinned at me while the laughter died down. He took a breath, and his Adam's apple bobbed as he glanced at his papers. A flicker of nerves flashed across his face before he covered it back up with his usual smug confidence.

"Avery, I knew I liked you the second I saw you." His voice rang out clear and loud in the room. "You were brand-new in town and serving at The Arbutus, and I saw a beautiful girl and wanted to sit in her section, but there were no available tables." He glanced up at me, and I tilted my head, curious. He had never told me this. "So I went back, but again, there were no available tables. I went back again. That time, I was finally in your section, but you were about to go on break." A few laughs among the guests. "Seven times I ate at that restaurant in a week until I got to talk to you." His mouth hitched with the memory. "And you wouldn't give me the time of day."

He glanced up at me and back down at his paper, and I watched with awe. I had to give it to him, that sounded so genuine.

"But after a couple years, I wore you down." He swallowed and blinked at his paper. "Avery Adams, you are the most hard-working, funny, intelligent, independent, determined person I know. You're fiercely protective of everyone in your life. You take care of your people, your staff, your friends, and me." When he met my gaze, his was full of sincerity and vulnerability. "I wasn't ready for that, and I wasn't ready for how hard I'd fall for you."

My stomach did a delicious roll forward. I gave him a small smile and reached out for the hand not holding the paper. He squeezed my fingers.

"I never expected to find someone I trust and respect so much, someone I want to talk to and see every day." He glanced up at me again, and my heart expanded at the vulnerable, open expression on his face. "Someone I want to wake up with every day. You are what my life was missing, and I didn't even realize it until I found you, but I have no plans to let you go. I love you, Avery Adams. I love you, and I'm never letting you go. That's the deal."

He leaned down and placed a soft kiss on my cheek. My heart beat in my ears. That sounded so real, and I wanted it to be, more than anything. His hands brushed mine, and my head swirled with both light, happy, delirious feelings and uncertain, surprised, confused feelings.

Wyatt nodded at me. "Go for it."

I turned to Hannah, who stood and passed me my vows. I unfolded them, aware everyone was waiting. My pulse raced.

Emmett smiled down at me softly, and when I smiled back, the tension within me eased. Right. This was going to be fine.

I reached out and slipped my hand into his. His warm fingers brushed against the back of my hand, and I took a steadying breath.

"I didn't like you when I first met you."

Emmett let out a bark of laughter. Some chuckles rose up from the guests as well.

I shook my head at him, grinning. "I really didn't like you. I thought you were the schmooziest, fakest, most insincere person I'd ever met. How could someone be friends with everyone?"

He gave me an amused, lopsided smile. I cleared my throat. "Then, I got to know you, and everything changed."

The paper shook in front of me. I sucked in a deep breath and closed my eyes for a brief moment while Emmett's warm hand squeezed mine. It was hard to say these things, even if this whole thing wasn't real.

I was just going to tell the truth.

"The Emmett I now know is the most selfless person." I glanced up into his eyes, so full of affection and warmth. Okay, this wasn't so bad. "You'd do anything for a friend, and you're friends with everyone."

Emmett laughed, and my heart burst with pride. I loved it when he did that.

I scanned the front row of guests and locked eyes with Elizabeth. We smiled at each other. "That's you, Emmett. I like spending time with you more than anyone. I used to like being alone. I valued my solitude, but I like being around you more. I love how warm and caring you are, how you take care of me, how you make me laugh, and how impulsive you are."

I met his gaze, and he was looking at me like I was the woman he was about to marry for real. My chest panged.

"It wasn't easy for me to trust you, but I took a leap and I'm so happy I did." I swallowed thickly, hesitating.

I promised myself I'd tell the truth.

"I want to spend the rest of my life with you. I want to

take as good care of you as you do of everyone else. I love you."

Emmett's hand came to my chin, and he covered my mouth with his. The soft brush of his lips over mine was such a relief I sighed against his mouth. I inhaled him, his intoxicating, masculine scent. His arm came around my waist to pull me closer to him and I didn't even care he crushed me against him, I kissed him back hard and my head swirled. My heart raced, not with nerves but with exhilaration.

I told the truth, and I said I loved Emmett.

I was deliriously happy.

He pulled my hair lightly, tilting my head back to deepen the kiss, and his tongue swiped mine. A soft moan escaped my throat. This was incredible, this kiss. My head spun. I could have done this forever. This wedding thing wasn't so scary after all. It was incredible.

We were two people in a crowd of over a hundred, but it felt like we had the room to ourselves.

"Kiss the bride," Wyatt said in a dry tone beside us.

The guests laughed and we broke apart. Right, the rest of the wedding.

Wyatt beamed at us. "I now pronounce you husband and wife."

Everyone cheered, and Emmett dropped another kiss onto my lips. I smiled into his mouth. My pulse still raced but I couldn't stop smiling. My cheeks hurt, I grinned so big.

Wyatt directed us over to a table on the side of the room where the marriage certificate sat. He told me where to sign and I did without even reading the thing. Emmett's hand rested on my lower back the whole time, sending shivers up and down my spine. I handed the pen to him and he signed his name before taking my hand.

Hannah signed as our witness and then Wyatt.

Wyatt gestured at the marriage certificate. "I'll file this."

Emmett shook his head. "Just leave it in my car. I'll do it

tomorrow." He glanced at me, the special *we've got a secret* look, before he tugged my hand and lead me down the aisle past our applauding friends and family. When we passed through the doors, he tilted his head down the hall.

"Come on." His eyes gleamed. He pulled me and we started jogging through the building.

"Where are we going?" I asked, laughing and trying to keep up with him.

He didn't answer, just led us past the receptionist who was still on FaceTime, and through the front doors. He stopped and scooped me up, and I let out a surprised squeal.

"What are you doing?" My face hurt from smiling. He threw me over his shoulder, and I gasped. "Emmett, you're going to rip my dress!"

"Good." His voice was gravelly. "Then we can go home and be alone."

He carried us around the side of the building and through the gardens before setting me down, right side up. We were in the rose garden beside town hall, surrounded by hundreds of varieties of roses in full summer bloom, and best of all, we were all alone.

He stepped into my personal space and looked down at me. "I want you to myself for a few moments before the reception." His hand came to my hair. "No one will bother us here."

I was breathless at his proximity. "That was very thoughtful of you." I narrowed my eyes at him. "And you had no ulterior motives?"

The corners of his mouth lifted. "Sure, I did. I wanted to do more of this." His lips dropped to mine and I sighed again.

I don't know how long we stood there, making out in the rose garden. Time seemed to stand still and I wasn't worried about anything else. Emmett's fingers brushed the back of my neck and my hand snaked around his waist inside his suit jacket. His kiss oscillated between soft and sweet, and demanding and bossy. Every slip of his tongue against mine sent a zing of electricity through my limbs and made me shiver against him. He nipped my lip with his teeth and a little gasp escaped my throat.

He pulled away from my mouth, leaning his forehead against mine. We were both breathing hard.

He blew out a frustrated breath. "I am so fucking hard right now."

I laughed a little. "They won't miss us."

"There you two are," Div called at the entrance of the garden.

A groan of frustration came out of Emmett's chest, and I sighed.

"We'll be there in a second." Emmett ran his hands up my shoulders and pressed a kiss to my forehead. "What's the grossest thing you can think of?"

I laughed in surprise. "What?"

"I need to get rid of this hard-on. Quick. Tell me about your grandmother or something."

I laughed again. "Think about Elizabeth."

His expression turned to revolt. "My mother?"

I laughed harder. "The turtle you almost made out with."

He gagged and I wheezed with laughter. "Oh god." He shuddered. "Yeah, that worked." He held a hand out. "Let's go."

Emmett and I met Div and the photographer he had hired at the edge of the garden, where we let her take a few pictures of us before she led us down to the beach. We kicked our shoes off where the sand started.

"You guys go ahead," she told us. "I'll hang back."

Emmett took my hand and led me along the trees at the edge of the sand. I inhaled the cool breeze coming in off the ocean and let the sun warm my skin. The late-spring temperature was just a little too cold, but I didn't mind since Emmett was happy to tuck me into his side to stay warm. Birds floated in the water, bobbing as the waves rolled in.

I gave him a sidelong look. "I thought this would be a lot harder."

"Getting married?"

I nodded.

"Me too." He squeezed my hand and my heart flipped in my chest.

We wandered down the beach for a bit before turning around and heading back toward where we started. I could hear the clicking of the photographer's camera but paid no attention to it.

"Get any good shots?" I asked her when we were ready to head to the restaurant.

She glanced up from her camera with a wistful smile. "One or two."

25

Emmett

MY MOM HELD her glass of champagne high in the air on The Arbutus patio. "To Avery and Emmett!"

"To Avery and Emmett," the guests on the restaurant patio chorused, and Avery met my gaze as we clinked glasses.

My hand was glued to Avery's low back, and it slid a couple inches lower on the soft fabric. Her eyes opened a fraction wider over her champagne glass.

"Stop that." The corner of her mouth pulled up.

I looked down at her. "I won't."

Fucking hell, I was hard again. I had been hard all goddamn day.

Avery's hair moved in the breeze, and she gave me a soft smile. Her eyes were so brilliantly blue in the light and my chest felt tight.

I had to give Div credit, he and Max had transformed the restaurant. It was decorated in tiny twinkle lights, inside and out. We were sitting out on the patio, overlooking the ocean while we ate dinner.

"Your mom and my mom are fast friends," I mentioned to Avery while dinner was being served. Our moms sat together, talking and laughing.

She nodded and gave me a lopsided smile. "I've noticed. Kind of makes me wonder what I was so worried about." Her gaze slid to me. "Thanks for telling me not to invite my dad." She winced and bit her lip. "I still feel guilty, but at least I'm not worrying about him doing something and ruining the night."

"Don't mention it. It isn't a big deal."

There was that lopsided smile again. "It is."

I leaned over and gave her a chaste kiss on the cheek, something to remind her I was here and on her side. I remembered the way she gazed at me during the ceremony, so sweet, open, and trusting, and my chest ached. I meant every word during my vows, and she had no idea. She thought it was all fake. I couldn't tell her yet, though. She had too much on her mind. Tuesday, she'd sign the papers to buy the restaurant. Once things had calmed down, in a week or two, I'd tell her how I felt.

I'd tell her I loved her and wanted to do this for real.

I blew a breath out. Holy shit. My heart raced with excitement and nerves, just thinking about saying those words to her.

I shook the thoughts out of my head. Soon.

"Big day Tuesday."

She laughed. "Big day today."

"How are you feeling?"

She glanced across the patio, a couple tables away at Keiko, who was talking with Miri, Scott, Will, and Nat. "I've waited so long to buy this place and now it's finally happening."

I placed my hand over hers and squeezed. "I'm proud of you."

She turned back to me with the most beautiful smile, and my heart twisted again.

Even if I wasn't running for mayor, I'd have cosigned on her loan. Anything to make this woman happy, I'd do it.

Avery and I ate dinner while watching half the town talk, laugh, eat, and drink. People came up to congratulate us and chat, wrapping us up in hugs and telling us how happy they were for us. The whole party felt like one big family reunion. After dinner was over and the plates were cleared, people began moving around from table to table, talking to their friends and taking pictures. Everyone was dressed up and looking their best. Music played and people danced on the corner of the patio.

Avery's hand squeezed my arm. "You okay, *darling*?"

I flashed a grin at her. "Never better, *peachy pie*."

She made a gagging motion. "Peachy pie?"

"Because you're so sweet." I stifled my laughter at her look of revulsion.

"I'm not sweet." There was a flicker of heat in her eyes.

I raised an eyebrow. "You sure as hell aren't." I winked, and a flare rose in me at the way her mouth parted. "This is so fun," I told her, gesturing at our guests. "Everyone should have a fake wedding."

Her eyes widened. "Shhh. Someone might hear."

I snorted. "Are you kidding? No one would believe us. Watch." I leaned over and tilted her chin to me before I brushed my lips across hers. Her eyes fluttered closed.

"Aww, that's so sweet!" Miri trilled, passing by with two glasses of champagne in her hands.

Avery laughed against my neck. "You're right. We've got them."

I glanced at the people dancing to the music and grabbed Avery's hand. "Come on, let's dance."

"Now?"

I hauled her up on her feet. "Yes, now. Come on, Adams, it's our wedding, let's have as much fun as our guests are having."

We were greeted on the dance floor with cheers and whoops. From then on, I kept one hand on Avery at all times

—holding her hand and spinning her in a circle, resting my hand on her lower back, wrapping my arm around her shoulders, and when the music slowed down, pulling her against me and letting my fingers tangle into her hair.

Div appeared at my side. "Do you want to talk to the Hendersons? They're here."

Bill and Patricia Henderson had been dodging my campaign calls for weeks. Patricia Henderson was the head of the local office of the electric utility and would be a critical part of making my campaign platform a reality. I glanced past Div, where they were gathered with some other people from town, drinks in hand. At that moment, Avery lifted my arm up and spun underneath it, wiggling her ass to the music and looking fucking hilarious and adorable at the same time.

I shook my head at Div. "I'll find them later."

Div gave me an *are you insane* look but I ignored it and spun Avery again, this time so she landed flush against my chest, laughing. I caught a whiff of her shampoo and my cock hardened.

This was fun, but I was counting down the seconds until we could be alone. Sex on the wedding night was a joke, I had thought. I'd always heard the couple was too tired to have sex. I could see how that happened, but I couldn't imagine being too tired to touch Avery.

Will and Nat danced past us, and Avery laughed at their goofy moves. I pulled her to me and dropped another kiss on her mouth. She leaned into me, and her hands came to my chest, sighing against my mouth.

There was no way I'd be too tired tonight.

The music lowered and everyone on the dance floor looked over to where a four-tier cake was rolled out. People began gesturing at us to step forward. When Avery grabbed my hand and led me to it, a little zing of excitement ran from my hand into my chest. A server handed Avery a knife, and she looked to me. The sun was setting across the water, casting pinks and oranges across the sky, and the twinkle lights hovered above us, giving her skin a warm glow. Her cheeks were flushed from dancing.

"I think we're supposed to do this together," she said, holding out the knife.

I placed my hand over hers and wrapped my arm around her. The photographer's camera clicked off to the side.

"I can't wait to smash this cake into your face," I murmured in her ear as we sliced into it.

I felt her laugh under me. A night of dancing had loosened her up. She was laughing easier, louder, and brighter tonight. It was like whatever anxiety had weighed on her had lifted.

"You absolutely fucking won't." Her voice was low, but she grinned. "Or I will smash a piece right into the front of your pants."

"I know you just want another excuse to touch me there," I whispered, and she gasped in annoyance but was still grinning.

I cut a slice and slid it onto a plate before picking up a small piece. I sent her a daring look.

Her shoulders shook with contained laughter. "Don't you fucking dare, Emmett."

I watched her steadily with a small, smug grin on my face. This must be what tigers felt like, stalking their prey, waiting for the perfect moment.

"Do you trust me?"

"Not one bit." Her smile took up her entire face.

"Do it!" someone yelled.

I raised my eyebrows, holding her gaze. "Come on, Adams. Say it."

She pressed her lips together and rolled her eyes, grinning. "Alright. I trust you."

Gently, I placed a small piece of cake into her mouth. She watched me the entire time with a heated gaze. Her tongue darted out to a smudge of icing on her lip and I inhaled sharply as all my blood rushed to my cock.

I wasn't the tiger, she was. I was the prey.

My theory was confirmed when she took a small piece of cake and smushed it into my mouth, smearing the icing all over my lips.

"Come here." I grabbed her, and she shrieked with laughter when I pulled her toward me and planted a kiss on her mouth. Our guests laughed as I kissed the icing all over Avery's mouth. "I'm going to make you pay for that later," I murmured, making her breath hitch.

Fucking hell, I wanted to leave right now. There was heat behind her eyes, and my balls tightened. It was like during the wedding ceremony, when it felt like we were the only people in the world, even though a hundred of our friends and family were watching us.

I had to get her alone.

We stepped away from the cake so the servers could cut it up and pass it out. The music volume increased, the dance floor flared to life again, and we were no longer the focus of everyone's attention. I grabbed Avery's hand and pulled her across the patio, toward the restaurant.

"Where are we going?" she asked.

Scott waved to get my attention. "Hey, Emmett—"

"Sorry, Scott, I'll catch up with you later," I told him as we breezed past. I pulled Avery into the restaurant. My hand gripped her small one as I hauled her into the quiet hallway where her office was and threw the door open.

"Oh, yeah, I was just thinking I needed to review the inventory levels." She hid a grin. "Thanks for the reminder."

I closed the door after her. "You need a few minutes of alone time."

She raised an eyebrow. "So why are you here?"

"A different kind of alone time." I pulled her toward me,

one hand in her hair and one around her waist, and kissed her.

A soft whimper escaped her and I groaned against her, tilting her head back to deepen the kiss. That little whimper of hers had already made me hard. I walked us backwards until I sat on the edge of her desk and she stood between my legs. Her hands were on my thighs and my cock throbbed.

Fucking hell, I wanted this woman. I wanted her so badly. I wanted to yank this dress up and tongue-fuck her until she screamed my name.

"Holy shit, Adams," I groaned. "I want you so badly." My hand skimmed up her waist over the rough sequins and beads and came to her breast, where I found her nipple through the thin fabric. It peaked under my touch and her breath became ragged. She broke our kiss and her mouth worked down my jaw and neck. My head fell back.

Her fingers worked at my tie, loosening it and undoing the top buttons of my collar as her mouth did incredible things. Her teeth scraped my skin and my cock pulsed.

"Shit," I rasped. I was so hard it hurt. My length rubbed against the apex of her legs, and when she rocked against me, a little gasp slipped out of her. I pressed my mouth in a tight line, trying to control myself. She was too soft and sexy and pushing all the right buttons and I couldn't handle it much longer.

"Are you going to take my virginity tonight?" Avery teased in between kisses on my throat before sucking on the skin where my shoulder and neck met. Her voice was raspy as well, low and husky and full of need. It sent a thrill through me. I needed to make her come.

I pinched her nipple and she gasped.

"I want you so badly," I told her and pulled her mouth back to mine, sliding my tongue over hers and tasting her. She moaned, and tension coiled inside me. Fuck. I couldn't take this much longer. "I've never been this turned on." Her mouth grinned against mine and I laughed. "What are you doing to me, Adams? I can barely think."

With a wicked smile, her hand slid up my thigh to my cock and she stroked me through my pants.

Need rocketed through me, and I nearly passed out. "Slow down, baby, you gotta slow down."

"I'm barely touching you," she murmured, still stroking me lightly. She looked at me with daring eyes. She knew the power she had over me, and she liked it. It excited her, and to my surprise, it excited me too.

I inhaled and exhaled slowly, trying to maintain control. "I'm going to make you come so hard you can't remember what it was like before we were together," I told her as her hand moved along my cock.

She shuddered and leaned up to kiss me, but the door to her office flew open. Her hand abruptly left my cock and we turned to see Wyatt at the door.

"Don't you knock?" I demanded.

He raised his eyebrows. "Busted."

"Do you need something?" I pulled Avery in front of me, partly because I enjoyed her pressed against me but also to hide my massive erection.

Wyatt snorted. "People were looking for you." He leaned out the door. "They're in here," he called.

"Oh my god." Avery leaned against me, and I laughed into her hair.

"There you are!" Miri appeared in the doorway. Hannah was behind her, followed by Holden and Finn. "What are you guys doing in here?"

"Taxes," Avery said.

I shook my head at them with an exasperated expression. "What do you *think* we were doing?"

Hannah winced.

"Hope we weren't interrupting," Will yelled from the hallway.

"You were," I yelled back.

Wyatt tossed me my keys and I caught them. "Your bags are all ready to go and in the car."

Avery and I frowned at each other in confusion.

She looked to Wyatt. "Our bags?"

Hannah looked pleased. "We booked you a room at the Emerald Seas Inn."

The Emerald Seas Inn was the nicest hotel in Queen's Cove. It faced the ocean, was newly renovated, and movie stars often retreated there to enjoy quiet, cozy getaways.

Finn snorted. "I didn't want to hear the bed banging against the wall all night."

I grinned. "Good call."

"You didn't have to do that," Avery said. She was still standing in between my legs with her hands on my chest, my arms around her keeping her close.

Wyatt shrugged. "Whatever. It's nothing. You're part of the family now."

Avery seemed to melt with happiness when he said that and I shot Wyatt a grateful look.

"Don't leave yet, though," Miri urged. "Come with us to the beach."

I looked down at Avery with a question in my eyes.

She smiled. "Let's do it."

My balls ached again with the need to make Avery orgasm, but I kept my mouth shut when I saw her eyes light up at Miri's suggestion. "Let's go."

The group of us left the restaurant, where people were still dancing and laughing, and walked down to the beach. Our shoes were left in a pile at the edge of the sidewalk, where the sand began. The moon was high in the sky and cast a glow over everything, and the lights from the restaurant illuminated our way. Avery pulled the skirt of her dress up so it wouldn't get dirty and walked to the edge of the shore. I walked alongside her with the cuffs of my pants rolled up so they wouldn't get wet.

"This was so easy," she told me. Her voice was low enough that the others couldn't hear us.

Finn was splashing Hannah and Miri with water, and they were laughing and running away. Holden sat on a log while Will and Nat held hands beside him. Wyatt was stripping down to his boxers. He dumped his clothes beside Holden and ran into the water before diving under.

I put my arm around Avery's shoulder. "It sure was. The easiest wedding I've ever had. I'm a genius."

She grinned. "The most modest, humble genius I know."

We walked up and down the beach as the waves lapped against our feet. The laughter from Finn, Hannah, and Miri followed us and the soft rumble of the waves rose up around us.

Tonight was one of the best nights of my life. I couldn't wait to tell her how I felt, but it wasn't time yet.

I pictured telling her that my vows were the truth, that I loved her and wanted to be with her, and I didn't want it to be fake anymore. Everything she had shown me in the past few weeks told me she would be receptive.

But what if she wasn't? What if she freaked out?

What if it was still fake to her?

I pictured us parting ways and going back to our regular lives. I couldn't even remember what my regular life was like, only weeks ago. What did I even do? What did I think about, being mayor? My business? Those things seemed so dull in comparison to thinking about Avery. One more week with her didn't seem like enough. Ten weeks didn't seem like enough. I wanted forever.

"Are you still good with our deal?" I asked her, glancing down and meeting her gaze as she looked up at me.

She hesitated, eyes narrowing slightly, and she bit her lip before nodding.

Well. There it was. Disappointment flickered throughout me, punctuated with something else. Pain, but I brushed it away too quickly to identify it. Moping wouldn't do any good. I was Emmett Rhodes, I didn't mope about things I couldn't control.

I blinked to myself. I was Emmett *goddamn* Rhodes.

For one, I was a fucking genius for cooking up this plan and somehow having the best damn day of my life with an incredibly gorgeous, funny, smart woman. I did that. So, who's to say I couldn't convince said incredibly gorgeous, funny, smart woman that we could do this thing a little longer? Why did it have to end after a week? We made that deal when we didn't even know each other. She couldn't stand me a month ago. This was different. She liked me now. She *really* liked me, if the way she responded when I touched her or kissed her was any indication.

My mouth hitched, and competition surged within me. Competition with whom? No idea. With myself, I guess, or with Avery's hesitation about us being more.

I was going to make Avery fall for me as hard as I had fallen for her.

The poor woman wouldn't know what hit her.

I flashed her my most charming smile, at which she narrowed her eyes.

"What are you up to?"

"Nothing. You're gorgeous, has anyone ever told you that?"

She raised an eyebrow. "What's going on with you? You're scheming."

"Me? Scheming? You're crazy, Adams." I sighed and pulled her close to me. The rest of our group now sat on the log, chatting, except for Wyatt, who was still swimming in the ocean while Holden watched on. If it was anyone else, I'd be more watchful and concerned, but Wyatt was a strong swimmer, and there was no keeping him out of the water. We had tried and failed many times.

"Come on, let's go," I said to her.

She met my gaze, and something passed between us. She shivered under my arm.

"Are you cold?"

She shook her head. "Let's go."

We were checking into the hotel when I realized I forgot to grab the marriage certificate out of the car. As soon as we had our room key, I turned to Avery. "I forgot something in the car, just give me one second."

She nodded. "I'm going to go up to the room."

"Sure." I gave her a quick kiss and headed outside.

I searched that car like I was a detective looking for clues in a murder investigation. I checked in the glove box, under all the seats, the trunk, behind the visors, everywhere.

The marriage certificate wasn't in there.

I blew a breath out and pulled out my phone to text Wyatt. He probably forgot to put it in the car. Maybe it was in one of my bags upstairs. I typed out the question to him and sent it.

When I opened the door of our hotel room, Avery stood in the dim lighting, wearing only a white lace bra and thong. The delicate lace fit her soft curves and her gentle cleavage swelled in the low light. My hands clenched at my sides, eager to touch her smooth skin and pull her to me. My heart began to beat harder as she bit her lip. She gave me a quick wink.

"That's my move." My voice was strangled. I was already at the edge of control, and all my woman had done was strip down to her underwear.

I was in deep trouble.

She gave me a wicked smile. "Get over here."

I did as I was told.

26

Avery

THE LOOK in Emmett's eyes as he saw me standing there in my lingerie, it could have burned me up from the inside, it was so heated. Anticipation and desire clouded my mind and all I thought about was how to get Emmett's mouth on me.

I didn't have to try that hard.

Within moments I was on my back on the bed, naked and gasping as he devoured me. His tongue slicked across my folds, dancing over my clit. I gasped and arched.

"Need this," he groaned against my wetness.

"Emmett," I moaned. My eyes were clenched closed, and I scrambled to find his hair. My fingers combed through his soft locks and gently pulled, and I felt his groan all the way to my center.

"Say my name so you know you're mine."

"Emmett." My voice was a gasp.

Pressure wound tight and hard inside of me and when he slipped a finger into my core and worked my G-spot, I unraveled underneath him, calling his name, paralyzed with overwhelming pleasure.

When I floated back down to earth like a feather, I gave him a shy smile and bit my lip.

Lust clouded his gaze. "I'm going to do that every day."

I nodded. My chest burst with joy at the idea, not just because of the orgasms but because the idea of seeing him every day was heaven. "Deal."

He climbed onto the bed and lay down beside me, propping himself up on his elbow, but I crawled over him, straddling him. The orgasm had taken the edge off but I still felt empty and hungry, and I needed more. His hardness pressed against my core, and I dragged myself up and down his length, pulling a shudder from his chest. His gaze darkened as he watched me over him.

When his hands came to my breasts and he touched the aching tips, my head fell back and something primal within me rattled her cage. More. I needed more.

I positioned him at my entrance, and he watched me with a gaze so dark it nearly shattered my soul. I lowered myself onto him and we moaned. He pulled me forward, flush against his chest, and I moved my hips slowly, taking all of his length deep inside me. I whimpered against him, and my body stretched around him in a delicious ache. My core thrummed with pleasure, and I slid up and down languidly, watching as his brow furrowed with delicious concentration.

"Stop holding back." I shuddered and he groaned, fingers digging into my hips as I bounced up and down on him. "Give up."

"Give me another one first. I can feel you clenching me." His voice was rough and it sent shivers down my limbs. "You're so close, I can feel it. I know you can do it again, baby."

His fingers pinched my nipples and I gasped. That familiar pressure built and the back of my legs tingled. My orgasm approached. Hot wetness flooded my core and Emmett groaned again and pulsed inside of me.

A moment later, it ripped through me, wrenching my soul from my body and wringing me out. Wave after wave crashed inside me, and stars exploded behind my eyes. God, I loved this man. I couldn't hold it in anymore and I didn't want to. What if one of us died tomorrow and he never knew how I felt?

Bravery surged within me and my head fell against his chest. "I love you. I love you so fucking much, Emmett." My voice was high and breathy, and I gasped against his chest as the last throes of the orgasm wracked my body and my muscles jerked.

I thought I'd panic when the truth was set free, but it didn't happen. My shoulders eased.

Emmett's gaze overflowed with heat. He watched me with a tense reverence before his arms came around me and he flipped me onto my back. "Really?"

I nodded. "Yes."

He made a noise like I was killing him. "I love you, too." He hovered above me to study my expression. "You're everything to me. I wanted to tell you, but I didn't want you to freak out."

He loved me too? I was worried I meant nothing to him. I laughed in relief and disbelief at my incredible luck. "Not freaking out." I shook my head and beamed at him. "Not freaking out one bit."

He leaned down to cover my mouth with his before he pushed his hips further into me and I groaned against his lips.

"I want to be married for real, Avery." His gaze was hungry, dark, and glazed.

I nodded against his mouth and whimpered as he thrust into me again. "We're doing this. It's real."

His hands grasped my hips and he tilted me so his arousal hit the right point, and with no warning, I came again, tipping back over that cliff of pleasure. He was right there with me, groaning my name into my hair and urgently shuddering his release into my soul.

The room was silent save for our breathing and my heart thumping in my ears.

All that worry about this being fake, for nothing. His vows sounded sincere because he *was* sincere. Emmett wanted me the way I wanted him. I could kick myself for keeping it a secret. What if I had never blurted out that I loved him?

At one point, I got up to use the washroom, and when I returned to bed, Emmett was studying his phone with a funny expression.

"What is it?"

He shook his head and put the phone down. "Nothing. Come back to bed."

I settled in with my head against his chest, listening to his heartbeat.

"I love you." He kissed my temple. "I mean it."

I nodded and turned my head to catch his mouth. "I love you, and I mean it too."

27

Avery

MONDAY MORNING, I sat in the kitchen reading the Queen's Cove Daily article about our wedding while Emmett made us breakfast. "There's a nice picture of my mom with your parents."

He turned. "She's coming back for Christmas."

"Who?" My eyebrows went up.

"Your mom. My mom invited her to stay with them."

Outside the window, a hummingbird hovered before it zipped off. Christmas was more than six months away. My gaze strayed to Emmett, where he stood with his back to me in his running shorts and t-shirt, and my mouth lifted into a soft smile.

This marriage was real. It wasn't just me who had gained family. My mom had, too.

Emmett's phone buzzed on the counter. He tapped a button to answer it on speaker.

"Morning, Div. You're on speaker in my kitchen with Avery."

"Hi, Div," I called.

"You both need to get to the town council meeting *now*." His voice was a sharp whisper.

I sat up straight. "What?"

Emmett froze, frowning at the phone, waiting.

"Chuck has put forth a motion to stop the sale of the restaurant to you, Avery." Div's words tumbled out. "He's speaking in a few minutes."

My stomach dropped through the floor, all the way to the core of the earth.

Hannah. The bookstore. The other day, with Cynthia. I still wasn't sure if she had overheard us but something heavy and ugly settled in my gut. I had a really, really bad feeling about this. I thought I was finished with Chuck when Keiko wouldn't sell to him.

I guess not.

"Max and I are here and we're going to try and stall, but you need to get here."

I jumped up. "I'll be right there."

Emmett turned off the burner and threw the spatula in the sink. "Five minutes." He hung up the phone. "I'll drive." He picked up my bag, grabbed his keys, and gestured for me to follow.

On the drive to town hall, my mind raced. Chuck wanted the restaurant, and he was getting increasingly persistent. If Cynthia had overheard us, what was he going to do? Tell everyone my relationship with Emmett was fake? I blew a long breath out and my knee bobbed up and down as Emmett turned the corner onto the main street. Even if he did that, he couldn't prove it.

My throat was tight when I swallowed. Everyone would know Chuck was telling the truth the second they looked at my face. There was no way I could deny it to a room full of people.

Fuck.

Chuck was warming up to take me down while I had been wrapped up in Emmett, frolicking and having sex and laugh-

267

ing. I'd been gallivanting when I should have been focused on the restaurant and the sale.

I swallowed and looked out the window. Emmett's hand came to my knee and squeezed.

"It's going to be okay," he told me, but I bit my lip with worry. I didn't know if it would be, and his tone said the same thing.

If Chuck outed us, it would ruin Emmett's campaign. The election was next week. He could never recover from something like this in time. No one would trust him to be mayor once they found out we lied to the town. The thought of disappointing Emmett and ruining his campaign turned my insides to granite. He had trusted me.

We pulled up to town hall, and I was out of the car before Emmett had even come to a complete stop. I sprinted into the building, through the halls until I found the large room used for town council meetings.

Everyone turned to look as I stepped inside.

There were about fifty people seated in folding chairs, mostly business owners from town. Hannah was near the back and shot me a worried look. Her face was flushed. Isaac and several members of the town council sat at the front of the room, facing everyone. Max turned and looked relieved when he saw I had arrived, but beside him, Div glared at Chuck, who stood at the front of the room, paused at my interruption with an annoyed expression.

I swallowed. My heart beat in my ears. There were no available seats so I leaned against the wall at the back.

The door opened beside me and Emmett slipped inside, taking the spot beside me against the wall. His hand found mine and squeezed. A tiny fraction of my nerves untangled. Emmett was here. I didn't know what he could do, but at least Emmett was here. I had someone on my team.

"As I was saying," Chuck shifted from one foot to the other, eyeing Emmett and me with a sour look, "if he's elected mayor, owning a business in Queen's Cove would be a conflict of interest."

Emmett's hand tensed around mine. His voice rang out strong in the room. "I have no plans to own The Arbutus."

Chuck's gaze was cold. "Your little wife will, and what's hers is yours. That's the way marriage works, buddy."

My throat clenched with fury. The way Chuck said *your little wife*, the condescending, disrespectful tone he used, it made me feel sick with anger. My stomach thrashed.

"Avery will be the business owner, and if I'm elected, I'll be mayor." Emmett dropped my hand and crossed his arms over his chest. "We'll have nothing to do with each other's roles."

"That doesn't mean you won't make decisions in her favor," Chuck pressed. Beside him, Cynthia was nodding with a smug look.

Cynthia glanced at me and then Hannah, and I knew she had told Chuck what she overheard in the bookstore. They didn't know every detail of our arrangement, but they knew. If they accused us of that, though, they'd be laughed out of town hall, so they'd found a different soft spot.

A soft spot that had merit.

Isaac wore a blank look but nodded as Chuck spoke.

"What if she needs a permit?" Chuck asked Isaac and the council. He snapped his fingers. "Approved. There's a dispute between her and another business owner?" He snapped again. "It's ruled in her favor. Oh, look, a complaint against The Arbutus?" He shrugged. "Magically gone."

"We would never do that!" The words burst out of me. My voice shook with fury and disbelief. The town council watched with rapt attention. Out of the corner of my eye, Hannah wrung her hands in her lap, looking stricken. "You know us. We would never do that. And when has The Arbutus ever had a formal complaint at town hall?"

"Chuck has made an excellent point," Isaac said, nodding and steepling his fingers in front of him.

No. This wasn't happening. This was a bad dream. I was still asleep, and I was having a nightmare. My mouth opened and closed but nothing came out.

"Are you kidding me?" Emmett shook his head and gestured at me. "She's wanted to buy the restaurant for years and now you won't let her because of me?"

"Our town prides itself in upholding the rules, Mr. Rhodes." Isaac glanced at the council on either side of him and they nodded with pensive looks.

My stomach flipped. I could see the conflict on the town council's faces. Sure, Emmett and I were well-liked around town, but what Chuck said had resonated with them. It was a conflict of interest. There was no doubt about it.

Isaac cleared his throat. "The issue is not with Ms. Adams buying the business but in Mr. Rhodes also running for mayor." He looked at Emmett and me with no emotion in his expression. Nothing. "It's one or the other."

My stomach shrank into nothing. "I'm going to sign the papers tomorrow. You can't throw this curveball at me now."

Isaac shook his head. "Sorry. There's nothing I can do."

Either I could buy the restaurant, *or* Emmett could run for mayor, but we couldn't have both.

I shot a glance at Emmett. He looked like he had been punched in the stomach, like he couldn't believe it.

"That concludes the town council meeting for today," Isaac said, gathering his papers. "We'll pick back up next month."

There was a tense, uncomfortable atmosphere in the room as people filed out. Emmett and I stood there, frozen and staring at each other.

His throat worked as he swallowed. "We're going to figure this out." He didn't sound like he believed himself.

I didn't, either. "How? How can we possibly—"

"Avery, I am so sorry." Hannah blinked in front of me, twisting her hands. Her face was red. "I can't believe he did that. I can't believe he would stoop to that level."

"What do you mean?" Emmett tilted his head at her. "Why are you sorry, Hannah?"

She bit her lip and glanced around to make sure no one would hear us. "Cynthia overheard us talking in the bookstore about—" She gestured between us with an emphasized expression.

Realization dawned on Emmett's face. He looked at me like I was a different person. "You told Hannah?" His mouth fell open and he shook his head in disbelief.

I threw my hands up. "She's my best friend and I didn't think this would happen."

Hannah buried her hands in her face. "I am so, so sorry."

The way Emmett was looking at me, like he couldn't believe I had fucked it all up, it broke my heart. He was right. I had done this. I told Hannah when I should have kept it a secret.

Emmett was changing his career, his whole life, so he could make this town a better place. It wasn't just for Will, it was for everyone living here. His intentions were pure.

I couldn't ask him to drop the campaign. I would never. Even if I wasn't head over goddamned heels for this guy, I couldn't ask that. This town needed Emmett as mayor.

Over his shoulder, I could see Keiko glancing across the room at me as Chuck spoke to her. She wore an expression of hesitance and her arms were crossed over her chest as he leaned down into her personal space, saying something. She and her family put everything into that restaurant. I was supposed to carry on their legacy, carry on the heart and soul of the place they had worked so hard for, but now she was realizing Chuck may be her only option.

This was too much. Keiko's legacy, Hannah's guilt, Emmett's disappointment, I couldn't handle it. I couldn't think in here. I couldn't get enough air. This room was too small. I was suffocating.

"I have to go," I told them and stepped through the door.

"Avery, wait." Emmett was right behind me. "Let's figure this out."

I didn't look back. "I need time."

His footsteps stopped and I barreled out of the building.

28

Avery

THE KNOCKING STARTED a few minutes after I closed my office door.

"I know you're in there." Max's voice carried through the door.

I sat frozen in my swivel chair, hands over my face, staring through my fingers at the door.

The doorknob turned but I had already clicked the lock closed. The doorknob rattled.

"Avery." Emmett's voice, this time. He sounded pissed. "Open the door."

Of course he was pissed. I had put him in this predicament. I couldn't keep my big mouth shut, so I blabbed our secret to Hannah. And now because I wanted my precious little restaurant, he wouldn't get to be mayor.

I heard him sigh in the hallway. "I'm going to fix this."

I didn't answer him. I didn't see how he could get us out of this mess. It was me or him, but not both.

"Nothing's changed, you know." There was a gentle thunk and I imagined his forehead resting on the other side of the door. "I still feel the same way about you. I'm going to go deal with this, but I just wanted you to know that."

I wanted to open that door, but seeing his face would make this so much harder. He wasn't going to let me give up my restaurant. I didn't want him to pull out of the race for mayor. I just needed time to think, by myself, without the intoxicating distraction of him.

Eventually, when I didn't answer, his boots thumped on the hardwood floors as he left the hallway, and I slumped into my chair.

Elizabeth's words from yesterday rang in my head. *He's the one who takes care of everyone else. I always worried he'd never have someone in his corner, taking care of him.*

I wanted to be that person for Emmett, the one who put his needs first. I didn't have a lot of practice at this relationship thing but I knew in my heart he needed that from me. He had always put others first, but I didn't want him to put me first for this. Being mayor was too important to him.

The photo of me and my mom sat on my desk, catching the glare from the light streaming in through the window. I pressed my lips together in an unhappy line as I studied my mom's face, so proud and excited to be opening her own restaurant.

If I threw the towel in now, history would be repeating itself. Maybe not in the same way, but I'd still be giving it all up for a man.

If I gave the restaurant up, my mom would be so disappointed. I could already see it on her face, the crushed look of confusion as I told her why. Would she understand? She and my dad, they were nothing like Emmett and me. They didn't laugh together like Emmett and I did. They may have loved each other deep down but they weren't friends the way Emmett and I were.

My mom would be disappointed. Keiko would be disappointed. Max, too.

Could I bear to see this beautiful heritage building turned into the next crappy tourist restaurant? No.

Could I watch as Chuck fired half my staff and made the other half wear low-cut tops to draw in more customers? No.

Could I watch Keiko's family's restaurant be stripped of all its character, its charm, its history? No.

But I couldn't bear to see Emmett crushed, either. I couldn't sit by and watch him go back to his company, knowing he could have won the election but gave it up for me. He was going to win, I knew he would.

My heart broke into fragments, because I knew what I was going to do. I knew it from the second I left town hall.

My phone buzzed in my pocket and I pulled it out and stared at the texts from Hannah:

Please call me.

Avery, I am so sorry.

I feel awful. I can't believe I did something so stupid. Please call me.

I dialed and she answered on the first ring.

"Hey." She was breathless.

"Hi." I twirled the ring around my finger, realized what I was doing, and stopped. I didn't want to look at it, not right now. It was just another painful reminder of what I was doing.

"You never should have told me about you two, I was supposed to keep it a secret and I let you down." Her voice broke.

I was silent a second, rubbing my face with my hand. Was I annoyed that Hannah hadn't locked the door? Sure. But Cynthia being in the bookstore at the wrong time wasn't her fault. It wasn't fair for Hannah to feel like this over a mistake I could have easily made.

"It's okay, Han. It easily could have been me saying it." I twirled the ring again before I forced myself to stop.

"Where are you? Emmett was looking for you."

"I know." I swallowed. Emmett's words from the other side of the door rang in my head. *I'm going to fix this.* How? How could he possibly fix this mess we were in? Of course he'd try, though, because he was Emmett. He was the guy who fixed everyone's problems.

"People are upset about this," Hannah whispered. "You should have heard Keiko giving Isaac a piece of her mind after you left town hall. Even the council looked upset."

I thought again about the words Elizabeth said to me yesterday, about how Emmett takes care of everyone, and no one takes care of him, until me.

"Married people work together all the time," Hannah continued, "and companies figure it out." She hummed. "You could sign a contract or something."

Emmett and I were married now. It wasn't a real marriage on paper, but I loved the guy. I told him that, and I meant it.

I wanted to fix this. Not just for me, but for Emmett. This time, I wanted to be the one in Emmett's corner.

Hannah's words registered and something clicked in my brain. "Wait. What did you say?"

"Uh." She sounded embarrassed. "I read it in a book. A romance novel. A boss wanted to date someone who worked for him so they signed a contract that said all the decisions about her employment would be made by other managers. She wouldn't report to him."

My scalp tingled and I could almost feel my neurons firing. "Hannah. You're a genius."

"I am?"

I smiled and stood, picking up my bag. "You sure are. I need your help, do you have some time today?"

"Of course! Yes. I want to help."

"I'll be at the bookstore in five minutes."

29

Emmett

WAVES CRASHED on the sand as the tide came in, and I sat on Castle Beach wondering how the hell I was going to get us out of this mess.

I love you, she had said.

My hands made fists, eager to call her, find her, pull her toward me and tangle my fingers into her soft hair, but she didn't want that. She wanted space.

Right now, she was probably regretting having anything to do with me.

I sighed and rubbed my hands over my face.

She wasn't going to give up her restaurant, I'd make sure of it. No fucking way. It was the only thing she wanted. The Arbutus was everything to her, and she was everything to *me*, so there was no way in hell I'd be the reason she didn't buy it. Not after what we'd been through to get here. Especially not after what she told me about her dad. I'd never do that to her. I'd made her a promise right here on this beach.

My heart twisted in my chest. I missed her. It had only been about eight hours but I missed her.

My phone buzzed again in my pocket and I shut it off

without looking at the messages. I didn't want to talk to anyone. I needed to be by myself so I could concentrate and come up with a plan.

Avery snuck into my thoughts, though. The soft, content expression on her face when I woke her up this morning. The way she rolled her eyes and bit back a smile when I teased her. And then the look of horror and confusion on her face at today's town council meeting, when she realized I stood in the way of her restaurant. What she was trying to avoid this whole time.

I wanted this marriage between Avery and me to be real, but if she didn't get her restaurant, I wasn't sure she'd be able to forgive me. I don't know if I could forgive myself.

I rubbed the scar on my lip and stared at the water. The only way I could help Avery buy the restaurant was to step out of the mayoral race. If I did that, this whole problem would vanish.

But what about Will? What about Kara and Nat? What about all the business owners in town who lost power every time we had a windstorm? What about Div, who had worked his ass off on this campaign so I would be elected?

No one would say a word if I quit. Will would understand. I'd feel like a failure, though. I made them a promise, too.

It was one or the other, though. Anguish tore at me and my chest ached. I couldn't keep my promises to both Avery and Will.

"You'd be a difficult guy to find—" Avery took a seat on the log beside me, and my heart shot into my throat. "—if I didn't have the top-secret directions to this place. I asked your brothers how to get here." Her pretty mouth pulled into a smile, and she dropped a kiss on my cheek.

I stared at her with confusion. She didn't look mad, worried, or upset. It was like the whole town hall thing never happened.

And then she did something that made my brain flip upside down inside my skull.

She laughed.

My mouth fell open.

"Emmett, I've got a proposition for you." She wiggled her eyebrows with a smug smile.

"*You* have a proposition for *me*?" I blinked. "We tried that and it didn't work."

She shook her head and fished a large envelope out of her bag. "Before you say it didn't work, read this."

I took the envelope from her, flipped it open, slid the papers out, and read.

"This emergency motion proposes the following," I read aloud. "If a conflict of interest exists between the owner of a Queen's Cove business and a member of the Queen's Cove town council, that council member will be exempt from decisions, input, and votes concerning that business. The remaining council members will oversee matters concerning said business. It is proposed that this motion be voted into effect immediately."

The paper was a photocopy of the original. HIGH PRIORITY had been stamped along the top, and beneath the text, every member of the town council except Isaac had signed. I stared at the signatures.

Avery nudged me. "They're voting right now." She reached out and flipped the page, revealing another long list of signatures. Hannah. Keiko. Holden. Wyatt. My parents. Miri. Scott. The owners of the hardware store, the grocery store, and several hotel managers and owners.

I glanced at Avery. My heart beat hard in my chest. "You did this?"

She nodded. "With Hannah's help. We got most business owners in town to sign in support." She smiled and my heart flipped over. "It's going to work, Emmett, I know it. There's no way Isaac could say no to everyone. The council will outvote him."

The earth had been ripped out from underneath me. Here I was, moping and staring at the ocean, when Avery was busting her ass to figure things out.

I searched her face. "You said you needed space."

She chewed her lip. "I did. And then I wanted to fix it." Her throat worked as she swallowed. "You take care of everyone, Emmett. Everything's always on your shoulders." She twirled the ring on her finger. Seeing her still wearing it eased something in me. "We're in this together. This is real for me."

This was new to me, this feeling that someone had my back like this. The light caught her deep blue eyes, and it occurred to me that for as long as I lived, I would never see a color more beautiful.

"This is real for me, too." I glanced at the list of signatures again. My chest filled with pride at her quick thinking and tenacity. "You think this is going to work?"

Her phone buzzed and she held up a finger once she saw who was calling. "Hold that thought." She answered. "Hey." She listened and I could hear a voice through the phone but couldn't make out the words. Her neutral expression told me nothing. "Okay. Thanks for letting me know." She hung up and looked at me with glittering eyes.

A smug grin grew on her face. "That was Keiko, calling to inform us the council voted the motion in, and our meeting at the bank tomorrow still stands."

"It worked."

She nodded. "Mhm. I'll accept your endless gratitude in the form of morning oral."

"It fucking worked." I couldn't believe it. The nightmare was over and my Avery had knocked it out of the park. "Get over here." I pulled her onto my lap and cut off her surprised laugh with my mouth on hers.

"I love you so much," I said against her mouth in between

kisses. Her hands felt so good, roaming my shoulders, raking my hair, sending shots of electricity down my spine. "I'm so grateful for you. You're everything to me."

"You're everything to me." Her breathlessness made my cock stiffen.

Something popped into my head. *It's real to me*, she said.

"Wait." My hands stilled on her ass. "There's something else."

A little frown creased her forehead. "Okay."

Out with it. I blew a breath out. "Wyatt filed the marriage certificate."

Her eyes went wide.

"I didn't ask him to," I added in a hurry. "I told him to put it in my car but he thought he was doing me a favor by leaving it at town hall."

Avery was frozen on my lap, eyes still wide and lips slightly parted.

"We can get it annulled if you want, that's fine with me. It's just a piece of paper and it doesn't change how I feel about you. I still want this to be real, but if you're not ready to make it legal, that's fine. After everything that happened with your parents—"

"No." Her hand covered my mouth and she looked down at me.

"No?" The word was muffled against her fingers.

"I don't want to get it annulled."

"You don't."

She shook her head, and the frown disappeared from her face. She took a deep breath and let it out before nodding once. "I want this to be real. This *is* real." She looked into my eyes with so much trust and love that I fell one step further in love with her. "You're nothing like my dad. And I'm not my mom. I trust you. Let's just leave the certificate where it is." She gave me a hesitant smile. "Let's be married for real. If that's what you want."

This woman. So fucking brave and sweet and smart and perfect for me. Made for me.

"It's what I want." I pulled her mouth back down to mine. "It's all I want. I love you, sweetheart."

She whispered the words I wanted to hear more than anything. "I love you too, darling."

Epilogue

"AVERY, you remember that table of tourists from last year? The mom had a sunburn." Max leaned on the doorframe of my office.

I looked up from my desk and squinted. "Two kids?"

He nodded. "They want to speak to the manager."

A grin crept onto my face. "Well, I guess you better get out there."

He rolled his eyes but I could see he was pleased. "They want to speak to *you*. Don't worry, they just want to say hi."

About six months after the sale of the restaurant went through last year, I had promoted Max to manager of The Arbutus. The whole *getting married* and *falling head over heels in love* and *nearly losing everything* sequence of events had shifted my life in a few ways. Now I had crossed my lifelong goal of owning a successful restaurant off the list, taking a day off occasionally didn't seem like such a bad idea. Especially when it was to spend time with the people I loved. Emmett. My mom, who had moved to town a couple months ago. Elizabeth and Sam. Hannah. My brothers-in-law, Holden, Wyatt, and Finn. Miri and Scott. Keiko, who I mostly chatted with via FaceTime now that she was living full-time in Vancouver.

I glanced at the photos on my desk. Keiko and the world's cutest chubby-cheeked baby girl, both smiling with bright eyes into the camera. Emmett and me, holding hands on the beach on our wedding day, me giving him a private little smile and him watching me like I was everything to him. One of Emmett and Kara at the beach, all tanned cheeks and freckles. And my favorite: the picture from Miri's turtle rehab, with Emmett and me holding the turtles up to our kissy faces, with Emmett's look of pure horror and mine of elated amusement.

Max looked over my shoulder at the picture. "That photo brings me joy. What time is the grand opening?"

"One o'clock. I should get going." I stood and grabbed my bag. "I'll say hi to the tourists on my way out."

In the restaurant, I grinned at my mom and Elizabeth as I passed their table. When they arrived earlier, I sat and chatted with them for a few minutes. Every Thursday, they had lunch together. It usually lasted a couple hours and was accompanied by several glasses of wine and laughter that had tears rolling down their faces.

Between lunches with Elizabeth, volunteering at the school with Miri, and the wine-making course she was taking, my mom had a full calendar. She seemed happy here, and that made me happy.

When I approached the table of tourists from last year, the parents' faces lit up. "We couldn't wait to come back all year," the mom said, beaming at me. "I follow The Arbutus on Instagram!"

My stomach fluttered with pride and I couldn't help the smile that spread across my face. "We're thrilled to have you back." I meant it. "I'm stocked up on aloe, too."

The parents laughed.

On my way out of the restaurant, something caught my eye. The framed picture of my mom and me in front of her restaurant years ago, the one that used to sit on my desk, hung in the foyer.

The Arbutus was Keiko's family's legacy, but now it was my family's legacy, too. Everything that had happened in my life had ushered me to this point: watching my mom's restaurant fail, experiencing the disappointment that was my dad, moving to Queen's Cove on a whim, and saying yes to Emmett's ridiculous plan. Some parts had been hard, but I wouldn't change a thing.

I smiled to myself as I walked the few blocks over, saying hello to people from town and enjoying the cool, sunny weather that was so typical for May in Queen's Cove. About thirty people gathered in front of the two-story building when I arrived for the grand opening of Miri's new turtle rehabilitation center. They had outgrown the previous center and this space was double the size. A banner reading *GRAND OPENING!* hung on the building and there was a small stage set up.

I spotted Emmett speaking to Miri at the side of the stage. Even after a year of being married, my heart flip-flopped at how handsome the guy was. His broad shoulders filled out that gray dress shirt and my fingers itched to rake through his thick hair. He nodded at something Miri said before he glanced up, caught my eye, and winked.

I bit back a grin. This man. It had occurred to me many, many times over the last year that Emmett and I were inevitable. I had always been affected by him, one way or another, even when it was just him teasing me in the restaurant, when we barely knew each other. I winked back at him, and a flicker of heat rose in his gaze.

"Hi, sweetheart." He pulled me under his arm.

I gave him a quick kiss on the cheek, inhaling his warm, masculine scent. "Hi, honey."

Miri clapped once. "Avery, good, you're here." She gestured at the turtle rehab employee rolling out a cart with a black cloth covering the contents. "You can hand Sarabeth to Mr. Mayor here when I give you the signal."

Emmett's grin dropped. "Who's Sarabeth?" His throat

worked, and I tried not to laugh. "Miri. We talked about this. Who is Sarabeth."

Miri gave him a look like *duh*. "One of our newest guests. We need to make her feel welcome." She pulled up the black cloth to reveal a googly-eyed turtle with its face pressed up against the glass.

Emmett gagged, his torso heaving. "Miri, no."

"Hi, folks, sorry I'm late." Don, the Queen's Cove Daily blogger, appeared at our side with his camera strung around his neck.

"Oh god, not again." Emmett pinched the bridge of his nose.

I rubbed his back. "It'll be okay, honey."

Miri's attention was caught by something and her face lit up. "Oh, perfect. And here's Carter."

I saw where she was looking and choked.

Carter, the early twenties stoner who lived in the basement of my old place, wandered up wearing a full turtle mascot costume, carrying the giant turtle head in his arms.

"Laser! Didn't know you'd be here. Hey, bro." His eyes widened when he caught Emmett's glare. "You don't look so good. Are you seasick or something?"

At least Emmett didn't look like he was going to puke anymore. He glowered at Carter and tensed up beside me. I squeezed his waist tighter to distract him.

He glanced down at me. "I don't like this part of being mayor," he muttered while Miri, Don, and Carter were in conversation about which way Carter would walk across the stage.

"It can't all be fixing the electrical grid and filing criminal charges against the last guy."

"Shhh." He looked around to make sure I wasn't heard before shooting me a grin. "You're not supposed to know about that."

Soon after Emmett was elected mayor by a landslide, Isaac relocated his family to Vancouver, and Chuck put his businesses up for sale. Emmett was looking for infrastructure development records and found some disappearing paper trails. Complaints against Chuck's businesses seemed to disappear once they were filed. The town infrastructure budget was used up every year by charges that didn't make sense. And there were a lot of expenses filed twice that somehow made it past the accounting department. Emmett suspected someone who had an interest in keeping the town's electric grid in the Dark Ages had been slipping Isaac cash under the table. A generator company or repair person, perhaps.

But I wasn't supposed to know any of this, because Emmett and the town council were still dealing with lawyers, and nothing had been formally filed yet.

Miri gestured at Emmett that they were ready to start and he leaned down to give me a quick kiss. His lips brushed mine and electricity zipped down to my toes.

"Love you, honey." His voice was low in my ear.

"Love you, too." I smiled at him.

"I hope you know I'm going to make you wear *that thing* later." He made sure no one was looking before giving me a quick smack on the ass. I laughed and he stepped on stage and up to the microphone.

"Good afternoon, Queen's Cove!" He beamed and the small crowd applauded and cheered. "Welcome to the grand opening of the new location of Miri's House of Turtle Horrors."

The crowd was silent and Miri's mouth fell open. Emmett's eyes went wide when he realized what he'd said. I covered my mouth with my hand to hide my laughter.

"I mean, Miri's Turtle Heaven." He coughed. "Let's give Miri a big round of applause!"

The crowd applauded as Miri stepped on stage, gesturing

for Carter to join her. The second he stepped up with his turtle costume, the crowd went nuts. He was wearing the turtle head so I couldn't see his expression but based on the way he was doing the robot and moonwalking around the stage, I knew he had a huge grin on his face. He danced over to Emmett and put his arm around Emmett's shoulders.

"Get off me," Emmett said, and I snorted. Into the mic, he continued. "Miri's organization has a long history of rescuing and rehabilitating turtles in the area."

Beside me, an employee unlatched the tank holding the turtles. Emmett's professional smile faltered and his eyes darted to the tank.

"And, um—" His throat worked. "And with the new facility, they'll be able to accept twice the guests."

The employee reached in and picked up the turtle, Sarabeth, whose arms and legs were splayed in the air. "Here you go."

"Thanks." I scooped up the turtle and glanced at Miri, who nodded and gestured for me to step on stage.

A look of nausea came over Emmett's face and his nostrils flared. His gaze darted between me and the turtle. "Miri's organization is mostly run off donations, and um, she would like to thank the residents of Queen's Cove for their generosity." He swallowed, staring at the turtle in my hands as I approached.

He looked up at me and gave a slight shake of his head. *No*, his eyes pleaded.

I grinned wider at him. *Yes*, I nodded.

"On behalf of the Queen's Cove town council—" Emmett gagged. "—I would like to present Miri's Turtle Heaven with a grant of twenty thousand dollars."

"Quick," Miri said in my ear. "Now."

I shoved the turtle into Emmett's hands and his face morphed into an expression of horror. Don readied his camera, Miri stepped up to Emmett's side and smiled, and on Emmett's other side, Carter began to twerk against him. Don snapped the picture and gave us the thumbs-up while the crowd cheered.

"Stop that," Emmett barked at Carter before almost tossing the turtle back to Miri. "Miri will be leading tours of the new facility all afternoon," he said into the microphone. "Congratulations, Miri. I need to leave now before I throw up."

Miri gazed into the eyes of her turtle with an adoring smile. "Okay."

Emmett pulled me off stage and slathered his hands in sanitizer. "I hope you enjoyed that. I need to go boil my hands."

I snorted as he grabbed my hands and smeared sanitizer on them too. "You did great up there."

He shuddered. "If Miri wants to open another turtle rescue place, I'm saying no."

I smiled at him. "No, you won't."

He sighed. "No, I won't." He pulled out his phone to glance at the time. "What does your day look like? I had booked off the entire afternoon for this. Want to play hooky with me?"

A sly smile grew on my face. "Mr. Mayor, you're a terrible influence on me. Always roping me into your grand plans."

He stopped and leaned down so his mouth was just above my ear. "Just wait until you see what we're going to do tonight."

A shiver rolled through me and my stomach fluttered. "I sure like being married to you."

His eyebrows went up. "Good. Get used to being my wife because I'm not going back."

We spent the afternoon at Castle Beach, sitting on a blanket we kept in the car for this very reason, watching the waves and the sparkling water, listening to the birds chirp at each other. The sun gently warmed our skin and Emmett's arm held me at his side while I leaned my head on his shoulder.

I glanced down the empty beach, then to the sea and the forest across the water. "This must be what heaven is like."

"Anywhere with you, Adams." His throat worked when he looked down at me. "Anywhere with you."

A familiar figure appeared out in the surf. "It's Wyatt," I said, squinting and pointing.

Emmett watched for a moment. "Who's with him? He's usually solo."

A second figure appeared, floating beside Wyatt. Their back was to me but I'd recognize that bright blonde hair anywhere.

"Is that *Hannah*?" I blinked. Hannah didn't surf. Hannah didn't leave her bookstore. Hannah could barely make eye contact with Wyatt.

Emmett made a thoughtful noise like *huh* and we watched them paddle off to another beach. I smiled to myself. Whatever was going on, Hannah would tell me when she was ready.

Finally, we headed home with plans to make pasta and sit out on the patio with our dinner and a glass of wine like we did most summer evenings. The second we stepped in the front door, though, Emmett ran up the stairs.

I was in the kitchen, pulling ingredients out of the fridge, when he reappeared with it in his hands and a huge grin on his face.

"Nope." I shook my head. "No way."

"Adams." His voice was teasing and cajoling. "You promised."

I took a step back but was blocked by the counter. "I did no such thing."

He shook out the mushroom hat, plumping it up to its

original size. It had been squashed in the back of my closet. Emmett wouldn't let me throw it out or incinerate it in a campfire the way I wanted to.

He put on an innocent expression. "I held that gross little turtle today, baby. I didn't want to do it but I did it for the greater good." He stepped closer with the puffy hat. "Now, your turn."

I made to bolt but he caught me and laughter tumbled out of me. I tried to wiggle out of his grasp but his arm was locked around my waist. I couldn't stop laughing.

"Marriage is about compromise." With one hand, he tried to shove the hat on my head.

My arms were pinned to my side. "Marriage is about trust," I wheezed, giggling and thrashing. "I don't trust you not to post a picture of me in this hat."

Emmett pulled the hat over my head, backwards at first so the head-hole was at the back. I sighed in defeat, straightened up, and he spun the hat around.

I tried to glare at him. He beamed back at me. "There she is. My beautiful wife."

"I hate you." I smiled, despite this fucking dumb hat.

The skin around his eyes creased and his eyes twinkled. "No, you don't. You love me."

My hands came to his chest. "Despite my best efforts, I have fallen deeply and madly in love with you, and we are destined to be together until the end of time."

A look of utter contentment passed over Emmett's face. "All I ever wanted, Adams."

———

WYATT'S MEANT **to find Hannah a boyfriend . . . but he wants her for himself. Read on for an excerpt from *The Wrong Mr. Right*, the perfect friends-to-lovers romantic comedy.**

———

WANT a bonus spicy scene with Emmett and Avery? Sign up for Stephanie's newsletter at www.stephaniearcherauthor. com/emmett or scan the QR code below.

Excerpt from The Wrong Mr. Right (Wyatt and Hannah)

"So you kissed him and there was no chemistry." Wyatt raked his hand through his hair, mouth in a hard line.

"Kissed him? No." I made a noise of frustration. "We never got that far. I spent the entire date talking about—" I broke off before I said something embarrassing.

"Talking about what, bookworm?" His dark gaze was back on me.

I shook my head, pressing my mouth closed.

He took another step toward me and I backed up, the backs of my knees hitting the bed. "Talking. About. What."

I threw my hands up. "You. Talking about you. Oh my god. You're so pushy." I rolled my eyes, when really, my heart raced, my skin tingled, and nipples pinched hard. I had all this energy and nowhere for it to go.

I put my hands on his chest to push him back a step but he grabbed my wrists. A smug grin grew on his features. Paired with his dark gaze, the effect was hypnotic.

"Me?" He raised his eyebrows, cocking his head. His hands scorched my wrists. It was like he ran hotter than normal people. Maybe that was why he was never cold in the water.

I rolled my eyes again. "You came up in conversation because of the surf lessons."

"Right. Because of the surf lessons." His gaze stayed glued on me, still heated. "So you didn't kiss him because it didn't feel right?"

I gave him another tiny nod.

"Interesting." His thumb brushed my wrist as if he didn't realize he was doing it. It sent tingles up and down my arm, making it hard to breathe. That could have been from his proximity, too. Or how he smelled freaking incredible.

He exhaled through his nose, and a muscle in his jaw ticked. "Are you disappointed?" His chest rumbled against my hands as he spoke.

I chewed my lip. "No. Beck's nice—" His hands clenched my wrists at the mention of his name. "—but he's just a friend." I swallowed and met his gaze. "I was looking forward to making out with someone tonight, but I don't want to do it with the wrong person."

Well, *that* sounded suggestive. Wyatt's eyebrow ticked up, still watching me with that dark gaze, and a shiver rolled down my spine. His warm hands seared my wrists. My heart hammered in my chest. I inhaled a shaky breath but it caught in my throat when Wyatt pressed his fingers into my wrist.

"Your pulse," he murmured.

I nodded again. Another flutter through my core, another clench around nothing.

He watched my face with heavy-lidded eyes. "It's been a long time since you've kissed someone, bookworm."

Another nod from me.

"I don't want you to be out of practice." His gaze dropped to my mouth and he cleared his throat. "You know, for when you meet the right person."

"Right. I don't want to be out of practice either."

I swallowed again, watching the curve of Wyatt's mouth, noticing the rise and fall of his chest against my hands. My hands tensed, my nails dug into him, and his breath caught.

"So we should practice." I lifted a shoulder in a half-shrug. Casual, so casual. Like Wyatt.

He frowned like he was torn. He glanced from me to the window, then back to me, then to the bed behind me. My core clenched hard again and I almost whimpered. My underwear was wet. That *never* happened, and definitely not from standing beside a guy for a few minutes.

I watched his mouth again. I wanted a taste of him. Just one. That would be enough.

You know what? Screw this.

I raised up on my tip toes and kissed Wyatt.

Read *The Wrong Mr. Right* or listen in duet audio!

Acknowledgments

I had a blast writing this book. I would write it before work, cackling to myself at seven in the morning as I taunted Emmett with turtles. Thank you times a million for reading it. I write primarily for myself, but I also write for you, because people like you and I? We love romance. Romance is fantastic. We don't let anyone tell us differently.

To my brilliant writer friends: Sarah Smith, Tova Opatrny, Maggie North, and Ashley Harlan. Thank you for always lending me your creative genius and your thoughtful words of wisdom. I feel lucky to know all of you.

To the members of FYS, you're the stuff dreams are made of. The sky's the limit with you bunch. Thank you for your enthusiastic support in all my endeavours.

Hello Clarice, my besties, my soulmates. One day, we will unlock ladies of leisure status. May our closets always be full of ethical faux-fur minks and martini glasses (for throwing).

To Kathleen. Thank you for never making me feel anything less than welcome and cherished in your family. The world needs more MIL's like you. Please don't read this book.

Tim. Every joke I tell is to make you laugh, every word I write is to make you proud. I send a silent *thank you* up to the universe every day that you're in my life.

**Turn the page to discover more spicy,
laugh-out-loud romances from Stephanie Archer.**

He's the hot, grumpy goalie I had a crush on in high school . . . and now I'm his live-in assistant.

After my ex crushed my dreams in the music industry, I'm done with getting my heart broken. Working as an assistant for an NHL player was supposed to be a breeze, but nothing about Jamie Streicher is easy. He's intimidatingly hot, grumpy, and can't stand me. Keeping things professional will be no problem, even when he demands I move in with him.

Beneath his surliness, though, Jamie's surprisingly sweet and protective.

When he finds out my ex was terrible in bed, his competitive nature flares, and he encourages and spoils me in every way. The creative spark I used to feel about music? It's back, and I'm writing songs again. Between wearing his jersey at games, fun, rowdy parties with the team, and being brave on stage again, I'm falling for him.

He could break my heart, but maybe I'm willing to take that chance.

Behind the Net *is a grumpy-sunshine, pro hockey romance with lots of spice and an HEA. It's the first book in the Vancouver Storm series and can be read as a standalone.*

The best way to get back at my horrible ex? Fake date his rival.

Being the team physiotherapist for a bunch of pro hockey players is challenging enough without my ex joining the team. He's the reason I don't date hockey players.

Vancouver Storm's new captain and the top scorer in pro hockey, Rory Miller, is the arrogant, flirtatious hockey player I tutored in high school. And he's just agreed to be my fake boyfriend. I get sweet revenge. Rory gets to clean up his image. It's the perfect deal.

Faking with him is fun and addictive, though, and beneath the bad boy swagger, Rory's sweet, funny, and protective.

He teaches me to skate. He sleeps in my bed. He kisses me like it's real.

But is there anything fake about our feelings?

The Fake Out is a pro hockey fake dating romance. It's the second book in the Vancouver Storm series but can be read as a stand-alone.

The hot, commitment-phobe surfer is the only one I can turn to . . .

In my small town bookstore, I'm surrounded by book boyfriends, but I've never had one in real life. At almost 30, I've never been in love, and my bookstore isn't breaking even. Something needs to change, and I know exactly who's going to help me: Wyatt Rhodes, the guy everyone wants.

He agrees to be my relationship coach, but his lessons aren't what I expected.

Between surfing, mortifying dates, and revamping my store, his lessons are more about drawing me out of my shell than changing me into someone new. But when we add praise-filled 'spice lessons' to the curriculum, it's clear he wants me. He's leaving town and I'm staying to run my store, so it can't work, but that doesn't seem to matter to him.

He's supposed to find me someone to fall for but instead, we're falling for each other.

A hilarious, small town, friends-to-lovers romantic comedy with lots of spice and an HEA. This is the second book in the Queen's Cove series but can be read as a standalone.

The deal is simple: the grumpy guy will pay off my debt if I find him a wife.

Holden Rhodes is grouchy, unfairly hot, and has hated me for years. He's the last person I'd choose to inherit an inn with. As we renovate the inn and put his dating skills to practice, though, I see a different side of him.

What if I was all wrong about Holden?

When we add 'friends with benefits' to the deal, our chemistry is so hot the sparks could burn down the inn. Holden's a secret romantic, and I'm secretly falling for him.
I'm terrible at bartending, a video of a bear stealing my *toy* went viral, and everyone in this small town knows my business, but Holden Rhodes is so much more than I expected.

I don't want him to find love with anyone but me.

A grumpy-sunshine, friends-with-benefits, small town romantic comedy with lots of spice and an HEA. This is the third book in the Queen's Cove series but can be read as a standalone.

The guy who broke my heart is now an arrogant, too-hot fire-fighter . . . who's hell-bent on getting me back.

This summer, I have one goal: field work. I need it to finish my PhD. I never expected Finn Rhodes to offer help. He broke my heart twelve years ago, and now that he's back in town, I want nothing to do with him. The only problem? He insists we're meant to be together.

I'll pretend to date him, but actually? I'm trying to get him to dump *me*.

Between hiking the back country and cringe-worthy dates designed to turn him off, I begin to remember why we were best friends. Despite how hard I try, Finn isn't interested in dumping me… and now I'm not sure I want him to.

Finn's always been trouble. The kind that might break my heart. Again.

Finn Rhodes Forever *is a spicy, second chance romantic comedy. This is the fourth book in the Queen's Cove series but can be read as a standalone.*